THE COMPLETE
BIRDER

JACK CONNOR

THE

COMPLETE

BIRDER

A Guide to Better Birding

Illustrations by
MARGARET LAFARGE

Houghton Mifflin Company
BOSTON   NEW YORK

LIBRARY OF CONGRESS CATALOGING-IN-PUBLICATION DATA

Connor, Jack
The complete birder: a guide to better birding/Jack Connor:
illustrations by Margaret LaFarge.
p.   cm.
Bibliography: p.
Includes index.
ISBN 0-395-38173-8   ISBN 0-395-46807-8 (pbk.)
1. Bird watching.   2. Bird watching — United States.   I. Title.
QL677.5.C72 1988
598'.07'234 — DC19   87-27217
CIP

PRINTED IN THE UNITED STATES OF AMERICA

FFG   12 11 10 9 8 7 6 5 4

The sonograms that appear as figure 4 (page 41) are adapted from *Birds of North America* by Chandler S. Robbins, Bertel Bruun, and Herbert S. Zim © 1966 Western Publishing Company, Inc. Used by permission.

The map that appears as figure 6 (page 110) is adapted from a map by Tom Will © Tom Will.

Portions of this book previously appeared in *Living Bird Quarterly*, *Bird Watcher's Digest*, and Blair & Ketchum's *Country Journal*.

For Blake, Colette, and Teal

ACKNOWLEDGMENTS

Lyn Atherton, Rick Bonney, Pete Dunne, Allen Fish, Steve Hoffman, Joe Morlan, Roger Tory Peterson, and Tom Rawls kindly reviewed chapters of this book in manuscript and offered many corrections and helpful suggestions. Clay Sutton read the entire manuscript, saved me from several embarrassing errors, and improved every chapter.

Thanks also to Tom Will for figure 6 and to Dick Morton for his help with the hawk counts in chapter 8.

Harry Foster, my editor at Houghton Mifflin, has had the patience of a saint. Margaret LaFarge has drawn like an angel. I am grateful to both of them.

Others whose understanding, encouragement, and assistance enabled me to write this book are Carson Connor, Penny Dugan, Kathy Hart, John Henry Hintermister, G. T. Lenard, Barbara Muschlitz, George Ovitt, Bob Repenning, and Kathy Easton Roig. My heartfelt thanks to each of them.

Finally, most of all, I thank Jesse, my wife, who has kept me going — and has done much, much more.

CONTENTS

FOREWORD *by Roger Tory Peterson* · XI

1. THE SPORTING SCIENCE · I

2. OPTICS · 9

3. ACOUSTICS · 36

4. MIGRATION · 58

5. WINTER · 81

6. SUMMER · 95

7. WARBLERS · 114

8. HAWKS · 133

9. SHOREBIRDS · 162

10. TERNS · 191

11. GULLS · 208

12. THE INNER GAME · 237

BIBLIOGRAPHY · 263

INDEX · 273

FOREWORD

by Roger Tory Peterson

Birding or *birdwatching?* By definition, what is the difference?

Birdwatching is much more inclusive, a blanket term covering the activities of almost everyone who looks at birds or studies them, from the watcher at the window who simply puts out sunflower seeds for the chickadees and nuthatches, all the way to the academic who belongs to the American Ornithologists' Union. Indeed, the observation of birds can be many things — a science, an art, a recreation, a game or a sport, an environmental ethic, or even a religious experience. We could call even the sportsman who shoots ducks or quail a birdwatcher, although he concerns himself with relatively few species.

On the other hand, the term *birder,* as we now use it, is more restrictive. It has come to mean the person who takes the identification of birds seriously; one who makes lists, keeps records of the birds in his neighborhood or in his travels; who monitors their migrations, their populations, their increases or declines; and who delights in spotting rarities. Jack Connor, who wrote this entertaining and instructive book, aptly calls birding the "sporting science."

But in olden days a birder was one who shot birds. That was Shakespeare's meaning when one of the characters in *The Merry Wives of Windsor* said: "She laments, sir ... Her husband goes this morning a-birding."

Audubon himself was a birder in that antique sense. He once

implied that it was not a really good day unless he shot a hundred birds. It was not until the early decades of this century that birders in increasing numbers began to rely on the field glass instead of the shotgun.

Birds are a perfect entrée to an understanding of the natural world. Some birders may ignore the butterflies, the flowers, and the other components of the ecosystem. To them, "the list is the thing." Listing is a perfectly valid sport or recreation, but most birders, those who have really done their homework and paid their dues, usually make good all-around naturalists and ecologists.

Field birding has gone through a remarkable metamorphosis in recent years. A greater sophistication has developed among the hard-core binocular addicts, and a polarization has taken place in the fine art or science of identification. Field marks, as exemplified by field guides such as my own, are simply the trademarks of nature, the patterns and special marks by which one bird can be told from another with some certainty. However, the experienced raptor watcher perched on a boulder on Hawk Mountain, or the seabird buff sailing the continental shelf, no longer relies only on the obvious field marks. While the bird is still half a mile away he intuitively puts shape, manner of flight, wing-beat, and a number of other subtle things together and comes up with an identification. He might casually use the term *jizz* — a British airman's acronym implying "general impression and shape." This approach is almost an art rather than a science.

At the other extreme we have those birders who use Questars and Celestrons. With these expensive telescopes designed for amateur astronomy, they can almost see the parasites on a peregrine or the mites on a merlin. In conversation these birders might refer to "worn tertials" and other bird-in-hand characteristics. So, in this category, field birding has come almost full circle back to the specimen tray.

Both extremes, the "holistic approach" and the "micromethod," are valid, but difficult to encompass in a field guide designed for the pocket.

Jack Connor confesses that he was a reluctant birder at first, resistant to the idea in his early teens, when so many of us got hooked. Obviously he has a very systematic mind and now he shows his readers how to do it. Assuming them to be already committed, he takes them beyond their field guides, which have already become dog-eared with use.

Not only does he give us the best advice on available equipment and how to use it, but he also presents an overview of the warblers, hawks, shore birds, gulls, and terns — those difficult groups of birds that have such a special fascination for the field glass fraternity.

Enjoy what Jack Connor has to tell you and upgrade your field skills. Good birding!

THE COMPLETE
BIRDER

1 · THE SPORTING SCIENCE

"BIRDING IS EASY," birdwatchers often tell their nonbirding friends. "You should try it some time. The only things you need are a field guide and a pair of binoculars. Birds are everywhere."

I wonder whether we'd win more converts if we used some reverse psychology: "Birding is impossible. You should try not to get hooked. Birds are hard to see. They hide in the bushes, they duck behind the trees, they fly into the sun. No matter how many field guides you own or how good your binoculars are, you're going to be frustrated."

2 · THE COMPLETE BIRDER

I wonder, too, whether the second speech isn't closer to the truth. Birding can be exhilarating, enlightening, evocative, or exasperating — and often all of these at once — but no birder I know, from raw novice to professional tour guide, finds it easy. It seems easy only to those who have never done it, and so the depth and complexity of birdwatching go unappreciated by nonparticipants.

Birds *are* everywhere, but that is precisely the reason they remain invisible to the uninitiated. John Hintermister, my wife, Jesse, and I drove to Kendall, Florida, one winter weekend to search for the red-whiskered bulbul. After an hour's walk through the suburban neighborhood, we spotted one perched in a tree next to a house fifty yards back from the sidewalk. We trespassed a few steps, two more bulbuls landed in the tree, and the owner of the house came out on his porch to pick up his morning newspaper. "What are you looking for?"

"Bulbuls," said John.

The man grinned and walked toward us. "Is that a bird or a flower or what?"

"It's a bird. The red-whiskered bulbul. This is a pretty special neighborhood you live in, you know. It's the only place in the United States bulbuls nest."

"Is that right? I've lived here for nine years and I've never heard anyone even mention that bird. I thought all the interesting birds were over in the Everglades."

"Well," said John, "you can't find any bulbuls in the Everglades, and you've got three of them in your yard right now."

As the man reached us, I handed him my binoculars and John pointed upward to the bulbuls. The man missed this signal, however, and aimed the binocs straight ahead, at a bird standing on his fence twenty feet away. "Wow!" he said, his eyebrows lifting as he adjusted the focus. "They're *beautiful!*"

He was looking at a blue jay.

And — mea culpa, mea culpa — when I try to remember the birds I noticed during the first twenty-seven years of my life, I come up with precious few. I can't plead ignorance either. My mother has been a birder all her life, and until I was old enough to refuse to go, she took me along on her field trips to the Kittatinny Mountains, the Newark Meadows, and Sandy Hook State Park and tried to point out birds to me. Today when she asks me, "Remember the time the pileated wood-pecker landed on our cabin at Lake Wallkill?" or "Remember that day we counted two hundred gannets from the beach at Sandy Hook?" I smile vacantly to hide my guilt. I remember the knickknacks at the cabin at Lake Wallkill, the phragmites at Newark Meadows, and the bitter wind at Sandy Hook. The birds are a total blank.

The only bird from my youth I can visualize today may have been the last one my mother tried to show me. I was shooting baskets in the driveway with some friends when she returned home, stepped out of the car, and pointed high into a pine tree. "What's that?" she asked. "Did one of you kids throw a coat up there?"

We looked. The coat blinked. "It's a great horned owl!" said my mother. She hurried into the house and to my dismay came back with her binoculars. Silver showed through the black of both barrels and the original strap, broken years before, had been replaced with a piece of chain from a dog leash.

My dismay changed to confusion when all three of my friends abandoned the basketball game to line up for a chance to see the bird.

"Don't you want a look?" one of them asked me.

"I can see it fine from here," I said, banking a jump shot off the backboard as loudly as I could.

Part of my resistance was ordinary adolescent fear. I wanted to be the average American kid, untainted by any eccentricity. Since no one I knew except my mother and her friends ever went birdwatching, I wanted nothing to do with it. It never occurred to me that birding was difficult. What could be easier and more boring than looking for birds? I used to think. They're everywhere.

Birders are bolder nowadays. Identifications are shouted to the skies, Christmas count teams exchange high fives after dis-covering a rarity, and raptor enthusiasts wear sweatshirts that read "I Counted 10,000 Hawks At Rockfish Gap." My mother and her friends celebrated their victories so quietly that, even when standing right next to them, I never realized anything dramatic was happening: "Goodness, look over here. Isn't this a harlequin duck?" "Well, so it is. Nice find."

Nowadays, too, the sporting nature of birdwatching is more widely recognized. Events such as the World Series of Birding and the various Big Day runs rate coverage in *Sports Illustrated* and the *New York Times*. In fact, if anything, the numerical aspects of birdwatching are now being overemphasized. Articles about birding competitions in the national press inevitably emphasize the miles driven, the hours of sleep missed, and the dollars spent, and pay scant attention to the birds seen. Even today, apparently, despite the increased publicity, you must be a birder to know that birding is no numbers game and is as much a science as a sport. Since its agonies and ecstasies are subtle and cerebral, they remain misunderstood by nonparticipants.

There's a ten-year gap between the owl in the driveway and the next bird I remember. My wife and I were living in Madison, New Jersey, half a dozen miles from the Great Swamp National Wildlife Refuge, and Jesse drove there once a week or so to hike in the woods. From time to time, about once every two months, when I couldn't find a baseball or basketball game, tennis match, track meet, or wrist-wrestling championship to watch on television, I went with her. She tells me now that she pointed out flickers, nighthawks, wood thrushes, and (once) a scarlet tanager on these trips. I remember none of them. I tagged along in the same yawning, absentminded mode I still use when following her through clothing stores.

The one bird I do remember is a great blue heron that flushed up in front of us while we were sitting in an observation blind near a muskrat colony. I was genuinely thrilled. The bird was so big! The next afternoon two friends came by, and I described it in such excited terms ("I've never seen anything like it! It's probably the only one in the state!") that they insisted we go look for it again. We did, and we found it again, but the next time Jesse went to the refuge there must have been a ball game on the tube. I don't remember going again. It didn't seem worth the trouble. I had lived in New Jersey all my life, and like the bulbul man in Kendall and nonbirders everywhere, I assumed all the interesting birds were somewhere else — in the Everglades or the Amazon. I just couldn't see wasting my time looking at ordinary birds on the remote chance that I might come upon another superrarity like a great blue heron.

My eyes and mind were forced open at long last when Jesse and I moved to Gainesville, Florida, in 1974 to finish our educations at the University of Florida. Neither of us had ever been south of North Carolina, and we had rented an apartment sight unseen. We arrived at noon on a Saturday to find that it was the upper floor of a two-story concrete and brick building surrounded by an asphalt parking lot. It had three small closets, three windows so tiny they looked like they belonged on a gun turret, and a toilet the landlord had promised to fix by Wednesday. It was 95 degrees outside and so hot inside that it hurt to hold your hand against the wall. Dejected and depressed, we spent several sweaty hours emptying our rented trailer. Late that afternoon, we yanked the apartment door shut on our unopened boxes, returned the trailer to the local U-Haul, and zigzagged at random through the city and out into the country. In a minute or two we passed a cow pasture, several fields of low-armed oaks, and another cow pasture. Then — suddenly, amazingly — we came upon a huge and beautiful lake, miles wide, bordered by cypress trees strung with sphagnum moss. "This must be Silver Springs!" I told Jesse.

We parked near a boat ramp, alongside a dock that extended far out over the water. A man stood fishing at the end. As we walked toward him, a giant brown and white bird spiraled down fifty yards beyond him, flopped awkwardly to the water, picked up a fish, and flew off. "Hey!" Jesse said. "That's a *bald eagle!*"

I looked at the bird, looked at her, and sprinted to the fisherman, who had hardly glanced at the bird. "Is this Silver Springs?"

"Silver Springs is about forty miles that way. You're in Gainesville. This is Newnan's Lake."

"But wasn't that an eagle just now?"

"Yeah, it was. We've still got a few pairs nesting around here."

The next afternoon we recovered Jesse's binoculars and field guide from one of our boxes and drove out to the lake again. I stopped at the same boat ramp and made sure to park in the very same spot. The fisherman was gone, replaced by a white bird with curling plumes. "It's a snowy egret," Jesse explained. "See? A black bill and yellow feet."

"You're right," I said.

Jesse showed me an osprey soaring over the lake on kinked wings and beyond it, over the trees, a trio of turkey vultures, their wings flaring upward. A second snowy egret flushed the first. A kingfisher rattled past us and then past a creature I would have called a pterodactyl, which was drying its wings on the next dock over. Jesse thumbed through her field guide and pointed to a picture. "That must be an anhinga," she said.

"No doubt about it," I said.

We walked to the end of the dock and passed the binocs back and forth. My next turn had just begun when I noted the vultures now numbered five, and two of them seemed to be coming right at us. One flapped, then the other, and even to eyes crusted by twenty-plus years of willful blindness, something looked wonderfully wrong. I had just enough time to think "Could they be . . . ?" when the leading bird's head flashed white against the blue sky. "Jesse!" I shouted. "Eagles! Eagles! Eagles!" They came right over our heads, two adults so close that their wings seemed as big as ironing boards.

"And that's the moment I became a birder" I always say when telling this story aloud, but you don't have to be a birder to appreciate an eagle. Walking home the next day, I spotted a woodpecker on a telephone pole, opened Jesse's field guide as soon as I came in the door, and was stunned to discover that

North America has twenty species of woodpeckers, and about half of them looked like the one I'd just seen. I grabbed the book and the binocs and raced back to the telephone pole. The woodpecker was gone. *That* was the moment I became a birder.

Red-bellied Woodpecker

I realize that in detailing all this I have been preaching to the converted. I promise not to do so again in this book. This book is written for people who are already intrigued by birds. It is intended to fit on your bookshelf between your field guides and your ornithology text. Chapters 2 and 3, "Optics" and "Acoustics," cover two topics that field guides and ornithology texts seldom have the space to discuss in any detail. Chapters

4, 5, and 6 discuss the rhythm of the seasons from the birder's point of view. Chapters 7–11 discuss the five groups of birds that seem to give intermediate and developing birders the most difficulty — warblers, hawks, shorebirds, terns, and gulls. Finally, chapter 12 examines "The Inner Game," the psychology of good birding.

For a time I considered calling this book "The *In*complete Birder," since no birder can ever be complete. All of us know of groups we have not yet mastered, behavior we have never witnessed, hot spots we have not yet visited, and birds we haven't seen. Indeed, much of the satisfaction in birding comes from the sense that the world of birds is larger than we can ever explore. No matter how expert we become, there will always be more to see and more to learn.

"Reality is an infinite succession of steps [and] levels of perception," Vladimir Nabokov once observed. "A lily is more real to a naturalist than it is to the ordinary person. But it is still more real to the botanist. And yet another stage of reality is reached with that botanist who is a specialist in lilies."

It seems to me that Nabokov's comment comes as close as any to suggesting the lure and joys of birdwatching. Blue jays, great blue herons, and bald eagles are more real to the novice birder than they are to the average person. They are realer still to the intermediate birder and even more real to the expert. Best of all, birds are more real to *every* birder this year than they were last year. The more experience we gain and the better we become at observation, the more birds mean to us. If this book helps you step up another level or two in your birding expertise, then it will have served its purpose.

2 · OPTICS

SINCE YOU ARE READING this book, you almost certainly own a pair of binoculars. If it's your first pair, chances are you bought it for $25–$75 in a camera or department store before you became a serious birder. If it's your second pair, it probably cost you $100–$250 and has earned your loyalty. The qualitative difference between a $50 pair of binocs and a $250 pair is akin to the difference between a tricycle and a 10-speed bike. In either case, however, you've seen birders in the field with more expensive equipment and have probably wondered whether the investment is worth the price.

"It's not the binoculars that matter," a friend I'll call Tim used to say, "it's the birder." Tim owned a pair of Brand X binoculars he couldn't have pawned for a lukewarm cup of coffee. The center-focusing dial had about three inches of play in both directions, and the left lens was held in place with a strip of black adhesive tape. Apart from his life list, which included well over 400 species, nothing gave Tim more pleasure than identifying some speck on the horizon before any of the better-equipped birders around him. And he performed this feat regularly: his eyes were sharp, and he knew his birds.

But one day on a pelagic trip off the coast of Florida, I was standing at the rail with Tim and another birder when a skein of ducks appeared far off the bow. "Scoters!" Tim shouted.

"I don't know," said the man on my left. "Their necks seem long."

"They're scoters all right," said Tim. "Probably blacks."

"Could they be fulvous tree ducks?" asked our companion.

"Fulvous tree ducks!? This far out? Be serious."

"Look at those necks and the rumps. *Fulvous tree ducks!*"

The rail crowded with birders, the flock came right at us, and finally there was no doubt: 23 fulvous tree ducks 30 miles off the coast. After they disappeared to the stern, I found Tim sitting down staring at the binoculars in his hands. "You know," he said, "I honestly don't know why I torture myself with these things."

Tim's old motto was only half correct. What matters is the birder *and* the binoculars. Finding the binoculars and other optical equipment that will best serve your needs involves some comparison shopping and careful analysis of the kind of birding you like most, but the best advice is one word: *upgrade*. There is no quicker way to improve your birding skills than to buy better equipment.

THE PRICE OF POWER

Magnification is the first thing most people consider when they evaluate a pair of binoculars. It's easy to understand why. Imagine you are walking among the mesquite and cholla of the Madera Canyon in southern Arizona one summer afternoon. It is the last hour of the last day of your trip, and you live in, say, Portland, Maine. The sky is empty in all directions, and you are growing desperate. A certain southwestern specialty has escaped you, one you've dreamed about seeing for years. You know that if you don't see it very soon, years more may pass before you have another chance.

A dot appears way out in the blue, a half mile off. You lift your binoculars to your eyes and see it's a bird riding a thermal. Slowly it circles closer, the wings in a dihedral, and then — yes — it rocks in flight, tilting left and right. Now your pulse picks up its pace. Only two birds in North America fly that way: the turkey vulture and the bird you're searching for, the zone-tailed hawk. You've done your homework and know that only one field mark separates the two species at a distance: the vulture's tail is dirty gray; the zone-tail's is banded with white and black. All you can do now is wait and hope.

In such situations every birder wishes for stronger binoculars. The bird is at the limit of visibility; the critical field mark is subtle; and behavior, voice, and habitat are no help. If your naked-eye vision is good enough to discern tail bands at 50 yards, with 7× (seven-power) binoculars you can identify a zone-tailed hawk at a distance of 350 yards (50 yards × 7). With 8× binoculars your range is 400 yards; with 10×, 500 yards. If the bird turns away at 475 yards and you are holding something less than 10×, you go home with only a might-have-been to remember. Why, then, don't all birders carry 10× binoculars or, for that matter, 12× or 15×?

One reason is the cost. Binocular prices have been resisting the tide of inflation in recent years, but the price of a pair of 8×'s is still significantly more than 7×'s of the same quality, and 10×'s are much more, generally close to twice the price of 7×'s. The price doubles again for high-quality 15×'s.

Linked to price is an important point of magnification mathematics, a kind of principle of diminishing returns. Imagine that, just as you've given up hope and have begun contemplating the long and depressing ride home, your possible zone-tail circles right at you. It soars closer and closer until it is only 100 yards away. This is still well beyond naked-eye range, but you can reach in your back pocket for your life list. Even with 7×'s

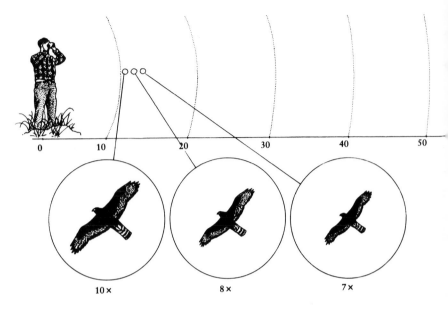

FIGURE 1. *Magnification Chart. A bird at a distance of 100 yards seems 10 yards away at 10× magnification, 12.5 yards away at 8×, and 14.3 yards away at 7×.*

you will have no trouble spotting those tail bands. In fact, you could easily identify the bird with your grandmother's 5 × opera glasses; 5 × magnification would cut the real distance of 100 yards to an apparent 20 (100 yards divided by 5). Magnification of 7 × would reduce the distance to 14.3 yards; 8 × to 12.5; 9 × to 11.1; 10× to 10; 12× to 8.3; 15 × to 6.6 yards (see figure 1).

Notice the diminishing returns. Each step up in power gains you less. The two-power step from 5 × to 7 × reduces the apparent distance by an additional six yards, more distance than you gain by the more expensive three-power step from 7 × to 10 × or by the extremely expensive five-power step from 10× to 15 ×. Only in a technical sense are 10× binocs twice as powerful and 15 × binocs three times as powerful as 5 ×. The way the eye and mind process visual information makes a mag-

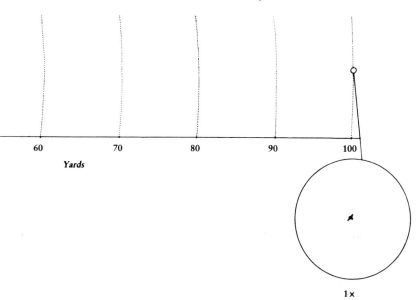

nified image seem closer rather than larger, and for this reason the 10 × 's seem just 10 percent more powerful than the 5 × 's and the 15 × 's only 13.4 percent more powerful. The 5 × 's reduce the apparent distance to the bird (or any object at any distance) by 80 percent; 10 × 's reduce it by 90 percent; and the 15 × 's reduce it by 93.4 percent.

Sometimes, of course, a small margin makes the difference. Every experienced birder has lost dozens of birds because of binoculars that were not strong enough. But most birding is conducted well inside the range of lower-powered binoculars, and so other factors must be considered.

BINOCULARS IN THE TWILIGHT ZONE

For an interesting experiment in optics design, stop for a few minutes as you go out the door on your next predawn birding trip to look at Venus, first through your binoculars, then through a spotting scope. Once your eyes have adjusted to the darkness, you'll find that the planet is brighter through the binocs and duller (though larger) through the scope. If the night is moonless and there are no ground lights, you may even find that it is brightest of all to your naked eye.

This effect is caused by a second principle of diminishing returns in magnification mathematics: *the higher the magnification, the lower the light transmission.* When all other things are equal, lower-power lenses allow more light to reach the eye than lenses of higher power. Even when other things are not equal, lower-powered lenses can be brighter. Most spotting scopes have an objective lens of 60 mm. If the magnification is 20×, the diameter of the light beam exiting the ocular ("eyeball") end of the scope is 3 mm. This *exit pupil* size is calculated by dividing the size of the objective lens by the magnification (60 mm divided by 20 equals 3 mm). Most binoculars have objective lenses of 50 mm or less and so take in less light than spotting scopes, but because they are lower powered, more light exits from the eyepieces. The exit pupil for 7×35 binoculars is 5 mm. For 7×42 binoculars it's 6 mm. Venus is brighter through your binoculars than through your scope because the beam of light reaching your eye is bigger.

Table 1 lists exit pupil diameters for eight sizes of binoculars. The two other measurements, *brightness index* and *twilight performance,* represent the two very different ways optics manufacturers calculate their products' performance in dim light,

TABLE 1. *Brightness Measures for Eight Sizes of Binoculars*

POWER/ OBJECTIVE SIZE	EXIT PUPIL	"BRIGHTNESS INDEX"	"TWILIGHT PERFORMANCE"	"T.P. RANK"
7 × 42	6	36	17.1	5
7 × 35	5	25	15.6	7
8 × 40	5	25	17.8	4
10 × 50	5	25	22.3	1
10 × 40	4	16	20.0	3
8 × 30	3.75	14.1	15.4	8
9 × 30	3.33	11.1	16.4	6
12 × 36	3	9	20.7	2

and both involve some debatable arithmetic. The exit pupil size, however, is a legitimate and certifiable measurement. You can confirm it for any pair of binoculars by holding them at arm's length and measuring the circle of the light at the ocular end with a ruler. The diameter of that circle will match the formula of objective size divided by power.

In sales brochures and other publicity information, many binocular manufacturers list a "brightness index" alongside exit pupil size. The formula is simple: exit pupil squared. Thus the brightness index for 7 × 35s is 25; for 7 × 42s it is 36. The mathematics is derived from the formula that astronomers use to calculate the light-gathering power of telescopes (the diameter of the objective lens squared). In binocular sales, however, the brightness index apparently serves mainly to accentuate the apparent differences between various models. Judged by exit pupil size, 7 × 42s seem to be 20 percent brighter than 7 × 35s; by the brightness index they seem more than 40 percent better. Actually, in most birding situations, they are neither.

An underpublicized fact is that in ordinary daylight *any* binoculars of equal optical quality will be equally as bright, *no matter what the differences are in their objective size and power.* The determining factor is the human eye. Your pupils contract to a minimum of about 2 mm in the blaze of the noonday sun and expand to their maximum diameter of about 7 mm in complete darkness. The only binoculars capable of delivering a 7 mm beam of light are the true astronomical binoculars (or "night glasses"), which are sized at 7 × 50, 8 × 56, or 10 × 70 and are generally regarded as too heavy for birding. Birding binoculars can be lighter because birdwatching is usually a daytime enterprise, and in ordinary light our pupils are about 3–4 mm in diameter. A pair of 7 × 42s always delivers more light than a pair of 7 × 35s, but except in dim light (when your pupils have expanded to wider than 5 mm), you literally can't see the difference. I haven't noticed many 7 × 42s in the field. Few birders seem to have found the occasional advantage in brightness worth the constant disadvantage in weight.

The analysis becomes trickier when we compare 7 × 35 with a size that has become very popular with birders in recent years, 10×40. Most companies that manufacture 10×40s and other high-powered/lightweight binoculars (none of which score well by the "brightness index") use a different formula: the square root of the product of power times objective size. Thus $10 \times 40 = 400$; the square root of 400 is 20. The gain in power, these manufacturers argue, compensates for the loss of light transmission. A given feature may be darker but more visible because it's bigger.

You can see on table 1 how the "twilight performance" formula scrambles the ranking of the eight binoculars. The 7×42s drop from first to fifth place and the 7×35s from second to seventh. The 10×40s climb from a distant fifth to a close third, and the 12×36s from last place to second.

What I find suspicious about the "twilight performance" mathematics is that exit pupil size has been eliminated from consideration. My 20×60 spotting scope with its tiny 3 mm exit pupil scores an apparently awesome 34.6 on twilight performance, but my scope is in no way as good as my 7×35s in what I consider true twilight. Through my scope I have several times been unable to see whip-poor-wills and owls that I could plainly see with my binocs. Even when I close one eye to make the comparison fairer, the view through my binocs is much brighter.

The logic of the "twilight performance" calculation — that bigger is better than brighter — seems to apply only while the sun is still above the horizon and the sky is at least red. Once the sky has turned gray, exit pupil diameter becomes the critical factor. For an evening search for owls or rails, you may even want to borrow a pair of 7×50s, the binocular size that amateur astronomers swear by.

"Listen," a binocular repairman who works for one of the best optical companies in the country told me, "if you want to give people the best advice, tell them to forget all about *both* those formulas.

"Don't use my name, but I've been in this business for forty years and I've got to tell you, the way people treat binoculars, all that twilight and brightness stuff is irrelevant. Ninety-five percent of the binoculars I get in here to repair look like they've been dragged through moose manure. How can people expect brightness and clarity when they never bother to clean the damn lenses?"

He's right, I thought as I hung up. Some birders are pretty careless. They're willing to spend good money on their equipment, but they're not willing to treat it right. It's a shame. Then I walked over to my bookcase, picked up my binoculars, and discovered that one of those slobs had actually sneaked into my house. My objectives had suddenly become encrusted with a thick gummy substance — apparently a composite of peanut butter, wet sand, and the crumbs from a granola bar I'd eaten on a trip to the Outer Banks in the summer of 1975.

FIELD OF VIEW

Birders tend to underrate the importance of field of view, probably because it is usually expressed as the width of vision at 1,000 yards. At 1,000 yards it hardly matters whether a pair of binocs has a 250-foot or 400-foot field of view. It is seldom a problem to track birds large enough to be seen at long range: not even a gyrfalcon at full throttle can jet across 250 feet faster than a birder can move a pair of binoculars.

Where field of view becomes crucially important, however, is *at close range,* and when you consider field of view, you should convert the measurement by moving the decimal point two places to the left. Binoculars that give you 250 feet at 1,000 yards are giving you 2.5 feet at 10 yards; a 400-foot-wide angle at 1,000 yards is 4 feet at 10 yards. At 10 yards a foot and a half of extra viewing space makes an enormous difference. Swallows, terns, and other aerial zigzaggers are hard to frame in narrow field binocs and are even harder to keep there. They are constantly flying out of your field before you can check for breast bands or determine bill color. The problem intensifies with woodland birds. Sparrows, thrushes, wrens, and warblers can hop out of a narrow field of view so quickly you can't even tell which direction they went. You'll find yourself dropping your binoculars to relocate a bird with your naked eye, framing it again in your binocs, losing it, dropping your binocs to find it again, and so on.

An even better way to measure width of field is by angular degrees (and a few enlightened manufacturers report this figure for all their models). To convert width in feet at 1,000 yards to degrees of angle, divide by 52.5. A full 180-degree field of view at 1,000 yards is 9,441 feet; each degree of field at 1,000 yards thus equals 52.45 feet. The birders I've talked to disagree about the dividing line between a normal field of view and one too narrow for birding, but it seems to lie somewhere between 6 and 7 degrees. At 7½ degrees (394 feet/1,000 yards), you should have few problems framing and tracking birds, even at close range. At 6 degrees (315 feet/1,000 yards), width of field becomes something you must learn to adjust for.

Although binoculars with larger objective lenses tend to have wider fields of view, width of view is more directly related to magnification. It's also another example of the principle of diminishing returns: *the higher the power, the narrower the field of view.* A typical 10× pair yields a field of view 2 degrees narrower than an 8× pair made by the same manufacturer. Internal design and optical quality are also important factors. Binoculars of the same size made by two different manufacturers may show as much as a degree and a half of difference in field of view.

The term "wide angle" is used loosely in binocular literature and can mean anything from 7 degrees upward. True wide-angle binocs (with fields of view above 10 degrees) are notorious for fuzzy optics, and I have yet to meet a serious birder who advocates their use.

GLASSES AND BINOCULARS

Eyeglass wearers have a special problem with field of view. Looking through glasses into binoculars with plastic eye cups necessitates holding your eyes an inch or more from the ocular lenses. The resulting tunnel vision — thick, black circles all around the field — is only one problem. Almost as distracting is the light that enters from the sides of the glasses and interferes with the image at the focal point.

Some birders flip their glasses away each time they look through their binoculars. This gives a wider field of view and closes out extraneous light, but it's time-consuming, tiring, and hard on eyeglass frames. In a full day's birding you may remove and replace your glasses several hundred times. This technique also costs you the magnifying power of your glasses and any weak eye/strong eye corrections in your prescription. If, like me, you have an astigmatism, when you look through your binocs without your glasses your brain may solve the problem of the doubled image by subconsciously shutting off the visual message from the weaker eye. Your focus becomes your strong eye's half of the field. Your binoculars are now a monocular, and you're a one-eyed birder.

If you wear eyeglasses and want to see as well as you can, fold-down rubber eye cups are a must. They are standard equipment nowadays on most medium- and higher-priced binoculars, but be careful: all binoculars with rubber eye cups are not equal. The ideal distance from ocular lens to eye is approximately the same as the distance from your eyeglass lens to your eye, which means you want eye cups that fold absolutely flat and ocular lenses that are not recessed.

Birders who do not wear glasses should also look carefully at any binoculars they are planning to buy to see how deeply the ocular lenses are recessed. Some poorly designed models have such deeply recessed oculars that full field of view is not possible even for people with 20/20 vision.

HOW CLOSE CAN YOU GET?

Another factor sometimes underrated by birders buying their first good pair of binoculars is close-focus range. The problem here is not that the various manufacturers present contradictory information but that they present no information at all.

You can read dozens of brochures and advertisements without finding a single reference to the minimum distance you can expect from a given pair of binocs. Hunters, sailors, and sports fans seldom use binoculars to look at anything closer than 20 yards, and so optics manufacturers have apparently not yet tuned in to birders' special needs.

Binoculars that focus near at hand are essential for successful woodland birding. In fact, a number of problematic pairs of small birds can be visually separated *only* at close range: Carolina and black-capped chickadees; sedge and marsh wrens; mourning and Connecticut warblers; LeConte's and sharp-tailed sparrows; Cassin's and Botterei's sparrows; and many others.

Fortunately, close focus is one binocular feature that can be tested in a store. Find the closest line or spot on the floor you can see sharply, then count your paces as you walk to it. For an accurate test, first adjust the dioptric-compensation ring for the different strengths of your two eyes. How far you need to turn that ring and how much play remains in the center-focusing mechanism will determine how closely you can focus.

A close-focus range of 15 feet to 18 feet is the least you should accept. If you can't look at birds closer than that, you'll find yourself stepping backward into cat briars and poison ivy to try to maintain distance.

If you are a particularly dedicated sparrow and warbler chaser, you're likely to be happier with a minimum range of about 10 feet. Depending on your eye strength, binoculars can be found with close-focus ranges down to 8 feet and even 6 feet. Within 10 feet, naked-eye identifications of even the smallest birds become reliable, but many veterans find looking at birds without an intervening optical instrument somehow unnatural, even unsporting. A Florida birder went to Maine one winter, and on her first walk in the woods a black-capped chickadee landed on her shoulder. Later she saw several others at normal distances, but that first one haunted her. "I'm not sure I should count it as my life bird," she said. "It flew away before I could see it through my binocs!"

THE FOUR DESIGNS

Although binocular models and styles are countless, there are
(at the moment) only four basic designs: field glasses, porro
prisms, roof prisms, and reverse porro prisms; see figure 2.

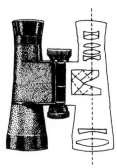

Roof prisms

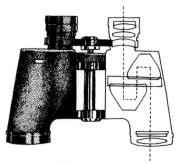

Porro prisms

Field glasses

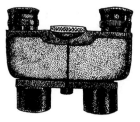

Reverse porros

FIGURE 2. *Four Binocular Designs*

1. *Field glasses* are the oldest, simplest, and sturdiest design: two monoculars held together by an otherwise nonfunctioning crosspiece. The lack of a central-focusing mechanism makes them light, durable, water resistant — and virtually worthless for birdwatching.

Each barrel of a pair of field glasses has an independent focusing mechanism at its ocular end. Binocular brochures being what they are, this feature is always described as a plus, for example: "An individualized focusing feature lets you align each lens separately for a clear, precise image." Truth in advertising ought to demand that these brochures also include the message "Caution: Field glasses are too darn slow for birdwatching." Individualized focus means that each time you look from the blackburnian at the top of the pine tree to the ovenbird at your feet you must close your left eye, reach up with your right hand, refocus the right barrel, then switch eyes, switch hands, and refocus the left barrel. Meanwhile the ovenbird migrates to Cuba. Beware: several of the superlightweight "minibinoculars" are actually miniature field glasses.

2. The first *porro prism* binoculars were developed by M. Porro in Italy in the mid-nineteenth century. The design features two right-angled prisms in each barrel and objective lenses that are set wider apart than the ocular lenses. Modern porro prisms have a center-focusing dial that moves both barrels simultaneously and a dioptric-compensating ring on one barrel to adjust for differences in the strength of the viewer's two eyes. Once you've adjusted the dioptric for your eyes, you should never have to change it, and you should see equally sharp images in each lens. Porros are much easier to use than field glasses, and they have been the design of choice for the majority of birders in America for most of this century.

In fact, though the roof prism design has become increasingly popular in the last 10–15 years, porros are still preferred by some of the best birders I know. Porro prisms usually have larger exit pupils than roof prisms, focus more quickly and more closely, and have wider fields of view. They are especially good for people who do most of their birding in woodlands (chasing small, fast birds at close range) or for birders who have the forearm strength to handle 10×50s. The primary disadvantage of porros is weight.

3. *Roof prism binoculars* have a reputation for representing the state of the art, but the design is almost as old as that of the porro prism. It was first developed by the Zeiss optical company in Jena, Germany, in the nineteenth century and was originally called the pentaprism because of its five internal lenses. Modern roof prisms combine the straight-line, letter H shape of field glasses with the center-focusing dial and dioptric-compensation ring of porro prisms.

Roof prisms generally have better power-to-weight ratios than porro prisms and can be focused more finely (though usually not as closely). They are especially advantageous at hawk watches and shorebirding sites, where long looks at distant birds through heavier porros can make eyes ache and wrists tremble. Because most of the focusing mechanism — all but the dial itself — is enclosed within the housing, roof prisms are also celebrated for their water resistance and durability. Their primary disadvantage is cost.

A number of people have told me that roof prisms are brighter than porro prisms because "the tubes are straighter and the light bounces around less." This statement is simply not true. Actually, roof prisms bend the light one more time than porros, five refractions to four, and if all other things were equal, a roof prism would yield a darker image than a porro prism.

Roof prisms are brighter than porro prisms only when the lens quality and lens coating are superior. Cheaply made roof prisms are bad binoculars, with dark and murky images in all lights. Lens quality cannot be judged in a store, but you can get some sense of the coating quality of any pair of binoculars by holding them at an angle to a fluorescent light and looking at the color around the exit pupil circle. An inexpensive coating reflects a yellowish light, a good coating blue. The roof prisms of two German manufacturers, Zeiss and Leitz, reflect a violet light. Both these optical companies use such superb lenses and lens coating that their 10 × 40s yield brighter images than the 7 × 35s made by many other companies. For this reason and others, Zeiss and Leitz roof prisms are widely regarded as the finest birding binoculars in the world.

4. Twenty-five years ago most pocket binoculars were plastic gimmicks advertised in the back pages of comic books. They magnified at 4 ×, distorted images like a funhouse mirror, and had a half-life of about a week.

Today most pocket binoculars are respectable optical instruments. They are appearing with increasing frequency at bird-watching sites all around the country. One optical company's marketing manager was surprised when my first question was not about their minis. "That's all anyone asks about lately," he said. "They're selling like crazy."

Some minis are down-sized field glasses (you don't want these; see above); most are very compact roof prisms. Several minis in the Bausch & Lomb line incorporate a new design: *the reverse porro prism.* Here the right-angled lenses of the conventional porro prism are turned inside out, so that the objective lenses are next to each other and the ocular lenses are on the outside. Once you stop trying to look through them backward, you'll find that the image is surprisingly good and the close-focus range is amazing. A monarch butterfly landed about six inches from my foot while I was holding a pair of Bausch & Lomb 8 × 24s, and I could count the dots on its wings.

All minis, whatever their design, share two obvious advantages and two not-so-obvious disadvantages. The advantages are weight and portability. Anyone who can lift a china teacup should have no problems with hand tremor or forearm fatigue with minibinoculars, and you can wear a pair of minis all day long without even noticing the binocular strap.

The compromises come in brightness and width of field. All minis have small objective lenses and consequently small exit pupils, usually 3 mm or less. As a result, the image will be somewhat darker than in larger binoculars on overcast days and significantly darker at dawn and dusk. Minis also have very narrow fields of view. Following warblers or sparrows with a pair of minis requires discipline and quick reflexes.

BRAND AND COST

Finding the model that fits your needs is more important than shopping for a particular brand name, but four optical companies deserve mention as representatives of the best in their classes.

At the moment, the middle of the price range is dominated by two companies that manufacture their binoculars in Japan: Nikon and Bushnell/Bausch & Lomb. Both produce a wide variety of field glasses, porros, roof prisms, and minis. If you haven't yet treated yourself to this level of quality, you really ought to do so as soon as possible. Your eyestrain headaches will disappear, and you'll suddenly be able to tell how the roseate tern, groove-billed ani, yellow-bellied flycatcher, and black-whiskered vireo got their names.

If magnification is your overriding concern, you may want to try Nikon's $12 \times$'s. Nikon seems to be the only international company marketing $12 \times$ binocs, and it offers two: a 12×40 porro prism and a 12×36 roof prism. Nikon's 9×30 roof prism is another model I've seen around a number of birders' necks. It combines minilike weight with an unminilike field of view, 6.7 degrees.

Bushnell's range of binoculars is even wider than Nikon's, and the company has a long-standing reputation in the United States for durability and good optics, especially for its porro prisms. Two Bushnell models popular with birders are the 7×35 Custom and the heavy (46 ounce) but bright and powerful 10×50 Discoverer. Recently Bushnell has been equipping many of its porros with an InstaFocus mechanism, a triangular lever that makes for very fast, very simple focusing — even in winter when the user is wearing mittens. The jury is still out on whether the ease of use justifies the loss of precision, however, and some birders prefer the more solid feel of the thumb-focus device on Bushnell's older models. Bausch & Lomb, Bushnell's sister company, has recently introduced a new model, the 8 × 42 Elite. This is a high-quality roof prism designed to compete with those of Zeiss and Leitz, the two German manufacturers that have dominated the top of the price range for decades.

I am currently addicted to a pair of Zeiss 10 × 40s, but my eyes were first opened to the wonders of German optics by a pair of Leitz's one day several winters ago on a New Jersey beach. I was squinting through my old, trusty 7 × 35s at a dark bird far out on a jetty when another birder walked up from behind me. "What have you got?" she asked.

"I'm not sure. A possible purple sandpiper."

"Yeah," she said immediately, "purple sandpipers. Three of them."

I turned around and gave her my best who-are-you-kidding stare.

She laughed, then looped her binoculars off her neck and handed them to me. "Try these," she said.

I took them and looked. Three purple sandpipers zoomed into view. "What are these — ten power?"

"No, seven."

I read the barrel in astonishment: "Leitz 7 × 35." I lifted my own 7 × 35s again. Two of the birds disappeared into the rocks, and the third was only a smudge. I lifted the Leitz's back to my eyes and there all three were again, no-doubt-about-it purple sandpipers. I went back and forth between the two pairs until I was sufficiently depressed. If you'd rather meet next month's mortgage than pay for a pair of Leitz or Zeiss roof prisms, you should try to avoid an experience like this one. On every field trip afterward you'll be left wondering how many more birds you would have identified had you been better equipped.

It is tough to compare Leitz and Zeiss. Both are superb, and distinctions are subtle. I have never met an owner of either who was dissatisfied or sorry to have spent the money. The birding journal *British Birds* surveyed its readers a few years ago and found that 16 percent of those who responded (119 of

732) owned Zeiss 10 × 40s, making it by far the most popular model. "The Zeiss 10 × 40B Dialyt came out very strongly as the most popular make among owners and non-owners alike, again reflecting its tremendous reputation." (This survey also found that 10 × in general is the size of choice among British birders: more than 60 percent of those surveyed owned 10 × 40s or 10 × 50s. Fewer than 5 percent used 7 ×, and the editors called it a "minority glass.")

The one weakness in both Zeiss and Leitz is the Achilles heel of the roof prism design: close-focusing range. Both companies offer a close-focus adjustment. While you're missing that mortgage payment, you should plan to default on your heating bill as well so that you can pay the extra $50–$75 for this option. It will narrow the close-focus range for the 10 × 40 from about 25 feet down to 15 feet or less, depending on your eyesight. The quality of the image is unaffected, and the lenses are not changed. The adjustment is made by squeezing a little room from the rarely used top end of the dioptric-compensation ring to allow for more play in the center-focusing dial. Recently Zeiss has begun making this adjustment in the factory on all rubber-armored 10 × 40 pairs.

Before buying any pair of binoculars, write to the mail order houses (advertised in *Audubon, American Birds, Smithsonian, Astronomy,* and most other natural history magazines) and ask for their complete catalogs. They will send you thick packets of brochures, reviews, price lists, and other information that will give you a much better sense of the full range of brands, models, and styles. This will also place you on their mailing lists so you can be informed of special sales and price changes, which are frequent. Mail order houses regularly sell optical equipment for about 50 percent of the retail price and sometimes for much less.

If there's a simple rule to follow, it's spend as much as you can afford. If you're an active birder, you'll be looking through your binocs for hundreds of hours each year. Why not treat yourself? A trip to Alaska will cost you more than even the most expensive binoculars. The trip will last a week or two. A really good pair of binoculars can last your lifetime.

SPOTTING SCOPES

Is a spotting scope necessary? By the same magnification mathematics described earlier, a 20× scope is only 5 percent stronger than 10× binocs. The 10× power cuts the apparent distance to any bird at any range by 90 percent; 20× cuts it by 95 percent. Above 20×, the principle of diminishing returns sets in strongly: the next 10-power jump, from 20× to 30×, reduces the actual distance by only 1.7 percent more, to 96.7 percent. Magnified 20 times, an eider duck 1,000 yards away seems 50 yards away. Magnified 30 times, the duck seems 33 yards away, and the difference from 20× is almost imperceptible. For a perceptible difference above 20×, you must jump all the way to 40×. At that power the increase in magnification (the thousand-yard eider seems 25 yards away) is less noticeable than the darkening of the image. Is it a king or a common? If you can't tell at 20×, you probably won't be able to tell at 40×.

Field of view is also much less in telescopes than binoculars and decreases dramatically as magnification increases. A typical spotting scope's field of view at 20× at 1,000 yards is 130 feet. At 40× the typical field of view is about 60 feet, barely 1 percent of the full horizon. For fixed-focus scopes, 60× eyepieces can be purchased, and zoom scopes usually go up to 60×, but at that power the field of view becomes so dark and so narrow (about 25 feet at 1,000 yards) that looking at birds through 60× is seldom worth the trouble.

Another potential problem with spotting scopes is not a factor at binocular magnifications. When you scan a field, marsh, or sod farm on a hot day or a lake or bay on a cold day, you are looking through air that is being disturbed by the warmth below it. The air is shaking in the heat. The lower and farther the bird, the more vibrations you're looking through and the harder it becomes to resolve a clear image. At spotting-scope magnifications, especially above 20×, these "heat waves" can make it impossible to tell a buff-breasted sandpiper from a mourning dove or a thick-billed murre from a lobster-trap buoy.

For these reasons and others, some of the very best birders never carry telescopes. They walk around unburdened by tripods and depend on their experience to identify distant birds by behavior, flight style, and context.

For most of us, however, a tripod-mounted scope is a necessary burden.

The scope's extra magnification is only part of its value. Just as important is the stability provided by the tripod. You can locate a peep or duck in your scope, twist the tripod handle to lock the view in place, open your field guide, lean back to the scope to reexamine the bird, look back at the field guide, turn a few pages, lean back to the scope, and so forth. You can study the bird as long as you want without hand tremor or arm fatigue.

For most of us, going scopeless means sacrificing birds that keep their distance and those whose field marks require close, long looks. Shorebirds, female ducks, and perched hawks are the most obvious examples. Pipits, longspurs, and ground-feeding sparrows must also frequently be viewed through a scope.

The good news is that spotting scopes are much easier to shop for than binoculars. Most spotting scopes have the same standard 60 mm objective lens (avoid anything smaller). Weight is not an important factor (the tripod will be bearing it). Close-focus range is not a consideration. The two main differences among spotting scopes involve eyepiece placement and magnification (fixed focus versus zoom).

Eyepiece Placement

Zoom scopes and some fixed-focus scopes have a *straight-through* line of sight: the eyepiece is directly behind the objective lens. The majority of fixed-focus scopes have their eyepiece sockets *offset,* or on a line parallel to the objective lens and above it. Either style is fine. You will have no more problem adjusting to the dogleg line of sight in the offset style than to the equivalent bend in each barrel of a pair of porro prism binoculars.

Birders should be wary, however, of the third eyepiece style — the *angled eyepiece* featured on some fixed-focus scopes. Here the eyepiece socket is set at a 45-degree angle from the objective lens. To see forward, you must hold your head above the scope and look down. These scopes are designed for competitive marksmen (who need to be able to take their eyes from their rifle sights and check their targets through their telescopes with a minimum of motion), not for birders. Because you must face away from your actual line of sight, panning the field searching for birds through an angled eyepiece is tricky. Tracking a flying bird requires the mind-over-matter concentration of a Zen master. You'll also probably find using an angled-eyepiece scope from inside your car not worth the contortion exercise. Finally, should you ever decide to buy a shoulder mount, you'll have to buy yourself a brand new telescope.

Fixed Focus or Zoom?

In fixed-focus scopes the magnification is set by the focal length of the eyepiece: the shorter the eyepiece, the stronger the magnification. To change magnification, you need only unscrew one eyepiece and screw in another, but most users of fixed-focus scopes own only one eyepiece (almost always 20×), so fixed-focus scopes are for practical purposes fixed-magnification scopes. Zoom scopes have internalized this lens-changing procedure. The distance between lenses can be adjusted by twirling the zoom control, and changing magnification is a simple matter.

There's no denying that zoom scopes have cleared their name of the gimmick label they carried a decade ago and are becoming increasingly popular with birders. The restrained and careful *British Birds* has called one zoom, the Bausch & Lomb Discoverer 15–60×60 mm, "arguably the finest [spotting scope] currently on the market." My friends who own zooms — the Bausch & Lomb Discoverer, the Bushnell Spacemaster II, and others — are even more enthusiastic: "You can see the eye color on an eagle!" "You can check the webs on a semipal!" Nevertheless, a few of us hardheaded, old-fashioned owners of fixed-focus scopes cling to the conviction that the value of zooms is more apparent than real.

Even zoom owners concede that there are two potential disappointments in store for anyone using a zoom for the first time. First, zooming up is not as easy as advertisements suggest. You can't simply focus on a bird and then quickly zoom in for a closer view. The focused image is usually lost with any increase in magnification. In effect, zoom scopes have two focusing mechanisms — one for magnification and one for clarity. Resolving a sharp, larger image requires patient and time-consuming adjustment of both.

Furthermore, increases in magnification often make disappointingly little difference. The increased image size when you zoom from 20× to 25× or 30× is almost imperceptible. Once you reach 40×, where the increase is perceptible, all the usual problems of high power set in: the width of field closes down, heat waves and other air disturbances create distortions, and the image darkens. Zoom scopes are subject to the same mathematics and exit pupil limitations as binoculars and fixed-focus scopes. Zooming from 20× to 40× shrinks the exit pupil size from 3 mm (60 mm divided by 20) to 1.5 mm (60 divided by 40). At 60× the exit pupil is a point of light just 1 mm wide. Since the human eye never closes to less than 2 mm, the image in a 60 mm spotting scope at 40× and 60× is always much darker than the naked-eye view.

"But so what?" zoom advocates argue. "You don't *have* to fiddle with the power control every time you look at a bird. What's important is that you have that option available when you need it."

"No," say fixed-focus owners. "What's important is image clarity, and zoom scopes don't compare to fixed focus in clarity."

"Do too!"

"Do not!"

The debate degenerates from there, and the ultimate judgment rests in the eye of the beholder who has invested a couple of hundred bucks in one style or the other.

In deference to my zoom-owning friends, and because zoom image quality has definitely improved in recent years, I won't recommend fixed-focus scopes over zooms, but I will say two things.

1. Don't buy a zoom because you're intrigued by the concept. Try one out in a situation — a club birding trip, for example — where you can look at the same bird from the same distance through both a fixed-focus scope and a zoom. Try it first at the same power and then zoom up. If you enjoy poking sleeping dogs with sharp sticks, ask the zoom owner to show you something in his scope that you can't see in the fixed-focus.

2. If you already own a satisfactory fixed-focus scope but want the zoom option, buy an extra eyepiece or two instead. A 40× eyepiece is the next most useful after 20×. The third most useful is 15×; its wider field of view can be helpful, especially if you are mounting your scope on a shoulder stock for use on a hawk watch or a pelagic trip.

TRIPODS AND ALTERNATIVES

The tripod is one piece of birding equipment you can test adequately in a store — and you should. Most tripods are designed for photography, not for birding. What birders would like is a tripod that could

- open to full, legs-locked extension in no more time than it takes to ask, "Hey, isn't that a wheatear?"
- hold the heaviest telescope rock steady on an 80-degree slope in a 50-mile-an-hour gale;
- fold down to the size of a pocketknife when not in use.

What we have to settle for is something less than that. More than any other birding essential, the tripod must be a compromise. The lightest tripods wobble in gentle breezes. The sturdiest models double the weight of the scope on your shoulder. The most compact, multijointed tripods take the most time to set up and tend to collapse at critical moments. The easiest-to-erect single-jointed tripods are hard to use from inside your car and in other cramped situations. Flip-locking joints are quick but breakable; twist-locking joints are durable but slow. No birders I know like their tripods. Those most satisfied hate their tripods only a little.

Finding a tripod that won't be entirely unsatisfactory involves patient shopping and hands-on testing. Tripods are sold in every camera store, however. If a salesman won't let you abuse his floor samples, you can walk right out and go elsewhere.

The first and most important test is the setup. You should go through this process from start to finish (from fully closed to fully open and back again) several times. Pay special attention to the joint locks. Do they click or screw smoothly and unambiguously into place with a minimum of resistance? Work the centerpost mechanism up and down. Some tripods have a centerpost crank; others have a twist lock. Try both styles and

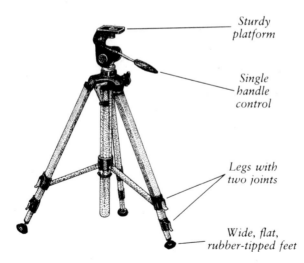

Sturdy platform

Single handle control

Legs with two joints

Wide, flat, rubber-tipped feet

FIGURE 3. *Tripod with Features Desirable for Birdwatching*

see which feels easier to you. After you've opened and closed your tripod 20 or 30 times on a field trip, every hitch in the sequence becomes an irritant.

One essential of tripod shopping: *bring your scope along and mount it on the platform.* You will gain a better sense of the weight of the whole assembly and will be able to test the strength of the tripod platform. Weak platforms will drop under the weight of the scope and will force you to overcorrect for this drift each time you focus on a bird. By bringing your scope along you will also be able to test the screw that will hold the scope to the platform. One friend of mine can't go birding without a screwdriver in his pocket, as he needs to re-tighten this connection about every 30 minutes. His tripod, like many others, was designed to hold a light camera.

Figure 3 illustrates some other features to look for, which include:

1. A platform that reaches your *eye level* when you're standing in a comfortable position without crouching.
2. A *single* handle that controls both vertical and horizontal movement and tightens down quickly to lock the platform in place.
3. The centerpost mechanism you prefer — twist lock or crank.
4. The joint locks you prefer — flip lock or twist lock.
5. Rubber-tipped feet that are *wide* and *flat* enough to resist slipping on rocks or sinking in mud and sand.

Legs that fold into three sections are probably the best choice for birders. Tripods with just two sections (one joint) in each leg are bulky and awkward to carry. Tripods with four (or more) sections tend to rattle and sag.

Selecting carefully pays off in the long run. In an odd way, the quality of your tripod is more important than the quality of your telescope. If you can't stand your tripod, you will climb out of your car near the end of the day, decide not to bother with the scope, walk down the path half a mile, and spot off in the distance — across a lake and two barbed wire fences — a dark and mysterious bird sitting on a telephone pole. Your binocs tell you only that it's something good, something you have never seen before (a South Polar skua? a Steller's sea eagle?). You squint and stare for all your eyes are worth, but it's no use. Just as you've decided that the bird might wait for you to run back to the car for the scope, it lifts up and flies off into the sunset. Thanks to your tripod, you'll never know what it was.

The two alternatives to the tripod are the *shoulder stock* and the *car window mount*. Neither is a complete substitute.

I most often see birders toting their scopes on shoulder stocks at hawk watch sites and on pelagic trips. Shoulder stocks are better than tripods for hawk watching because the birds are often directly overhead and moving too quickly to be followed with a tripod. They are better on boats because the floor is so unsteady. In most other situations, however, tripods are superior to shoulder stocks, and the average shoulder-stock-equipped birder probably looks through his scope for less than five minutes per hour. Shoulder stocks are harder to hold steady than binoculars, and the extra magnification of the telescope accentuates hand tremor. For a view steady enough to be valuable, you must find a tree or car roof to rest against, which neutralizes the advantage of portability, or you must lie down, which means losing a lot of your vertical angle of vision and getting cold and wet.

Birders who do a lot of birding from inside their cars sometimes find car window mounts useful. These are tripod heads with clamps designed to tighten around the window glass when the window is rolled up three or four inches. Before spending your money on this accessory, try toting a pillow along in your car and resting the scope on it — or use a folded jacket. You might not get quite as steady a view, but you'll be able to move your scope quickly to the opposite side of the car, and since you can leave your scope on your tripod, you can hop out and chase after birds with far less fuss.

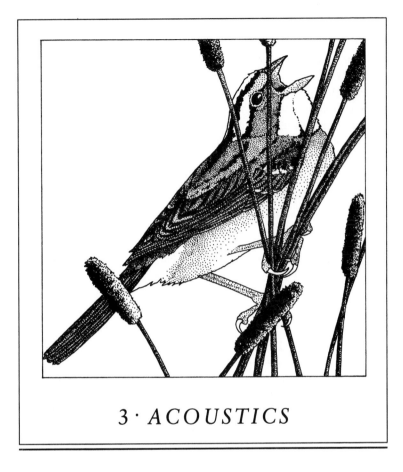

3 · ACOUSTICS

I FIRST REALIZED that there was more to birdwatching than bird *watching* on my second official field trip, "An Introduction to the Spring Migration," led by Frank Mead of the University of Florida.

I was standing in a circle of fellow novices, awaiting Dr. Mead's arrival at the lakeside rendezvous spot, when the trees overhead suddenly filled with birds.

"What are they?" someone asked.

"Chickadees," someone answered. "Or maybe sparrows."

They looked like flying blots to me. It was one of those Florida mornings when the haze is so bright that it hurts to lift your eyes. Fumbling with my new binoculars, I managed to follow one blot as it worked its way to the end of a cypress limb, threw back its head, and sang: *buzzy-buzzy-zip!*

"What's that one, a goldfinch?"

"It's tiny. Is it a kinglet?"

Dr. Mead pulled up alongside us, his window rolled down. "Good morning," he said. "What've you got?"

I shrugged. "Can't tell. It's at the top of the tree and right in the sun."

Buzzy-buzzy-zip!

"Parula warbler," Dr. Mead announced, without looking up. He pulled his car to the side, opened his door, and while lacing his boots, reeled off a dozen identifications: "There's a prairie . . . There's a pine . . . a great-crested . . . cardinal . . . prothonotary warbler . . . yellow-billed cuckoo . . . summer tanager . . ."

What an amazing trick, I remember thinking. He hasn't even glanced at one bird yet!

Perhaps only a beginner as green as I was that day can appreciate how lucky we are to have birdsong. More experienced birders tend to take for granted two odd facts: first, that the most visible animals on our planet are also the most vocal; and second, that the vast majority of them have voices we can distinguish and identify. It didn't have to be that way. Evolution might have led birds to develop like bats and to rely primarily on ultrasonic frequencies. In a slightly different ecological system, under a different set of evolutionary pressures, birds might have developed smell or some other sense as their means of individual recognition. Instead we live in a world where the sounds of birds are as inevitable as the rising of the sun, and the first problem faced by novice ear birders is acoustic overload.

On a typical spring morning in a typical patch of northeastern woods, you will hear three or four times as many birds as you will see. Of those you do see, probably half are birds you would not have seen if you hadn't heard them first. In all but wide open habitats, ears are far more effective instruments for detecting birds than eyes. Ears don't need clear lines of sight, and of course, most woodland birds seem to prefer being heard to being seen.

Passerines are particularly determined singers. Individual song sparrows, black-throated green warblers, Kirtland's warblers, brown thrashers, and mockingbirds have been recorded singing more than 2,000 times in a day. In 1954 L. de Kiriline and a very determined red-eyed vireo set a world record that has stood for more than thirty years: 22,197 songs counted from a single wild bird in a single day.

Birding by ear is not easy, however. One problem is sensory. As we age, our ears lose their ability to hear high pitches. Many adults have difficulty distinguishing pitches above 4,000 hertz (cycles per second), approximately the pitch of the top note of a piano and the call of the killdeer. Yet the killdeer's call is 1,000 hertz *lower* than the average frequency for the songs of North American wood warblers, 5,400 hertz. Many passerines hit notes above 7,000 hertz. The eastern kingbird and brown-headed cowbird peak at more than 10,000 cycles per second.

Another problem is conceptual. Humans are visually oriented creatures. Most birders find it far easier to remember a bird's shape and colors than its calls and songs. Only people who have had musical training seem able to memorize birdsongs as pure sound. Most of us must convert them into something else.

SONOGRAMS

The closest things we have to visual pictures of birdsongs are sonograms, which are featured in the Robbins field guide and in most ornithology textbooks and which appear frequently in journal articles about birdsong. For birders who have the patience to study them, sonograms can be helpful analytical tools.

A sonogram is a plot drawn by a recording instrument called

the sonograph. The darkness of the trace indicates volume; the vertical axis indicates pitch in hertz or kilohertz; and the horizontal axis indicates times in half-second increments.

The first variable, volume, is the least useful and can be deceptive. Since the loudness of any recorded song is determined by the circumstances of the recording — primarily how close the microphone was to the singer — trying to compare the volume of one species' song to that of another by comparing the darkness of their sonograms is a mistake. You'll note in Robbins, for example, that the pretty whistle of the white-crowned sparrow has traced as dark a pattern as the bugling call of the herring gull. As an identification clue, the only value of the volume measure is in its indication of changes of volume *within the same bird's* song.

Reading sonograms for pitch can also be deceptive — first, because most birders who have not had musical training have difficulty determining absolute pitch, and second, because even musically trained human ears do not hear differences and changes in pitch with the same accuracy throughout the entire range of birdsong. The rule to remember is: *the higher on the scale it is, the larger the change of pitch must be to be perceptible.* Below 2,000 hertz, relatively small changes in pitch are discernible. Most of us can easily distinguish the call of the northern raven from that of the common crow, for example, although their sonograms are similar and show that both calls are pitched at about 1,000 hertz. Much more concentration is required to hear equivalent differences in the range above 2,000 hertz — distinguishing the common flicker's call from the pileated woodpecker's, for instance. Above 4,000 hertz (again, this is the pitch of the highest key on the piano), things really become difficult. If you can hear differences in pitch in this range, you have excellent ears. The first note of the golden-winged warbler's song, at about 7,000 hertz, is nearly 1,000 hertz higher than the blue-winged warbler's, but it's a rare birder who can hear a difference in pitch.

The problem is that many passerines sing their whole songs in pitches above 4,000 hertz: the brown creeper, the eastern kingbird, Bewick's wren, the blue-gray gnatcatcher, the grass-hopper sparrow, the Tennessee, Nashville, Cape May, protho-notary, worm-eating, blackburnian, blackpoll, golden-winged, and blue-winged warblers, and others. Most of us can hear most of the notes in these songs, but we cannot separate one song from another on the basis of pitch.

The key to using sonograms, Joseph C. Beaver has noted, is paying careful attention to the third variable — duration, the length of the song across the horizontal axis of the graph — and interpreting that in conjunction with whatever relative changes of pitch can be heard to get a precise sense of different species' song patterns. "Though many birdsongs are far too high to conclude anything about absolute pitch, it is evident that they go up or down relative to themselves, and on the so-nogram, the pattern of ups and downs, and the pattern of noise and silence, is [also] evident."

Beaver recommends reading sonograms while listening to a tape or record of the songs and learning to time the alterations of noise and silence in each. "Here's an old piano-tuner's trick: whisper 'from Milwaukee to Chicago' over and over again as fast as possible with the stress on the second syllable of 'Mil-waukee.' The time between successive 'wauk's' will be approxi-mately one second." This technique can enable you to distinguish between a number of otherwise similar songs. The worm-eating warbler's song, for example (see figure 4), is often compared to (and confused with) the chipping sparrow's, but it's actually much shorter. The sparrow's trill, the sonogram shows, is two and one-half seconds long; the warbler's is barely one and one-half seconds. The songs of the field spar-row and the prairie warbler are even easier to confuse. Both sing a steady, rising trill. Again, though, the sparrow's song is longer than the warbler's, three seconds to one and a half.

By considering the song's length and the frequency with which the bird sings in one minute, you can frequently make surprisingly accurate identifications. On Sanibel Island, Flor-ida, Beaver once identified a life bird before he ever laid his eyes on it. He'd noticed that the sonogram of the black-whis-kered vireo's song showed a pattern of two pairs of doubled

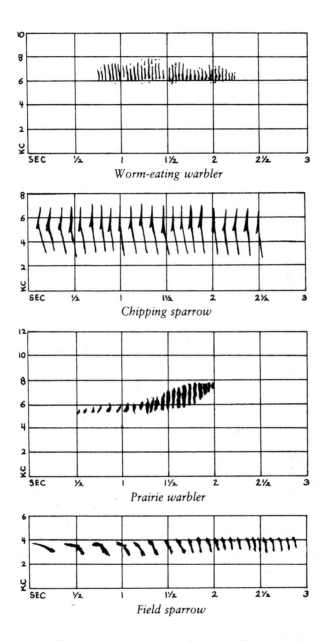

FIGURE 4. *Four Sonograms. Darkness indicates volume, the vertical axis indicates pitch, and the horizontal axis indicates time.*

notes separated by a space of exactly one second, and his field guide told him the song was repeated twenty to thirty-two times a minute. "I heard a vireo-type song of this time pattern in some trees in the Bailey tract of the J. Ding Darling Refuge, and immediately knew it was the bird."

"It is a simple fact," Beaver concludes, "that one can identify a heard song by reading the picture of the song, just as one may identify a seen bird by looking at a picture of the bird."

Beaver admits, however, that his is a minority opinion. Most ear birders rely on other techniques.

PHONETICS AND MNEMONICS

Most field guide descriptions of birdsong combine a verbal sketch of the song's general characteristics with a phonetic transliteration. These descriptions are best used only to confirm birds you've already identified by sight. They are rarely useful for identifying unseen birds. Here are three such descriptions (from Edgar M. Reilly) of the songs of a trio of related songbirds. Can you identify the three species?

1. The call is a simple *click;* the song is variable but consists of many short, quick notes interspersed with long, clear, down-slurred whistles, [such] as *wheeeoo.* Each individual may have 2–3 songs.
2. The song is a series of clear, sweet, high-pitched phrases separated by short pauses and delivered at a slow pace; the notes are a harsh *see-a* or *see-eep* and a sibilant, almost chattering *she-she-she-she-she* series.
3. A complaining *queee* call; the song is a series of short, monotonously repeated phrases from a repertoire of 20–40 robinlike notes, separated by distinct pauses. One series has been transliterated as *cherry-owit, cheree, sissy-a-wit, tee-oo.*

One problem with phonetic transliterations is that birds are under no obligation to articulate proper consonants. The phonetics must be conceived in the ear of the listener, and so transliterations vary widely from one source to another. Here, for example, are two more interpretations of the song of bird 1.

John K. Terres: "One [call] is sharp *chick! ticha wheeyo chick!*, another, *chick-ah-per-weeoo-chick.*"

Witmer Stone: "The simplest songs run: *tick, che-weeo, sick; chuck, che-wee-ju; ill, che-wheo, chip; see it, see, wee-ah;* and a shorter: *chick wissa.* Other more complicated phrases are: *chick, che-weary-o-wissel; chuck, see, chur-a-lury, stick; chewirra; chu, wee, che switz, ah, wee; pechitcha wirra, wee; swee-a, spititulia, sip.*"

These renditions are so good that you may have guessed bird 1 by now. It is the white-eyed vireo. Bird 2 is the solitary vireo, and bird 3 the red-eyed. You probably won't be able to use these phonetics, though, the next time you're out in the field. Phonetic transliterations are nearly impossible to remember. They are strings of nonsense sounds and so fly out of the mind like swallows leaving a barn.

Writing down your own phonetic transcriptions is a good first step to learning any new bird's song, because the note taking will encourage you to listen closely. But if you want a practical and reliable identification clue, you must eventually convert your notes into something shorter and more memorable: a *mnemonic.*

The simplest form of verbal mnemonic (pronounced "nihmon-ick") is the acoustic analogy. The red-breasted nuthatch's call sounds as if it came from a toy horn. The rusty blackbird's is like a squeaky hinge on an old fence. The kingfisher's flight call is like a baby's rattle. The wood thrush plays the scale like a flutist. The Virginia rail oinks like a pig. The call of the yellow rail sounds like two pebbles being tapped together. The call of the ring-necked pheasant sounds like someone reeling in laundry on a rusty clothesline. The call of the boreal owl drips like water.

A more sophisticated form of mnemonic works by species-to-species association. The song of the rose-breasted grosbeak,

Roger Tory Peterson has observed, is like the robin's but seems to be sung with more feeling — "as if a robin has taken voice lessons." An evening grosbeak's call, Peterson has noted, is like a "glorified house sparrow's." The scarlet tanager, Arthur Allen taught his students at Cornell, sings like "a robin in a hurry with a cold."

Another common mnemonic is the English "translation." The rufous-sided towhee's "Drink your tea" may be the best known of these, or the ovenbird's "Teacher, teacher, teacher!"

"Trees, trees, murmuring trees," sings the black-throated green warbler.

"Pretty, pretty Rachel," the magnolia warbler sings sometimes. Its longer song sounds like "She knew she was right; yes, she knew she was right."

"Sweet, sweet, sweeter than sweet," sings the yellow warbler.

"Pizza!" shouts the acadian flycatcher.

The olive-sided flycatcher's whistle is usually transliterated as "Quick, three beers." This apparently applies to eastern breeders only, however. Rich Stallcup has pointed out that the western breeders' whistle sounds more like "I say there."

A good mnemonic does two things: (1) it condenses and highlights the most distinctive elements of the song; (2) it links you back to the bird's identity. If there's a call that identifies the novice ear birder, it's "I know that bird! I know that bird! What *is* it?" Generally, this call is accompanied by gnashing of teeth and desperate binocular stabs into impenetrable greenery. What has usually happened in these cases is the mnemonic has helped with step 1 but not with step 2.

When you memorize a mnemonic, always try to incorporate a mental image that will take you back to the species. "Drink your tea" is a successful mnemonic for you only if it generates a picture of the towhee. To memorize the cue, picture a towhee wearing teabags around its neck or sitting in a teacup. Or you might think of the call as "Drink tow-hee" and imagine lifting the teacup to your mouth with the bird inside.

Absurd and ridiculous images are the most memorable. Picture a kingfisher flying with a baby's rattle stuck in its mouth.

Mnemonic: Towhee in a Teacup

Picture a red-breasted nuthatch blowing on a toy horn — and make it a *red* horn; otherwise, you'll be out in the woods saying, "I know that's a nuthatch! I know that's a nuthatch! Which one is it?"

To remember that the evening grosbeak sounds like "glorified house sparrow," notice how it behaves at backyard feeders: it is the only bird that gobbles down birdseed faster than the house sparrows and one of the few backyard birds that house sparrows will not challenge. The evening grosbeak is, in a sense, king of the house sparrows.

The red-eyed vireo's song can be translated as: "Here I am. Where are you? Here I am. I'm up here. Where are you?" On and on the *monologue* continues *monotonously,* and (if you live east of the one-hundredth meridian) the red-eyed vireo is one bird you should encounter with monotonous frequency. It is believed to be the most common bird in deciduous forests, and it sings endlessly.

Think of the yellow warbler as a piece of candy — bright yellow with cherry stripes. "Sweet, sweet, sweeter than sweet."

Birds whose visual appearances are not striking are the hardest to incorporate into mnemonics. The veery, for example, has a loud, beautiful, and distinctive song that seems to whirl down into a well, echoing off the sides. The bird itself, though, is drab and hard to picture. Here the trick is to play on the bird's name: "The veery sings a *veering* song."

Someone taught me to memorize the fish crow's call as if it came from a crow with a clothespin clipped to its nose. But the fish crow is visually identical to the common crow, and out in the field, hearing that nasal "caw!" I kept forgetting which crow it was that was supposed to wear the clothespin. I had to modify the mental image so that it was a picture of a crow with a *fish* pinned to its nose.

Inventing your own mnemonics is usually better than memorizing someone else's. Then the linking images will spring quickly from your subconscious, polished and sharpened by your own personal references. For the ovenbird my reference is the mental image of the cardboard oven we had in my kindergarten class; the bird jumps out of it, calling "Teacher, teacher, teacher!" My mnemonic for the white-eyed vireo is "Check! Pierre, check!" and "Check! Hey you, Pierre, check!" I picture a little man at a Parisian outdoor cafe — James Joyce, I guess it is — wearing thick, wire-rimmed glasses (so that his eyes look white) and trying to get some service. "Pizza!" is linked in my mind to the acadian flycatcher because I don't like green peppers on pizza and the acadian is the greenest of the *Empidonax*. The connection is crooked, but it works.

An excellent exercise is to list the twenty most numerous and vocal birds in your area and then try to write down your own mnemonic or phonetic translation for each. You'll probably discover you identify most on your list without thinking, but by forcing yourself to describe *how* you know them you will gain a basis for memorizing others.

Once you've learned the key species for your area and have built up your repertoire of references, you can move on to more elegant and powerful mnemonics. Randolph Little, who grew up in Ithaca, New York, and has been contributing re-corded bird sounds to Cornell's Laboratory of Ornithology for more than twenty years, recalls how Arthur Allen taught his students to distinguish two of the most difficult of warbler songs. "Doc Allen taught us to remember Tennessee warbler by thinking of a tennis ball bouncing. 'Tennis' suggests 'Tennessee' and when you bounce a tennis ball it first bounces several times distinctly, then accelerates toward the end as the bounces shorten and finally blur together: *see......see.....see..... see..see..see..see-see-see.*

"The way he taught us to remember the Nashville's song was to remember the association of Nashville and Tennessee, and notice that the Nashville's song is like the Tennessee's — the same beginning, with spaced notes then acceleration, but it doesn't have the third part, the blurring together. *Nashville is only a part of Tennessee.*"

THE SECRET TRICK

Four S's are part of every ear identification, and only one of them is sound. The other three are site, season, and situation. In the majority of aural identifications they are critical factors. Site, season, and situation form the context for every bird sound, and depending on them is the secret trick of ear birders everywhere.

1. You are canoeing on a lake in Minnesota under a full moon in May and hear the yodeling wail of a loon. Which loon is it?
2. A hummingbird sings from a telephone line in California. Which species is it?
3. It's 2:00 A.M. on an October night in West Virginia, and flocks of birds are passing overhead, honking. What are they?
4. In Connecticut on a bright afternoon in January a bird the size of a sparrow is singing a long, complicated song from a television antenna. What is it?

Your score on this quiz will have nothing to do with your sense of pitch or your mastery of mnemonics. If you guessed question 1 correctly, you knew that only one loon occurs inland south of Canada in late spring: *the common loon.* If you were right on question 2, you knew that the only North American hummingbird likely to sing from a perch is *Anna's hummingbird.* For question 3 you needed to know that only one honker can be expected in numbers in fall in West Virginia: *the Canada goose.* Question 4 is more difficult because dozens of birds the size of sparrows sing long and complicated songs. If you live in New England, though, you've probably learned that only one such bird sings regularly from television antennas in January: *the house finch.* In each of these cases, as in most aural identifications, the precise acoustical qualities of the bird's sound — pitch, rhythm, texture, and so on — are secondary. The key is *context:* site, season, and situation.

Take a Minnesotan who believes he knows the call of the common loon, and fly him to the Mackenzie River delta in the Yukon. There *two* species of loons call in yodeling wails — the common and the yellow-bill. Can the Minnesotan tell the difference? Probably not. Does this say anything about his ability to identify common loons on the lakes back home? Absolutely not. Making identifications by context ("I'm in Minnesota, so that must be a common loon") is a basic operating principle of ear birding.

How do most birders distinguish the *peter, peter, peter* of the tufted titmouse from the *ti-wee, ti-wee, ti-wee* of the plain titmouse? By looking at their range maps! In Ohio, it's *peter, peter, peter;* in Nevada, it's *ti-wee, ti-wee, ti-wee.* By the same logic, an elongated black bird clacking and whistling in Oklahoma is the great-tailed grackle; in Georgia it's a boat-tailed grackle. In Kentucky in the middle of winter a bubbly trill from the banks of a mountain stream is the song of a winter wren. In Idaho in the middle of winter a bubbly trill from the banks of a mountain stream is the song of a dipper.

And those distinctions are easy. An experienced ear birder relies on much more subtle contextual clues on every trip into the field. Walking in a wooded, wet swamp in coastal Delaware in the first week of April, she hears a metallic *chink* coming from low in a bushy tangle, and she names the bird: "Louisiana waterthrush!" Walking in the same swamp two months later, in the last week of May, she hears a metallic *chink* coming from the same bushy tangle and calls out, "Northern waterthrush!"

"How did you *do* that!?" asks the stunned novice. "The two waterthrushes sound identical to me."

The expert only smiles and shrugs, following the unwritten tradition of expert ear birders everywhere: *keep the secret trick secret.*

The truth is that the expert knows the two waterthrushes have different migration schedules. An early waterthrush is more likely to be a Louisiana, a late one more likely to be a northern. In different circumstances — for example, the same place, same bush, in the *middle* of the migration period — the expert wouldn't have been able to pull off her trick. In that context, the two waterthrushes would have sounded identical to her too.

Some contextual clues can be picked up in an armchair. Studying migration timing and breeding range maps will dramatically improve your "ears." But there's no substitute for raw experience. The most useful clues are locally specific and won't be found in field guides. Is the flicker or the pileated woodpecker more likely in your backyard? Are fish crows possible in woods across the street? Do solitary vireos ever sing in your area? When do the juncos leave your county on spring migration? When do the chipping sparrows arrive?

You don't need to do a focused exercise to collect this knowledge. You'll absorb the answers to these questions and hundreds of others without even realizing it. They simply come with time. You need not even worry about identifying all the sounds you hear. It is enough at first just to tune into the sounds. Birds are singing or calling outside your door every day of the year — morning, noon, and night, winter, spring, summer, and fall.

EAR BIRDING AFTER DARK

For a consciousness-raising experience in nocturnal birding, try spending a night or two in a sleeping bag in your backyard. You're likely to be very surprised how much the walls of your house have been blocking the sounds of the birds in your own neighborhood.

It's often said that owls are detected less frequently than they should be because most of us sleep with our windows shut during late winter and early spring, when owls do most of their calling. Actually, though, in most areas of the country, opening your windows will not increase your chances of hearing an owl very much. The only North American owl that frequents residential areas and has a call loud enough to penetrate open windows from long distances is the barred owl. It is the barred's resonant "*Who* cooks for *you*? *Who* cooks for *you-allll*?" that is the archetypal owl call of Hollywood soundtracks and that has given many nonbirders the impression that all owls hoot.

Our largest owl, the great horned, has a call so low pitched and softly textured that you're not likely to hear it from indoors unless one lands in a tree within fifty yards of your house. The sweet tremolo whistle of the screech owl doesn't carry much farther. The maximum distance for detecting a screech owl through an open window is probably less than a hundred yards.

Naturally, the more time you spend outdoors at night, the better your chances for hearing an owl. For the best chance, you have to be outdoors all night, listening at 3:00 or 4:00 A.M., after car traffic and other human sounds have stopped and night's natural sounds have taken over.

Even birds with louder calls can pass undetected by birders who spend their nights indoors. I used to wonder why I never heard any whip-poor-wills in my neighborhood in New Jersey. The species is a common breeder nearby in the Pine Barrens, and its famous three-note call is loud and persistent. I thought any migrant that stopped for the night in the woods at the end of our street, a hundred yards from our house, would certainly make its presence known. Then one May night, house guests and a shortage of bedrooms forced me to sleep on the porch. I woke past midnight to a strange sound, something like a muffled hiccough: *ip* (ten-second pause) *ip* (ten-second pause) *ip*. I couldn't identify it, and it seemed to be coming from deep in the woods. Was a walk down the street and a search in the dark worth a try? I sat up and spotted a whip-poor-will in the moonlight, thirty feet from the porch, perched on the fencepost next to our mailbox. What luck, I had time to think — a mystery owl off in the woods and a whip-poor-will right here. Then the bird on the post called again: *ip . . . ip*. The call was so restrained and ventriloqual I had to close my eyes again to be sure it was the same one I'd been listening to.

Of the diurnal birds that sing at night, one is notorious. Under a full moon in May, June, or July, the mockingbird will sing all night, apparently taking one breath just before dusk and the next sometime long after dawn. On and on the song goes, so piercing and steady that insomniacs regularly retaliate with sticks, stones, and even gunfire.

The other diurnal birds that sing after dark have quieter voices. They include the yellow-billed and black-billed cuckoos, the eastern wood peewee, the ovenbird, the yellow-breasted chat, the wood thrush, and at least five sparrows — field, swamp, vesper, grasshopper, and Henslow's. To hear these you need to be out in the open air.

Sleeping outdoors in April, May, September, or October will also give you a new perception of the passerine migration. If it's a clear, starry night with a cold front pushing through, the air can be filled with the cheeps and chirps of migrating birds. Some sound so close it seems you could reach up and catch a veery or a grosbeak in your hand. These are the birds you will not see by day — the "flyovers" who are bypassing your area for points south.

"Flyovers" outnumber the birds you will see by at least one order of magnitude. A nocturnal census conducted in Canada in the fall of 1982 proved this point. On nine nights in September, migrants were counted by call notes as they passed over four different observation points in Ontario. The averages at each site varied from 3,000 to 7,000 songbirds per *hour*! The counts on September 10–11 and 27–28 were particularly interesting, since Swainson's thrushes were heard in the thousands over Sudbury and Kingston on those two nights, yet observers couldn't find a single thrush in either place the following morning. "If the night calls had gone unnoticed," wrote Paul Lehman in summary, "the thrush migration would have been seriously misjudged."

WINTER AND FALL

Winter, the quietest season, is the best time to begin training your ears. Since the calls of all songbirds are simpler and more repetitive during the winter, they are more easily mastered. Also, the lack of foliage means it's much easier to make a visual match of call to caller — a crucial element in memorizing the sound. Birds with species-distinctive voices that call throughout winter include all North American crows, jays, chickadees, titmice, and nuthatches, almost all woodpeckers, and most finches and wrens. Good ear birders can also identify unseen sparrows in winter by subtle differences in their chips, but this usually requires experience and heavy reliance on context.

The end of winter can be heard before it is seen. On bright days in late January or early February, house finches, titmice, cardinals, robins, chickadees, white-throated sparrows, and other birds begin tuning up for spring with "subsongs," abbreviated or muted versions of the songs they will shortly be singing in full.

Paying careful attention to the sounds of the woods in late winter will radically improve your efficiency when the southern migrants return in April and May. "It's doing your homework while the snow's still on the ground that will make or break you as an ear birder," says Randolph Little. "Getting out in the field for the eight weeks before the spring migrants arrive to listen to the nonmigrants is crucial." When the migrants do arrive, the woods are so filled with sounds that it's just not possible to track down every call. If you've done your "preseason" training, though, you won't even notice the calls and songs of the resident birds. Your ear will tune them out, and you'll be able to focus on the unfamiliar sounds — the calls of the birds that *are* worth tracking down.

Knowing the calls of the residents helps you again in fall when the migrants pass back through your area on their way south. Warblers, vireos, and thrushes are generally silent in autumn and much harder to spot — but most of them will associate in mixed feeding parties with the resident birds that are still calling, especially nuthatches, titmice, and chickadees. One theory is that the migrants follow after the residents because the local birds know where the best feeding areas are. Whatever the reason for the phenomenon, there is no better way to find woodland migrants in autumn than to track down the call notes of nonmigrants.

FIELDS AND SHORES

Ear birding can be helpful away from the woods too. The water pipit, Sprague's pipit, the bobolink, the four North American longspurs, the snow bunting, and many other open-area birds call in flight and can be identified more accurately and at much greater distance by sound than by sight. "I'll tell you how to identify a water pipit," a cynical veteran once announced. "Pick out a dot flying away, wait until it's at least half a mile off, and then shout, 'There goes a water pipit, everybody. I heard it!'"

Several shorebirds are more readily identified at a distance by ear than eye. The killdeer, the snipe, the willet, and the two yellowlegs are obvious examples. Experienced birders can also separate by ear the piping and snowy plovers (two notes versus three), the golden and black-bellied plovers (a tinny *kweee-eee-a* versus a rich and mellow *pee-a-wee*), and the most problematic pair of common shorebirds in North America: the short-billed and long-billed dowitchers. Some birders claim the short-billed says its name, *dow-wu-cher;* others hear the call as *tu-tu-tu* or *phew-phew-phew.* In any case, it's usually a lower-pitched, three-note call. The long-billed's call is generally a higher-pitched single note, universally transcribed in field guides as *keek*. A mnemonic that might help you with this difficult pair is, "The short has the long call, the long has the short call."

In 1975 Allan R. Phillips sparked a controversy that still burns when he claimed in a carefully documented and very pointed article in *American Birds* that birders had been confusing western and semipalmated sandpipers for years because they'd been depending on a visual field mark, the supposed difference in bill length and shape, to make the distinction between the species. After examining and measuring specimens in more than a dozen collections, Phillips argued that the overlap between short-billed male westerns and long-billed female semipals meant that "most semipalmated sandpipers are safely distinguishable from western sandpipers only by voice or by bill measurements combined with careful determination of sex." Since the second option is not possible for anyone without a collecting license, those birders who accept Phillips's analysis must rely on their ears to identify two of the most numerous birds on the North American continent.

Few shorebirding experts seem to share Phillips's belief that the visual distinctions are as useless as he claims (and we'll return to this debate in chapter 9), but most do agree that he is right about the voice difference. It is the most reliable way to separate these two peeps. "To me," Phillips notes, "[the semipalmated's] call or location note has a *chit-chit* quality, lower pitched than the almost shrill *cheep* of a western."

FOR YOUR EARS ONLY

A number of other pairs of problematic species are so visually similar that they are ordinarily inseparable except by voice: the trumpeter and tundra swans, western and whiskered screech owls, common and Antillean nighthawks, Couch's and tropical kingbirds, eastern and western peewees, and other species. In areas where both members of any of these pairs appear, you are only fooling yourself (and undermining your credibility) if you claim an identification without hearing a call.

North America's most notorious "ear only" birds are the

Empidonax *Flycatcher*

Empidonax flycatchers. This single genus has eight species generally separable from each other only by voice. The eastern complex includes the least, willow, alder, and acadian flycatchers; the western complex includes the least, the willow, and the four western empids — the dusky, Hammond's, western, and gray flycatchers. Adding to the confusion, each half of the country has another empid that is separable by sight from all the others only under ideal conditions: the yellow-bellied in the East and the buff-breasted in the West.

The icing on this rock-hard cake is the fact that all ten species are frequently silent on migration and refuse to give any clue to their identities away from their nesting grounds. Several birders I know reserve just two places on their year lists for the *Empidonax,* one for the local breeder and the other for all other members of the group, labeled "*Empidonax* species." Some don't even bother with that distinction.

"Uh-oh," I announced on a recent bird hike. "Here's an empidonax."

"What's the problem?" said my wife. "Just keep walking."

IS HEARING BELIEVING?

It would be nice to end this chapter with a claim that birders who learn to use their ears will live happily forever after.

Unfortunately, it just ain't so. Starlings can call like killdeers, blue jays can scream like red-shouldered hawks, catbirds can sound like thrashers, thrashers can sound like mockingbirds, and mockingbirds can sound like a Big Day in a nightmare. Birders who depend too much on their ears are just as susceptible to error as birders who depend too much on their eyes. What *is* true is that following your ears will lead you to discoveries you would never make by eye alone.

My brother Greg was walking hand in hand with a female companion along a forest trail in Illinois one afternoon when he heard a familiar sound: *Kah-erk!*

"Hear that?" he said. "Ring-necked pheasant."

His friend gave him a warm look of admiration. "You know bird calls?"

"I know that one. It's supposed to sound like someone reeling in the laundry on an old rusty clothesline."

Kah-erk!

"Let's cut through the woods," said Greg. "You've got to see this bird. It's huge and beautiful."

Greg led the way into a thick and tangled brush. There was no path. Ten steps into the woods, they were forced to walk backward to keep the briars out of their faces. Fifty steps in, they were creeping on their hands and knees.

Kah-erk! Kah-erk!

The brush parted at last, only to reveal a cyclone fence that seemed to mark the park's boundary. There was no going back now, though, and Greg persisted. He led the way along the fence, following the call of the bird, until they found a break, squeezed through, and staggered out to the road beyond.

By this point the friend had lost some enthusiasm. "Where the hell are we?"

Kah-erk! Kah-erk! The sound was louder than ever.

Greg hurried across the road, looked down a knoll, and spotted his pheasant: a woman in curlers reeling in the last of her laundry from her old, rusty clothesline.

4 · MIGRATION

A STRING OF SWALLOWS on a telephone wire, a V of geese against an autumn sky, a cluster of kinglets in a backyard pine, a solitary eagle drifting down a mountain ridge. Our clearest mental images of birds are most often pictures of migration. For many of us, birdwatching *is* migration watching. And the beauty surpasses the understanding. Of the how, where, when, and why of bird migration, only the why is easy to answer.

Why do birds migrate? *Because they can.* "Nature abhors a vacuum," Chris Mead has written. "If there were [for example] no birds in higher latitudes to exploit the flush of insect food, there would be a vacuum on a huge scale." Other animals migrate — crabs, fish, turtles, caribou, whales — but birds have flight, the speediest and most cost-efficient means of travel, so migration is an especially rewarding ecological strategy for them. Birds have left no "vacuums" on Planet Earth. They live in all the habitable regions we know and in many that would otherwise be considered uninhabitable.

Nearly half of all avian species in the world migrate. Most that don't live year-round in the tropics and subtropics. Of the 800-plus species that have been recorded in North America, more than 600 are migratory. Generally, the colder the winters in your area, the higher the percentage of birds you see will be migrants and the more your birding will involve tuning in to the migration seasons. Of the 215 birds that nest in Michigan, only 20 are nonmigrants. Of the approximately 300 species seen annually in North Dakota, only a dozen are nonmigrants. In Churchill, Manitoba, only 5 of the more than 200 species found annually do not migrate.

Migration has developed in species after species because it is, apparently, the natural consequence of two phenomena — the tendency of all populations to expand and the seasonality of the earth's climate. As a species expands away from its home base, it eventually encounters autumn or winter weather that is too cold for it. The colonizers must retreat until the urge to breed and the crowded conditions in the home base force them to move again. Evolution takes over from there. Those individuals whose biological clocks happen to coincide most closely with the springtime warming breed with the most success. Those that move too soon risk death by starvation; those that move too late find the good territories already occupied and their potential mates taken. The offspring of the successful breeders are selected to breed themselves.

After many millions of years of evolution, each species has developed its own routes, and most have fine-tuned their migration timing with extreme precision. Each individual migrant is competing with all other members of the same sex and species. Each year's race is won by those that follow just the right routes to arrive at just the right spot at exactly the right moment. Off-course vagrants, early arrivals, and late-season lingerers are the birds that get the exclamation marks in local birding reports. The migrants that deserve our awe are those we take for granted — the oriole that appears in the sycamore across the street every spring in the first few days of May, the flock of juncos that returns to our feeder each year in the second week of October, the two loons that come spring after spring to the same corner of the same lake right on schedule.

I once listened to Alan Brady tell a carful of birders about an experience he had with a saw-whet owl that had wintered in his yard for several years. One November evening, knowing the owl was due back, Alan went out to its favorite tree and broke off some branches to give the owl a good roosting spot. The next morning he walked out to check his work, and there was the saw-whet staring back at him.

"That's amazing," someone said. "That you knew just when he'd come."

"Well, I've got a calendar to look at," Alan said. "How about the owl?"

PHYSIOLOGY I:
BRAINS, BODIES, AND FLIGHT STYLES

How birds navigate on migration is the subject of dozens of books, hundreds of doctoral dissertations, and thousands of journal articles and is a mystery still largely unsolved. At the moment the cues used by various birds are believed to include visual landmarks, internal clocks, smells, polarized and ultraviolet light, infrasound, stellar and solar movements, barometric pressure, wind direction, the earth's magnetic fields, wave patterns of the sea, and gravitational variations caused by tides. How birds process and interpret all this information we don't know. In orientation ability, bird brains are far superior to human brains. "Birds are not living in the same sensory world that we live in," Stephen Emlen of Cornell has observed. "They are hearing, seeing, and sensing a world expanded from ours."

The most famous of migratory species is the arctic tern, and the most famous of arctic terns is a juvenile that was captured and banded at Disco Bay on the west coast of Greenland on July 8, 1951, and was found dead on the east coast of South Africa on October 30, 1951. It had covered 11,000 miles (as the crow never flies) in fewer than ninety days. This record has stood for almost forty years as the most distant recovery of any banded bird, but observation and other banding records indicate that arctic terns regularly fly back and forth the length of the planet, from their breeding grounds around the top of the world to their wintering areas south from South America and Africa to the edge of the antarctic pack ice.

The arctic tern is built for long-distance travel. It has swept-back wings, a long forked tail, a light torso, and a strong and steady stroke. The regular arrival of juvenile birds in the species' wintering areas three months after birth proves that these birds are able to navigate "instinctively" almost as soon as they can fly.

The gull with the shape most like that of the arctic tern is Sabine's, and it too is an extraordinary migrant. It breeds over much of the same area as the tern — actually at the northern limits of the arctic tern's nesting range — and flies south to winter off the coasts of Chile and South Africa, making the longest migration of any gull in the world.

Two land birds with the arctic/Sabine's swept-back wings, forked tail, and small torso are the common nighthawk and the barn swallow. Both are champion migrants. The nighthawk's annual migration back and forth from Argentina to the Yukon makes it the most migratory member of the nightjar family. The barn swallow has as long a migration as any American passerine, from Argentina to Alaska.

All four of these birds have similar flight styles. They flap their wings with buoyant, regular strokes, and they can fly in a wide range of weather conditions — from heavy winds to dead calms. None of them soars or depends on thermals.

At the opposite extreme from these distance champions are a few migrants that cannot fly well in any conditions. All grouse, ptarmigan, and quail have heavy bodies, short and rounded wings, and weak, fluttering flights. Most members of these groups do not migrate; those that do tend to do so on foot. When winter comes, the mountain quail of the Pacific Northwest, for example, descend in single-file marches from the highest altitudes. The distance covered is so minimal that some authorities do not consider it migration; others observe that air temperature rises about 1 degree for every 150 yards subtracted in altitude, and the quail's vertical descent of about 1 mile is the climatic equivalent of a 2,000-mile flight south.

Aerodynamic structure frequently determines the routes that migrating birds must follow. The albatrosses of the southern oceans fly very long distances between breeding seasons, but their movement is primarily east/west, not north/south. Shearwaters, storm petrels, and other tubenoses that breed in the high southern latitudes migrate each year to the North Atlantic and North Pacific to spend the austral winter off our coasts. The southern albatrosses occur here only accidentally, however. Their narrow, glider-plane wings are designed for dynamic soaring in heavy winds, and albatrosses are weak flappers, poorly equipped to cross the equatorial doldrums under their own power. The wandering albatross, the longest-winged of all birds, has been recorded fewer than half a dozen times in the Northern Hemisphere. Its inclusion on the American Birding Association's *Checklist of the Birds of North America* is the result of a single occurrence, a female photographed off the coast of Sonoma County, California, in July 1967.

Other gliding birds' migration routes are restricted by their weak powered flight. You'll never see a vulture or any of the buteo hawks on a pelagic trip. Since these large soarers depend on thermals — rising bubbles of heated air — and on winds deflected off mountain ridges to carry them from their nesting grounds to their wintering ranges, they must avoid large bodies of water on migration. Nearly the entire world population of the Swainson's hawk is squeezed through Costa Rica and Guatamala twice each year, and single flocks containing tens of thousands of birds ("railroad trains of raptors," hawk watchers call them) can take more than an hour to pass.

The Swainson's route south from the prairies of Canada and the far western United States down through the land bridge of Central America to the plains of southeastern South America looks like a smoothly curving dog's leg on a migration map. The bird's reliance on thermals means that the movement is actually a countless series of looping, overlapping glides, and the actual distance covered must be three or four times the linear distance traveled. A couple of dozen Swainson's appear each winter in the southern tip of Florida; these birds are inevitably immatures who seem to have missed the route south through Texas and to have been funneled to the farmlands near the Everglades.

The hummingbirds' general reluctance to cross water develops from the opposite aerodynamic weakness. Their full-steam-ahead, straightforward flight is entirely self-powered. Their short wings and proportionately heavy bodies make them unable to glide at all. They must earn every yard they travel with ceaseless, energy-depleting wingbeats. Until the 1960s, ornithologists were unconvinced that the ruby-throated hummingbird could cross the Gulf of Mexico. Although observers along the coast regularly reported seeing birds apparently heading straight out to sea, it didn't seem possible that these birds could store enough fat to fuel the nonstop 600-mile flight needed to reach the Yucatan peninsula. R. C. Lasiewski's work with hummingbirds in metabolic chambers eventually demonstrated that the ruby-throat's flight range was more than 600 miles, given ideal wind conditions. Still, the ruby-throat seems to be the only hummingbird to make regular overwater migrations. This may be one reason why it is the single member of its large family to breed in eastern North America.

The annual autumn occurrence of western hummingbirds — rufous, black-chinned, buff-bellied, and others — along the Gulf coast from east Texas to the Florida panhandle is probably linked to their reluctance to cross water. Many of these individuals are juveniles making their first migration; like the

Swainson's hawks that winter in Florida, they seem to have missed the overland route down through Texas and Mexico and to have been forced to release their migration urges flying east rather than south.

One other consequence of aerodynamic shape is the tendency of some birds to migrate in V-formations. The birds that do so — pelicans, cormorants, cranes, swans, ibis, geese, and some of the larger ducks — share the same general shape and flight style. They are all heavy, big-bellied birds with broad wings that they flap in steady movements. The turbulence generated by their wings creates a slipstream behind and above each bird that gives the following bird extra lift. Like the lead rider in a bicycle race, the first bird in any V is in a disadvantageous position. Generally no one bird will hold the point for long. Keep your eye on these flocks as they cross the sky, and you'll often see the V shift or break into a W as the leader falls back.

PHYSIOLOGY II: FOOD AND FEEDING STYLES

Food preferences and feeding styles have a direct effect on migration patterns. The most omnivorous birds tend to be nonmigratory. Because one kind or another of the various food items they live on is available all year long, many pigeons, doves, crows, and jays are sedentary. When autumn comes, it is simpler and safer for these and other omnivores to change diets than to embark on migration flights.

Birds that depend on specific, temporary food sources are the most migratory. The arctic tern's migration enables it to specialize, feeding on certain crustaceans that live only in very cold ocean waters. This strategy also helps to minimize competition with other terns which prefer fish. The barn swallow and common nighthawk feed only on flying insects, not available in the colder months.

Most woodpeckers are nonmigratory because their chiseling beaks enable them to dig out insects from their winter hiding places. The few woodpeckers that do migrate all have specialized feeding styles. Our three sapsuckers — Williamson's, the red-breasted, and the yellow-bellied — need a warm sun to keep the sap moving at the holes they make, and so they must retreat from northern areas in winter. The yellow-shafted flicker is actually a ground-feeding bird whose favorite prey is terrestrial ants. As a result, its northern populations are migratory and its southern populations sedentary. One other migratory woodpecker is the Lewis', whose favorite prey is flying insects, which it captures flycatcher style, darting out from its perch.

Yellow-shafted Flicker

Food preferences also determine the route and timing of migration for many birds. Ospreys, like buteos, can ride the winds deflected off mountain ridges, but unlike the buteos, they're more often seen following coastlines and river valleys, where the fish on which they depend are more available. The merlin and peregrine falcon are both swift, strong fliers and are perfectly capable of following the interior ridge routes flown by the buteos, but both prefer the coastline, apparently because their favored prey — passerines and shorebirds — is more plentiful there.

Several insectivorous shorebirds — lesser yellowlegs, golden plover, white-rumped sandpiper — fly elliptical migration routes each year. Northbound in spring, they tend to follow the inland routes and are rarely seen along the coasts, apparently because the interior areas warm up faster than the coasts and insects are more numerous and active. In fall, they can circle back down the coasts because insects are more widespread by that time.

The spring arrival of the red knot on the Delaware Bay shore is timed to correlate precisely with the annual egg laying of the horseshoe crab. At the highest tide of late May (under either a new moon or a full moon), the horseshoe crabs come ashore to mate and lay billions of eggs. The red knots arrive just in time to take advantage of the situation. "The scene is primeval," Linda Leddy has written. "The coast appears to be paved with cobbles, each one a horseshoe crab clambering to secure the right spot for laying its eggs. Add to this scene tens of thousands of gulls, sandpipers, and dense flocks of knots, all lined up along the shore to feast on crab eggs. It's amazing that the revolution of the moon around the earth, the reproduction of horseshoe crabs, and the hemispheric migrations of shorebirds are so closely linked."

After fueling up on crab eggs, the knots fly nonstop to the southwestern shore of James Bay, where they arrive just in time for the annual peak of the Macoma clam population. They fuel up again and then fly to their nesting grounds in arctic Canada. Brian Harrington, one of the world's leading authorities on the species, has observed, "The patterns and timing of knot migration from Tierra del Fuego to the arctic reflect a coordination that must have developed over the eons on a remarkable geographic scale of trial and error."

ORNITHOMETEOROLOGY

Birders love to talk about weather. Some talk about it ceaselessly, and every birding group seems to have at least one self-proclaimed expert on weather's influence on migration. "This low-pressure system is moving northwest," he tells us on Friday night, "which means that a back-door high from the south is going to reach us tomorrow afternoon. By Sunday morning, the warblers are going to be dripping out of the trees at River-side Park." On Sunday morning, when the only birds at Riverside Park are three starlings and a rock dove, he tells us: (1) the low-pressure system was stalled by an arctic air mass over Greenland; (2) the high-pressure system was pushed through too fast by tail winds from Mongolia; or (3) Riverside Park has never been good for warblers, and he doesn't know what we're doing there. The truth is: (4) both birds and weather are highly unpredictable.

Weather obviously has an enormous influence in determining which birds we see in the field, especially during migration. The problem is that we can know what the influence has been only *after* we've had the weather and have seen the birds. Trying to predict where the migrants will be next weekend by studying the maps on the local weather forecasts is like trying to predict which baseball team will win the pennant next year by studying the statistics on bubblegum cards. There are simply too many secondary factors and unforeseeable circumstances to be considered. There are several very important and complex considerations.

The same weather conditions can have different effects in different localities. Studying nocturnal migrants in coastal Louisiana and the Piedmont Plateau of Georgia, Kenneth Able commented, "Surprisingly, the songbird migrants nearly always flew downwind, regardless of the appropriateness of the wind's direction." Later Able continued his study in upstate New York and discovered that the songbirds did not usually fly downwind when winds were blowing away from their intended destination. "This surprised me since many of the species in New York were the same as those we had observed in the south. Apparently," he concluded, "how birds respond to directional cues may vary from region to region and the response in a particular region may vary from one kind of bird to another."

The same weather conditions at the same localities can have different effects at different times of year. In spring, for example, offshore winds at coastal and lakeside sites sometimes bring down migrating passerines and create good birding conditions. The birds must battle the wind to reach shore. When they come over land, they often drop into the first trees they find to rest and refuel. In fall the same winds often trigger the migrants' departure and generate empty trees. Onshore winds in spring usually encourage woodland migrants to continue inland and to overfly coastal localities. Onshore winds in fall often pin down the migrants that reach the coast and create huge congregations of woodland birds forced to wait for the weather to change.

More subtle differences can also occur within the same migration season. Ducks and geese do not ordinarily migrate through rain and snow, but late in fall hundreds can sometimes be seen in the midst of storms, flying hard south despite the cold and wet. These are sometimes called "forced departures," as the birds seem to recognize that time is growing short and delaying their leave-taking will only make things worse for them.

Distant weather systems can outweigh local conditions. The 1983 invasion of brown pelicans up the Columbia River on the Washington/Oregon border was apparently caused by the "El Niño" equatorial current off the Pacific coast more than a thousand miles to the south. Normally, surface waters of the equatorial Pacific move away from the coast of South America, and marine plants are drawn up from the deep, cold waters below. These plants are the base of the food chain of plants, fish, and birds that makes these waters ordinarily some of the richest in the world. "El Niño" is an irregular reverse current that pushes *toward* the coast, trapping the plants below and indirectly starving the seabirds. The pelicans, Heermann's gulls, elegant terns, and Cassin's auklets that appeared off the North Pacific coast in 1983 during El Niño of that year were believed to be birds pushing north in an effort to find food.

The same local weather can have a different effect on different birds. Even closely related birds respond differently to the same local conditions. El Niño drove elegant terns up to Oregon and Washington in unprecedentedly high numbers in the fall of 1983. More than 200 were seen in a single flock on the Rogue River in Oregon. Meanwhile the usually resident Caspian terns had virtually disappeared.

Hawk watchers know well that no one set of conditions is good for all species of hawks at any one lookout. At ridge sites like Hawk Mountain, Pennsylvania, broad-winged hawks are most likely on windless days, as they prefer to ride thermals; red-tailed hawks are most likely on windy days, when they ride the turbulent air deflected off the mountains.

The source of a weather system can be more important than its individual characteristics. Harry LeGrand studied the effects of four kinds of cold fronts in autumn at Cape May Point, New Jersey, and found that each seems to bring a different selection of raptors. Cold fronts from the Canadian prairies and Great Lakes bring the best variety, with sharp-shins usually the most numerous. Cold fronts from eastern Canada and New England bring the largest numbers of peregrine falcons. Cold fronts from the south generally produce good buteo counts, especially on the second day after the front's passage, and cold fronts from the Great Plains generally produce few hawks of any kind.

No single weather pattern in any area generates all migrants. Rain, for example, generally ends all hope of watching a hawk migration, but a hard rain can bring down migrating passerines by the thousands. It can also create temporary pools in pastures and fields, attracting shorebirds that would otherwise pass unseen overhead. Ducks too can be drawn to such pools. Something often forgotten by birders is that most migration is invisible. Most passerines migrate at night, and many diurnal migrants fly too high to be seen. In many areas, the best weather for birding is the weather that's worst for the birds. "It was an excellent migration season" often means that the birds had a terrible time trying to get where they wanted to go, and they were forced down all along the path. Conversely, "This season's migration was dull" usually means that the birds reached their destinations with few hardships.

The list above is only a small sample of the most important

complexities. In his exhaustive review of the scientific literature on the subject ("Timing and Amount of Bird Migration in Relation to Weather," *Oikos* 30 [1978]), W. John Richardson lists more than two dozen different factors that researchers have identified as influencing migration. These include conditions en route, conditions at takeoff site and destination, pressure systems, warm fronts, cold fronts, wind speed, wind direction, barometric pressure, temperature, relative humidity, atmospheric stability, updrafts, rain, fog, clouds, visibility, moon phases, magnetic disturbances, atmospheric electricity, and tides. People who think they understand where the birds will be tomorrow on the basis of today's weather forecast ought to read this article. Richardson pointedly notes how often researchers have reached contradictory conclusions. Most generalizations seem to depend on where the research was done, which kinds of birds were being studied, and which secondary variables were factored into the equations.

For birders, the one rule worth remembering is that birds migrate in all kinds of weather — or, more precisely, that different birds migrate under different conditions in different localities, and in spring and fall there are always some birds moving somewhere. To know where that somewhere is, you must be out in the field, looking for it. The only useful weather reports are those that persuade you to grab your binocs and head out the door; the useless reports are those that persuade you to stay home.

"There is really no such thing as bad weather," John Ruskin once wrote, "only different kinds of good weather."

GEOGRAPHY I:
CORRIDORS AND FUNNELS

Geography is a more reliable indicator of migration patterns than weather. In fact, geography, not weather, has apparently determined the direction of the major migration patterns on the planet — the movement of long-distance migrants north to North America and Eurasia to breed during the Northern

Hemisphere's summer and south to South America and Africa to winter during the Southern Hemisphere's summer.

Why do so few transequatorial migrants breed in the Southern Hemisphere's summer? If warmer weather were all these birds needed, half — by chance — should winter here in the Northern Hemisphere and breed in the south. It is just as warm in Tierra del Fuego in December as it is in Manitoba in June. The answer to the puzzle is geographical: the coincidental shape of the earth's four major land masses. Both North America and Eurasia widen at their northern ends. South America and Africa taper to points at their southern ends. Breeding requires more space than wintering, and there's simply more land available in the Northern Hemisphere. The only birds that breed in the austral summer and winter here during our summer are seabirds — storm petrels, shearwaters, and southern skuas.

The particular shape of our continent also determines the flight paths of many migrants. The old idea that there are four North American "flyways" — the Atlantic coast, the Mississippi valley, the central prairies, and the Pacific coast — has fallen into disfavor in recent years because it is too simplistic. Most birds migrate on broad fronts much wider than is suggested by the term "flyway." Nevertheless, the geography of the continent gives migration its dominant grains. Our two coasts are heavily traveled by migrating birds, not only because of the food sources available there, but also because the ocean fronts running north/south are directional guides and warning markers to birds flying too far east or west. South Texas is a superb area for birding partly because it stands above the Central American bottleneck. In spring, land birds that have wintered in Central or South America come north up the isthmus and fan out east and west through Texas. In fall, Texas is a funnel for birds returning overland to winter retreats south of our border. To a lesser extent, Florida is also a bottleneck and funnel. In spring, warblers and other passerines that have wintered in the West Indies "island hop" to Florida before fanning northeastward toward New England or northwestward toward the Midwest.

The "funnel effect" generally makes peninsulas running north or south excellent migrant traps. Ontario's Point Pelee (figure 5) jutting southward into Lake Erie may be the most celebrated migrant trap north of Texas. "No other spot in the interior of the continent," Roger Tory Peterson has noted, "can offer the bird lister more action on a good day in May or in September." More than 340 species have been recorded there and more than 200 in a single day. Of North America's 52 wood warblers, 42 have been seen at Point Pelee — 34 in a single day in 1979. Migration watching is all the easier because the peninsula tapers to a very fine point. The most productive area is usually right at the tip, where birds arriving in spring descend before fanning northward and where in fall they are squeezed together by the water on both sides as they come south.

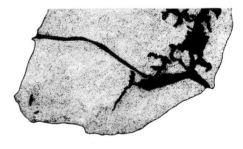

Cape May Point

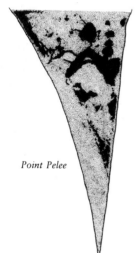

Point Pelee

FIGURE 5. *Point Pelee, Ontario, and Cape May Point, New Jersey, Two of North America's Most Celebrated Migrant Traps*

Whether a peninsula is a better migrant trap in spring or fall depends on the surrounding geography. New Jersey's Sandy Hook, a peninsula extending northward into New York Bay, is a more productive hawk-watching spot in spring than in fall. The sharp-shins and other raptors found there in spring are funneled up the Hook as they try to avoid crossing water coming north up the Atlantic coast. In fall, hawks heading south apparently turn west when they come upon Long Island Sound or New York Bay and so never reach Sandy Hook.

By the same principle, Cape May Point (figure 5) is a better hawk-watching spot in fall than in spring. Buteos coming north in spring must turn inland to avoid crossing the Delaware Bay, and those seen at the Point probably appear there "against their will" — as reverse migrants or overshoots heading back south. The falcons and accipiters that do cross the Bay in spring can come across at any spot on the southeastern New Jersey coast. Cape May does not jut out in the water as Point Pelee does, and so it is less often the first point of land a migrating bird will see. For birds coming south in fall, however, the Point is at the bottom end of the funnel that is the state of New Jersey. Hawks heading south are pressed in by the Atlantic on one side and by the Delaware Bay on the other. When they reach the Point, they turn back and circle over the Point's hawk-watching stations. Many don't actually cross the Bay at the Point. They turn west as they come upon the water and head north up the Delaware River to find narrower crossings. Cape Henlopen, Delaware, directly south of Cape May, sees few southbound hawks.

The next good hawk-watching spot to the south of Cape May is Kiptopeke at Cape Charles, Virginia, at the bottom of the Delmarva Peninsula. How many of the hawks seen at Kiptopeke are the same as those seen at Cape May is a matter of debate among local hawk watchers. It may be very few. The species mix is certainly different. In 1985, for example, Kiptopeke counted 166 black vultures; Cape May had 1; Cape May had nearly 3,000 Cooper's hawks, Kiptopeke fewer than 300. (See tables 8–14, in chapter 8.) Banding studies and radio telemetry have improved our understanding of how hawks and other migrants change their flight paths in response to geography, but the puzzles are far from solved, and the human eye is still our most important instrument.

Alan J. Ryff recently researched records of visual sightings of Sabine's gulls going back to 1859 and concluded that Sabine's is not as exclusively a pelagic migrant as has commonly been supposed. The various east/west river systems of the Pacific Northwest and Canadian prairies may be its primary spring corridors to its nesting grounds on the Hudson Bay. Ryff's analysis of reported sightings indicates that the gulls turn inland as they come north up the Pacific coast to follow the rivers of British Columbia, Alberta, and Saskatchewan across the Canadian prairies overland to their breeding areas on Baffin Island and Southhampton Island. This route is obviously far shorter than the pelagic route around Alaska, and the gulls are often seen flying low over the rivers, apparently searching for fish and other food while they travel. The juvenile Sabine's seen each fall over the Great Lakes are probably funneled in that direction by James Bay, the southward extension of Hudson Bay, and by the north/south rivers leading from James Bay and pointing toward the Great Lakes.

Even away from large bodies of water, the "corridor effect" can be a factor. The Huachuca and Chiricahua mountains of southeastern Arizona are at the northern end of the western Sierra Madre chain and so host a number of Mexican species seen nowhere else in the country: the elegant trogon, magnificent hummingbird, berylline hummingbird, buff-breasted flycatcher, sulphur-bellied flycatcher, olive warbler, and several others. All of these birds stay close to this corridor of high-altitude habitat on their spring and fall migrations. If the geology of the region were different and the mountain chain stopped short of the Arizona border, these species would probably not be members of North America's avifauna.

Another entirely terrestrial corridor is the Goshute mountain chain in eastern Nevada. Steve Hoffman, who directs the autumn raptor census there, theorizes as to why the Goshutes seem to be one of the few hawk migration concentration points in the Far West: "Birds of prey migrating through the West obviously concentrate along north-south ridges. The problem is that there are so many, the migration is rather dispersed. The Goshutes are an exception as the Bonneville Salt Flats form a fifty-mile-wide barrier to raptor migration. Most accipiters, buteos, and eagles prefer to avoid this vast, flat, and treeless terrain."

Not all migration corridors run north and south. This fact is especially evident at the local level. Depending on the geographic features of your area, the migrants you see over your house may tend to fly east or west or even south in spring and north in fall. Over my house, most migrants fly west, in both spring and fall. The Delaware River is twenty-five miles to the west, and the birds I see may be heading there to follow the river north or south.

One last important point about migration corridors is that paths followed in fall are not generally simple reversals of the paths followed in spring. Fall corridors tend to be wider and more variable, primarily because of the abundance of juvenile birds in fall. All species that nest in summer have their populations at a peak in summer and fall, and far more migrants head south each year than come back north in spring. The first fall migration and the first winter are the toughest seasons in most birds' lives. Only the lucky survive. Migration can be a hit-or-miss situation for young birds. The paths they follow are usually more dispersed and less straightforward than the corridors that the adults follow. More than nine out of ten of all accipiters and buteos seen at Cape May, for example, are immature. The adults have apparently learned to avoid this funnel.

GEOGRAPHY II:
ISLANDS, OASES, AND BLACK BOXES

After peninsulas, the most reliable spots for finding migrants are islands. The Dry Tortugas is celebrated among birders for its tropical specialties — sooty tern, brown noddy, brown and masked boobies, and white-tailed tropicbird. Less well known is the Tortugas' status as a springtime refuge for migrating land birds. The island is the last in a chain of small islands extending west from the Florida Keys, and it is perfectly placed as a rest station for birds crossing the Gulf of Mexico. Almost every day from early April to late May, the few short trees inside Fort Jefferson host spectacular collections of warblers, vireos, tanagers, thrushes, and grosbeaks — all at eye level and with nowhere else to go. Fall migration is less diverse and dependable, probably because the Tortugas is too close to the coast to be a way station for southbound birds. Migrants departing from the mainland apparently fly over the islands before they begin to tire and look for a place to rest.

The position of the Farallon Islands about thirty miles west of San Francisco makes them also a migrant hot spot, but for different reasons. These islands play host to more eastern accidentals annually than any area of similar size in the western United States. The gray-cheeked thrushes, catbirds, blackburnian warblers, and other purely eastern birds that reach these islands have strayed far west from their regular routes and must come down on these islands out of desperation. Any bird overshooting the coast has one last chance to save itself as it flies over the Farallons. After those islands, the next land mass is Hawaii, 2,300 miles away.

The Aleutian Islands of Alaska serve as a refuge for migrants overshooting in the opposite direction, birds flying east in spring past their breeding grounds in Asia and Siberia. The regular appearances of Asian breeders — Temminck's stint, the red-breasted flycatcher, the eye-browed thrush, the Siberian rubythroat, and dozens of others — make the Aleutians a mandatory stop for any birder who hopes to see 700 species in North America. Birders on Attu, the westernmost island, spread out in small groups and carry CB radios to stay in touch with each other and to relay news of good finds. With the possibilities list so exotic, spring migration watching there is as tense — and as rewarding — as it is anyplace in North America. On his visit to Attu in 1986, Brad Williams found himself at one end of the island when a Terek sandpiper was discovered at the other. "Hearing this, I start out immediately, but it still takes two hours of hard bike riding and cross-country hiking to get to the spot where the bird should be. No one is there. Needless to say, I am upset. But after a minimum of cursing, I start walking the beach. First to the east as far as possible. No bird, no people. Then to the west. Same thing. And then I return to where I started and finally notice an unattended Questar set up on the shore. I walk up, look in, and there is the bird quietly feeding within the field of this scope."

The Aleutians, Farallons, and other islands are often called migrant traps and are sometimes even credited with exerting a magnetic effect on vagrants. These descriptions are misleading. A peninsula can act as a trap; the birds found there are often present against their will, having been squeezed into the peninsula's point by the surrounding water. Islands are more properly considered refuges than traps, since birds ordinarily land on them by choice. Then, too, the word "magnet" suggests that the island leads birds off course. The Farallons cannot draw a blackburnian warbler away from its regular migration route thousands of miles to the east. How do lost birds find these tiny islands in the immensity of the Pacific? Most probably don't. The magnetic effect is an optical illusion. The eastern birds found on the islands are probably a tiny fraction of all misoriented individuals — the lucky few who happened to have taken their wrong turn in just the right direction. The majority of land birds overshooting westward elsewhere along the Pacific coast are never seen by birders, and tens of thousands of them must drown at sea.

Isolated patches of good habitat, oases both literal and figurative, also exert an apparent magnetic effect on migrants. As with islands, an oasis's attractiveness to birds is actually created by the "antimagnetism" of the surrounding area. New York City's Central Park is an 800-acre rectangle of greenery in a desert of concrete and asphalt. Migrants forced down over Manhattan by exhaustion or bad weather have few woodlands to choose from, and so the park is a surprisingly good birding spot in spring and fall. More than 270 species have been recorded there. The Big Day record for the park is 101.

The Salton Sea, a new oasis of greenery and water in the Colorado Desert of southeastern California, serves as a migrant refuge in both spring and fall. It was formed in 1905 when a flood on the Colorado River caused a man-made canal to overflow and refill an old lake basin that had been dry for more than 400 years. "What had been a land of burning sand with a few rock wrens," James Lane notes in his *Birder's Guide to Southern California* (Denver: L&P Press, 1979), "became a lush valley filled with birds." Today the Salton Sea is one of the most reliable spots in California for Mexican breeders straying north — wood storks, black skimmers, and yellow-footed gulls — and for shorebirds, ducks, and swallows descending from their regular migration paths between the coast and the interior.

On the other side of the Colorado Desert, even further inland, is another oasis with an apparent magnetic effect — Lake Havasu on the border between Arizona and California. This is a forty-six-mile-long lake created by Parker Dam on the Colorado River and is situated in one of the hottest and driest areas in the country. Its specialty? *Pelagic birds.* Brown and blue-footed boobies and all three jaegers have been seen there; magnificent frigatebirds are considered "casual"; common terns and northern phalaropes are regular. All have perhaps been funneled northward by the Gulf of California.

One other connection between geography and migration routes might be called the black box effect. We don't know why certain areas attract migrants, only that they do. These places attract migrants year after year, although — to the human eye, at least — they seem no different from the surrounding areas where birds are few. The black box effect is especially evident on the local level. All experienced birders can lead you to their favorite secret spots — the one acre in a hundred acres of woods that the warblers like best, the one pond the ducks always choose in a cluster of ponds, or the one sod farm in a county of sod farms where golden plovers and buff-breasted sandpipers appear each fall.

The marshes of Pedricktown, New Jersey, are an especially intriguing black box. Since the mid-1970s this rather mundane patch of wetlands a half hour's drive from Philadelphia has been the only regular migration staging area for ruffs and reeves known in North America. As many as a dozen birds appear each spring, and they can be found daily from late March to the end of April. Although a few ruffs and reeves appear elsewhere on our continent, the species has been found breeding in North America only once — in Alaska. If it weren't for the Pedricktown birds, the species could be considered a vagrant in the Lower Forty-eight. But it is very unlikely that the Pedricktown migrants are straying birds. Their appearance is too regular, and because the male ruffs show individual variations in colors, Jim Meritt and other local birders have been able to track individual birds as they reappear each year. Several have returned three or four springs in a row. In 1986 one ruff, conspicuous because of its white collar, appeared in Pedricktown for the sixth successive year.

Experts have speculated that the ruffs are breeding somewhere in eastern arctic Canada and that those seen in New Jersey and elsewhere along the Atlantic coast may winter somewhere in South America. Even if a nesting location or wintering site were found, however, the special attractiveness of the Pedricktown marshes would remain unexplained.

In a sense, all migration is a black box. Most researchers admit that they know much less about it than they'd like. The mysteries still to be solved far outnumber those that have been solved.

The recent work of "radar ornithologists," who have borrowed the equipment of satellite and missile tracking systems to study nocturnal migration, has demonstrated that the birds we can see from the ground represent only a tiny fraction of those on the move. On a good migration night, tens of millions to hundreds of millions of birds are in the air over North America, all leaving from different points, heading in different directions. Most will never be seen.

Even if we limit the discussion to the few birds we do see,

the more migration "hot spots" we explore and the more carefully we study the birds we find in them, the more we seem to discover how much more there is to learn. If no birders had ever carried their spotting scopes to the Pedricktown marshes, would we know today that certain ruffs migrate regularly up the East Coast? Probably not. If no birders had ever rented motorboats to ride to the center of Lake Havasu and the other deep-water lakes on the Colorado River, would we know that pelagic birds regularly cross the southwestern deserts? Almost certainly not. And discoveries like these are made every season as some birder somewhere notices something no one else has ever noticed before. Of course, that's all part of the magic of watching migration. The phenomenon is so immense and multidimensional that there is always something new to be learned — and next season's discovery could be yours.

5 · WINTER

NOTHING MAKES A BIRDER appreciate winter more than a long Indian summer. At first it's fun as phoebes and gnatcatchers linger into November, and out in your shirtsleeves, you set all kinds of personal "late dates." But then one day in December you wake up, the sun is shining again, and the truth hits home: warm is dull. The birds outside your window are the same birds you've seen for months, and by this time you'd gladly trade a dozen phoebes for a snow bunting and a couple of hundred gnatcatchers for one pine grosbeak.

"Nice bird!" I said to Brian Moscatello when on a 60-degree day in December he found the first barn swallow ever seen in the thirty-year history of the Oceanville (New Jersey) Christmas count. "I don't know," he said with a shrug. "A barn swallow is a barn swallow."

Birds are designed for cold weather. The growing consensus among paleontologists is that feathers originally evolved not for flight but for insulation. The line of two-legged reptiles that eventually evolved into the birds apparently developed feathers first to maintain their warm-blooded bodies and only later learned to fly. The best evidence for this theory is *Archaeopteryx*, the oldest fossil bird, which was fully feathered but almost certainly could not fly and probably could barely glide. It lived by running down its prey on foot in the style of its closest relatives, the small, warm-blooded bipedal dinosaurs. "The dinosaurs never died out completely," the paleontologist Robert Bakker has argued. "One group still lives. We call them birds."

Today, the insulating properties of feathers enable *Archaeopteryx*'s relatives to survive in the coldest regions on the earth. Skuas and storm petrels have been observed flying over the South Pole, and emperor penguins actually incubate their eggs through the antarctic winter. At the other end of the planet, the ivory gull lives year-round at the edge of the pack ice in the high arctic, surviving in winter by eating, among other things, the frozen dung of seals, walruses, and polar bears. Even more remarkable is Ross' gull, whose winter diet is a total mystery. Ross' gull nests in Siberia in June and July, moves east across the Bering Sea onto the Arctic Ocean in fall, and then, in November, when the pack ice moves south, flies *north* — straight into the absolute dark and unimaginable cold at the top of the world. How it feeds itself through the months of polar night we may never know.

It is food, not cold, and internal temperature, not external, that determine most birds' winter habits. Lapland longspurs and snow buntings seem to be such erratic visitors to midlatitude birders in part because they come south in numbers only when there is heavy snow on their regular wintering grounds. If the weather is dry and their feeding areas are clear, most members of both species will stay in Canada and the border states no matter how cold it gets.

By the same principle, the birds least likely to linger in winter beyond the first hard freeze are the insectivores: cuckoos, swifts, flycatchers, vireos, most warblers, and most nightjars. Once their prey has taken refuge for the winter, most insectivores must head south. Some obvious exceptions are the woodpeckers and the brown creeper, which have bills modified to dig insects and larvae from their hiding places, and the yellow-rumped warbler, the most winterized member of the warbler family, which feeds on berries, sap, and even birdseed in the cold months. One odd exception is the poor-will, which — alone among all birds — hibernates.

As the insectivores depart in fall, the northern waterbirds arrive. One pattern to watch for in late fall and early winter is "shortstopping" by swans, geese, ducks, and gulls. Some individuals of each of these groups fly quickly all the way to their southern wintering grounds, but many come down short and loiter in the central tier of states from October through December. When the freeze-up comes, they move again. Once they have been forced south, they tend to stay there until their spring migration. A midwinter thaw will not bring them back. Consequently, in areas north of the Mason-Dixon Line, November is the best month for duck watching, and a cold day in December just before freeze-up will be better than a warm day in January.

Two other things to keep in mind about the northern waterbirds:

1. Salt water freezes later and at lower temperatures than fresh water, so oceans and bays generally make for much more productive birding than inland areas at the same latitude.

2. The last open water in an otherwise frozen area will be an oasis for these birds and will concentrate their numbers enormously. Ducks and gulls will cluster in the tens of thousands at the deeper lakes, large rivers, tidal inlets, and warm-water outflows at power plants. Niagara Falls is a gull watchers' mecca in winter — as many as twelve species of gull may be present simultaneously — because the movement of the river keeps it open long after other areas nearby have frozen solid.

Between the insectivores and the northern waterbirds on the winter spectrum is a loose association of birds sometimes grouped under the term *half hardy*. The term is relative — one area's half hardy is another area's regular winter resident — but it is generally applied to birds whose numbers fluctuate with temperature, especially with hard freezes. Land birds often included in the group are the catbird, mockingbird, brown thrasher, both kinglets, and the Carolina wren. The half-hardy shorebirds include the willet, oystercatcher, marbled godwit, and both yellowlegs; half-hardy herons include the black-crowned night heron, the great blue, and the great egret. All seem to be pushing the upper extremes of their wintering ranges northward in our latitudes but will retreat (or die off) during the hardest winters.

WINTER AS CONTEXT:
THIS IS JANUARY, SO THAT MUST BE A ———

Many birds' responses to cold weather are so patterned and regular that the coming of winter can be a contextual key to distinguishing closely related, lookalike species. Some examples follow.

Terns. Despite its name, the arctic tern is the least likely of the white terns to be seen in cold weather. Arctic terns generally withdraw from our latitude by the end of September and are seldom recorded anywhere in the United States after mid-October. By the end of October the common tern is almost as rare. After November 1, if you see a medium-sized tern north of Savannah, Georgia, or Los Angeles, California, you can bet it's a Forster's. A large tern on the East Coast north of Georgia in November or December is almost certainly a royal; eastern Caspians do not linger. In the West the situation is reversed. North of Los Angeles in winter a Caspian is more likely than a royal.

Thrushes. Differentiating between the four *Catharus* thrushes may be the most underrated identification problem in North American birding. All four — veery, Swainson's, gray-cheeked, and hermit — appear in a bewildering mix of plumages, and every year Christmas count participants report seeing one or another of the first three. Christmas count editors generally append a "??" or "dubious" to these reports. Any *Catharus* thrush — red, brown, or gray — seen after November 1 anywhere in the continental United States is in all probability a hermit thrush, the only one of the four to be half hardy. See the *National Geographic Guide* for an excellent illustration of the hermit's variable colors.

Buteos. Another reported species that raises the eyebrows of Christmas count editors is the broad-winged hawk. Because the broad-wing migrates in such huge numbers, it is the most familiar small buteo to most eastern birders. After November 1, however, the ordinarily less common red-shouldered hawk is far more likely. When perched, an immature red-shoulder is virtually identical to a broad-wing. If on your next winter walk you think you've found a broad-wing, wait until it flies and study the underwings — or lie down until the feeling goes away. Broad-wings are very rare north of the Florida Keys in winter. In the West in winter, one common buteo that you can cross off your possibilities list is Swainson's hawk. The few immature birds that are funneled to the Everglades (see chapter 4) are the only Swainson's hawks to be found in North America in winter. All the rest migrate out of the country.

Swallows. The only half-hardy swallow is the tree swallow, which feeds on berries and seeds in winter and frequently lingers into January at midlatitudes and overwinters in the South. The violet-green might be considered one-quarter hardy. Its diet is apparently restricted to insects, but some members of the species overwinter each year in central California. No other swallows are at all probable in winter anywhere in the United States north of southern California or the Texas coast. Purple martins are early spring migrants (February–March) in the southern states, but beginners should be aware that the "first martin" of the year frequently proves to be a misidentified starling.

Eiders. Although the common eider is generally considered the more numerous of our two eiders, the king is actually more likely to stray south of New York on the East Coast and the border between the United States and Canada on the West Coast. The principle involved here is sometimes called "leap-frogging," where the more northerly of two closely related species heads farther south. The king eider has strayed as far south as Alabama and California.

Plovers. The principle of leapfrogging applies to our large plovers also, but in this case the more long-distance migrant continues down and leaves our area. On the East Coast in winter a large plover can safely be assumed to be a black-bellied plover; the species regularly overwinters as far north as Virginia, while the golden plover retreats to Argentina. The golden plovers that winter on the West Coast may actually be a third species of plover, the tentatively labeled Pacific golden plover, or *Pluvialis fulva*.

Hummingbirds. Anna's is by far the hardiest of our hummingbirds. It has survived subzero winter nights in Alaska (drinking sugar water during the day at electrically heated feeders). Any hummingbird seen in the West north of San Francisco in late fall or winter almost certainly belongs to this species. Southeastern birders should be aware that after October 1 the ruby-throated, a summer resident, is apparently less likely than several western strays — especially the rufous and black-chinned.

Pelagics. It is easier to distinguish phalaropes in winter because on both coasts red phalaropes linger significantly longer into December and January than red-necked ("northern") phalaropes. The Atlantic skua problem is also less problematic in cold weather. Any skua on the East Coast after December 1 is much more likely to be a great than the lookalike South Polar, which should be on its breeding grounds by that time. In the Pacific, the winter shearwaters are the sooty, the short-tailed, and (south of San Francisco) the black-vented. In the Atlantic, the most likely shearwater after December 1 is the Manx, more adapted to the cold than its lookalike, the Audubon's. "It's usually easy to tell the Manx and Audubon's shearwaters apart," claims pelagic veteran Alan Brady. "If the water temperature is above seventy degrees, call it an Audubon's. If it's below sixty degrees, call it a Manx. In between, hope to see some field marks."

WINTER IRRUPTIVES — IN THEORY

Some ornithologists use the term "irruptive" to describe any species whose numbers fluctuate widely from year to year. The word has been applied to temperate forest species, such as the pygmy nuthatch, the yellow-bellied sapsucker, and the cedar waxwing, and to seabirds such as the fulmar, the sooty shearwater, and the brown pelican. More often, however, the term is reserved for northern birds that winter only intermittently and in erratic numbers south of the boreal forests. In North America the most celebrated irruptives are the rough-legged hawk, snowy owl, northern shrike, bohemian waxwing, boreal chickadee, black-backed woodpecker, three-toed woodpecker, and the eight "winter finches" — the pine siskin, purple finch, evening grosbeak, pine grosbeak, common and hoary redpolls, and red and white-winged crossbills.

Actually, *all* raptors that winter regularly in Canada, with the apparent exception of the pygmy owl, show irruptive tendencies. Although the specific causes are complex and not fully understood, the general principle is clear: because they are specialized animals living at the top of very simple food chains, northern raptors lead precarious lives.

The classic example is the snowy owl. Through most of its range, the snowy owl feeds primarily on voles and lemmings; in winter in the Far North, there simply aren't many other animals living above ground. Both of these rodents have strongly cyclical populations which at a periodicity of about four years reach very dense numbers and then "crash," dying off by the millions. When the crashes come, snowy owls must move south to avoid starving. In 1945 V. E. Shelford linked the irruptions of snowy owls in New England in 1930–1931, 1933–1934, 1937–1938, and 1941–1942 with the simultaneous population crashes of the collared lemming recorded in Churchill, Manitoba. In 1947 Alfred O. Gross traced records of snowy owls in

Immature Snowy Owl

the United States and found a pattern of irruptions at intervals of approximately four years going back to 1833.

The cyclical nature of these irruptions is accentuated because in the breeding season immediately preceding the crashes, when the rodent populations are peaking, snowy owls lay more eggs (as many as thirteen have been found in a single nest) and fledge more young. It is the immature birds, the least experienced hunters, that suffer the most during crashes and account for the vast majority of the owls seen south of the Canadian border. Immatures are identifiable by the dark horizontal markings on their breasts and the dark-tipped feathers throughout their plumage. Adult females are lighter, and adult males are almost pure white.

It is interesting to contrast the ecology of the snowy owl with that of the most widespread winter bird in Alaska and northern Canada, the common raven. The raven, too, hunts voles and lemmings. Because it soars like an eagle and stoops like a falcon, birders sometimes call it an "honorary raptor." But in its ability to survive in an enormous variety of arctic and subarctic habitats under any circumstances, the raven is superior to any raptor and probably to any bird on the planet. When behaving raptorially is not to its advantage, a raven can pick berries like a grouse, gobble acorns like a jay, or crack open shellfish like a gull. Because ravens are so adaptive (or "unspecialized"; the terms are interchangeable), they do not irrupt. A few migrate short distances, but most stay home, no matter what the winter brings.

Our most regular irruptive predators are the snowy owl, the rough-legged hawk, and the northern shrike. All of them feed heavily on voles and lemmings and show some tendency to irrupt together at four-year intervals. The rough-leg is also an annual fall migrant. Some members of the species can be found each winter in the central and northern United States. During irruptive years, however, rough-legs come across the border in much higher numbers, disperse more widely, and fly farther south, sometimes all the way to the Gulf coast.

Two raptors that irrupt about once a decade are the goshawk and great horned owl. Some goshawks migrate into the United States every fall, and we have a large resident (nonmigratory) population of the great horned, but about one winter in ten, these two species appear in much higher numbers. Their usual prey on their Canadian wintering grounds is ruffed grouse and snowshoe hares, which feed on the same winter berry crop and experience population crashes every ten years or so. As a result, goshawks and great horneds are pushed south of the Canadian border. The gyrfalcon, which feeds heavily on ptarmigan in winter, also irrupts at about ten-year intervals, though never in the numbers of the gos and great horned.

WINTER IRRUPTIVES — IN REALITY

None of the statements made above is as neatly definitive as college biology textbooks usually make it seem, however — or as regular and predictable as birders might like it to be.

Different populations of snowy owls, for example, feed on different populations of lemmings. In eastern Canada, depending on the local habitat, snowy owls feed on one or two of *five* different species of lemmings — the Labrador collared lemming, the Greenland collared lemming, the southern bog lemming, the northern bog lemming, and the brown lemming. Crashes of a particular species in a particular area will push only the owls of that particular area south, so that snowy owls may irrupt on one coast and not the other, or in the central states but not on the coasts, or even in Maine but not in Massachusetts, or in Minnesota but not in Illinois. Moreover, not all snowy owls depend on lemmings. They will eat hares, too, in areas where they are available. This may be one reason why shrikes move south in some winters when snowy owls do not: during a lemming crash, the owl can move up to capture hares; the shrike, which is much smaller, cannot. There are also cycles within cycles; a simultaneous crash of snowshoe hares and lemmings will drive more owls south.

The ten-year cycles of goshawk and great horned owl, though linked in most textbooks, are likewise not a perfect match. The fluctuations in populations of the two prey animals — the ruffed grouse and the snowshoe hare — are not always synchronous, and so the hawk (which feeds more often on the grouse) and the owl (which prefers the hare) are not always in sync with each other.

How should we understand the pattern of irruptions of the great gray owl? The invasion of 1978–1979, when an estimated 334 great grays moved south of their usual wintering range into southern Ontario, Maine, Massachusetts, Connecticut, and Long Island, was believed to be the first major invasion of great grays since the winter of 1890–1891. An eighty-eight-year-cycle? Hardly. Four years later, in the winter of 1983–1984, an estimated 407 great gray owls moved south, the largest irruption of the species on record.

"The complex interactions between predators and their prey," raptor expert Leslie Brown has noted, "is a subject which has fascinated and largely defeated a number of very able scientists."

Winter-finch irruptions are apparently even more complex. At the moment, researchers seem generally to agree upon only two principles: first, the invasions have little, if anything, to do with the severity of the winter, and second, all finches do not respond in the same way to the same conditions.

The back-to-back hard winters of 1976–1977 and 1977–1978 proved these points. According to the U.S. Weather Service, 1976–1977 was the worst northeastern winter in the 200 years that records have been kept. Lake Erie and Lake Champlain froze solid, as did Pamlico Sound in North Carolina. The ice on the Hudson River was so thick that commuters from New Jersey walked across it to New York City. Wind chill factors in northern Minnesota were estimated at − 80 degrees. Snow was six feet high in Maine, and snowstorms reached the Everglades and the Bahamas. Yet only the purple finch came south into the United States in irruptive numbers. The other winter finches stayed home in Canada.

The following winter, 1977–1978, was also colder than normal but nowhere near as extreme as 1976–1977. Purple finches irrupted again. This time, however, they were accompanied by enormous flocks of compatriots. Evening grosbeaks reached Florida and southern California. Pine grosbeaks reached College Station, Texas, and pine siskins were everywhere, swarming over feeding stations throughout the South and appearing for the first time ever in the Florida Keys. But two finches were conspicuous by their absence. Whatever drove the other finches south had little effect on the crossbills. White-wings were seen only in small numbers, and red crossbills — usually far more numerous than white-wings during irruptions — were virtually unreported south of the Canada border.

What conclusions should be drawn by the birder interested in adding the irruptive species to his or her life list?

1. *Invasions cannot be predicted.* Since we don't fully understand the specifics that cause the invasions, we don't know where or when they're coming. It would be a mistake to head

north during a bitter winter in the hope of spotting a redpoll, or to plan a winter trip to some border state to search for a northern shrike or snowy owl simply because it's been four years since the last invasion.

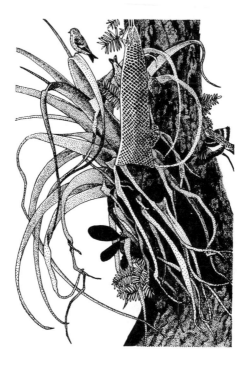

Pine Siskins in Florida

2. *"Irruption" is a relative term.* During an irruption of pine siskins it's difficult to walk through a suburban neighborhood without encountering several flocks. The largest recorded irruption of gyrfalcons, in contrast, in the winter of 1971–1972,

involved only an estimated sixty individuals, and they were
spread out over forty-eight different locations from British Columbia to Virginia. Raptor enthusiasts called the event an "ex-
plosion," but almost all the sightings involved a single gyr seen
one time on one day.

3. *Irruptions are usually localized.* Because the conditions
that trigger an invasion may occur in only part of a given species' normal winter territory, irruptives may appear only in
scattered parts of the species' "regular" irruptive territory.
How far south the irruptor comes also depends on factors
other than lack of food. Both the hawk owl and northern
shrike feed on lemmings and tend to irrupt during lemming
crashes. The hawk owl, however, seldom ventures more than a
couple of hundred miles south of its usual wintering grounds
and has rarely been found south of the border states. The
shrike, in contrast, flies thousands of miles south in irruption
years, especially in the western United States, where it has appeared as far south as New Mexico, Arizona, and southern
California. The snowy owl has reached California, Louisiana,
Texas, and Bermuda.

4. *Irrupting birds tend to wander in fall and early winter,
searching for good feeding areas.* Unlike annual migrants, irruptives have no regular established wintering territories and
so must spend some time searching for good areas. In most
cases, it's best to wait until at least mid-December before chasing after any reported on birding hotlines. Snowy owls are particularly notorious for being "you should have been here
yesterday" birds during October and November. One reported
in January or February, however, is likely to be on its wintering territory and will probably have established a predictable
and regular daily pattern. The same is generally also true for
rough-legged hawks, northern shrikes, and boreal owls. Goshawks are more secretive and, like all accipiters, difficult to
stake out. Even in irruptive years, you'll have a better chance
of seeing a gos flying past a hawk watch site during fall migration than of finding one on its wintering territory. Winter
finches seen in fall are also generally on their way elsewhere.

By mid-December, though, evening grosbeaks, siskins, and red-polls are easy to stake out, as they sometimes return to the same backyard feeders for weeks. The crossbills have a strong preference for hemlock stands and will return day after day to the same area once they have found a good one.

5. *Many irruptions are not evident until mid-January or later.* Christmas counts, which are conducted in the last two weeks of December, can be misleading as indicators of some winter bird populations. Some regular migrants and many irruptives are still loitering north of their eventual wintering area during this period and will not move south until forced to do so by snow, ice, or lack of food. Not until January 20 did the first great gray owl appear on Amherst Island in southern Ontario in 1979, and not until February 17 did the numbers build to the point where observers knew that a major incursion was in progress. It was March 4 before the invasion had peaked. Winter finches, too, often move south long after the New Year. In the two redpoll irruptions of the 1970s, in 1972 and 1978, redpolls apparently did not cross the Mason-Dixon Line until the first week of February.

6. *Some kind of irruption occurs in every northern state every single winter.* If the snowy owls don't come, the shrikes may. If the shrikes don't come, the crossbills may. If the crossbills don't come, the bohemian waxwings may. No matter how bleak the winter or how empty the skies, there's always good reason to be tramping around in the snow with your binoculars around your neck and hope in your heart.

6 · SUMMER

BIRDING IS NOT EASY in the summertime through most of North America. Spring and fall are more exciting seasons everywhere. Only in Alaska, in Canada, in the northern border states, and at high-altitude sites are birds much easier to find in summer than in winter. From the midlatitude states south, the month of June and the first two weeks of July are the doldrums of the birdwatcher's year. Two rules are worth following in summer.

1. *Get out early.* Early in the day, while the birds are their most active. And early in the season, while the males are still singing, pursuing females, and disputing territories — and before heat, glare, and leaf cover make searching for nesting birds an exercise in exasperation.

2. *Trust the range maps.* Of all the seasons, summer provides the strongest contextual clues to identification. Virtually all birds will be in the proper habitat on their established nesting grounds in June and July. Heat in summer does not generate vagrants as the cold of winter sometimes does. Southern birds are not coaxed north by a summer hot spell in the way that northern birds are pushed south by winter's snow and ice. A breeding-aged adult out of territory during its nesting season is the rarest of rarities.

JUNE IS THE CRUELEST MONTH

Summer strays are rarer than winter strays because the costs are much higher and the chance for profit remote. A winter vagrant must expend extra energy flying a longer migration route and must also solve the problems of finding food in foreign territory, but occasionally the gamble pays off. If a severe winter should decimate the population in the usual wintering range and the vagrant survives in its different retreat, it will return to the breeding grounds the following spring to find fewer competitors, more available nesting territory, and much better chances for breeding success — and so the lucky vagrant's genes will be passed on to the next generation.

The primary cost for a summer stray is the obvious one: an individual who lingers in the south, overshoots to the north, or otherwise fails to return to the species' breeding range generally finds itself alone. It can't pass on its genes because it has no mate. The lives of most birds are so short and the ordinary odds against successful nesting so high that one lost breeding season can be disastrous. Many birds have only one chance to nest. Second, if by wild luck a summer wanderer does manage to find another vagrant of the same species in the same territory, and if by further luck the second vagrant happens to be of the opposite sex, there is another price to pay. The pioneering pair must find a nesting site and food for their young in a foreign territory and unfamiliar habitat among unfamiliar predators, parasites, and other dangers. Finally, even if the pair manages to buck these odds and fledge their young, there is a hidden, additional cost. Any of the second generation who inherit their parents' oddball sense of nesting territory will return to the same area in future years, where dangers will be high and potential mates few or none.

The spread of the starling, the house sparrow, and a couple of other artificially introduced birds and the recent, explosive growth of a few birds that are natural range expanders — especially the cattle egret and the glossy ibis — can give the impression that, when a species nests outside its traditional range, prosperity is imminent. Actually, the vast majority of nesting attempts out of range are failures. Even most artificial introductions, with man standing by to provide mates and sometimes even food and nesting sites, have been failures. More than 100 species of birds have been introduced by man in North America. Only 7 have become widespread: the starling, house sparrow, rock dove, mute swan, ring-necked pheasant, chukar, and gray partridge. The budgerigar, Eurasian tree sparrow, and about a half dozen other aliens persist in very limited populations, mostly in southern cities. All other introduced species have quickly died out.

The only summer vagrants seen regularly in North America are *postbreeding wanderers*, birds that can afford to wander in June and July because they have completed nesting by that time or because they are juveniles trying out their wings and exploring the world before the weather turns cold. Southern waterbirds are the most frequent summer wanderers. They nest early in the year, have the whole summer free for exploration, and are capable of long, sustained flights. Frigatebirds have wandered to Alaska and Nova Scotia, wood storks to Tennessee and New Jersey, and roseate spoonbills to Nebraska, Colorado, and Indiana. The only states east of the Mississippi where the brown pelican has *not* appeared are Vermont and New Hampshire.

Still, these appearances are few and far between. If tracking down strays and accidentals is your favorite birding game, summer will be your least favorite season. Summer is for census taking.

BREEDING BIRD CENSUSES

Some summer censuses are conducted in the manner of Christmas counts. Participants divide up a territory and fan out to count all birds seen or heard on a single day. Although these counts are good for a rough approximation of local populations, ornithologists generally regard them as the least accurate form of breeding bird census. A single day count in summer invariably produces skewed data. Those species whose courtship period happens to coincide with the count day tend to be overcounted because their singing and displaying make them easy to find. Those who have already fledged their young or are nesting and sitting quietly tend to be undercounted. Another problem with summer Christmas counts is that there is usually no attempt to note how many birds were seen in actual breeding behavior. A dozen robins flying overhead count as twelve times as many "breeding birds" as one robin seen on its nest.

A more scientifically valid form of census is the study area survey. Here one or two observers return to a given small area (usually less than 100 acres) at weekly intervals to count all birds seen on each visit. Counting repeatedly throughout the breeding season minimizes the problem of skewed data and increases the chances that all breeders will be observed. Territorial males are counted separately, and the total number of birds observed is divided by hours in the field and size of the plot to give a truer indication of population status. *American Birds* and its predecessor, *Bird Lore,* have been gathering and publishing the results of such censuses since the 1930s. Some areas have been surveyed annually for twenty, thirty, and even forty years. The data compiled form a historical record often used in avian and environmental studies and certain to be treasured by ornithologists of the twenty-first century.

The newest form of bird census came to us from Europe and has been spreading across North America even faster than the lesser black-backed gull. It is the breeding bird *atlas,* first developed in 1968 by British birders and ornithologists to map the distribution of all breeding birds in the British Isles. In an atlas census the area to be surveyed is divided into grid blocks of uniform size. In the British study, the blocks are ten kilometers square; in the United States they are usually twenty-five kilometers square. Teams of observers are sent into each block to record all the species seen and to search for evidence of breeding behavior. The resulting compilation is an atlas because each species found breeding is individually mapped, with its occurrence or nonoccurrence in each grid block noted. The British effort required 1,500 observers and four years of surveying. The product is probably the most complete and accurate study of breeding bird distribution ever completed for any country in the world.

Chandler Robbins organized the first atlas effort in the United States in a survey of the breeding birds of Montgomery County, Maryland, in 1971. The Massachusetts Audubon Society organized the first statewide atlas in 1974 and completed it five years later, in 1979. Vermont, Maine, New Jersey, New York, Connecticut, Rhode Island, and the province of Ontario soon followed. Although the United States and Canada are a long way from matching the British effort, mainly because we have far fewer birders per square mile, most other eastern states and several western states are currently compiling atlases.

Breeding bird atlases have the double value of pleasing ornithologists who want good hard data and inspiring birders who want competition and the thrill of the chase. In an atlas survey, identification is just a preliminary step. A bird seen in suitable breeding habitat is considered only a *possible* breeder. Even a singing male may be counted only a possible breeder unless it is seen singing in the same area for several days simultaneously, when it is regarded as a *probable* breeder. Other criteria for *probable* breeder include active territorial defense, courtship display (with both sexes present), or nest building. Evidence of *confirmed* breeding includes a nest with eggs or young, adults feeding young, fledglings seen, or an adult observed in a distraction display. The number of birds in each grid block is not recorded. The atlaser's challenge is to find new species and to upgrade the status of each, promoting "possibles" to "probables" and "probables" to "confirmed." A success rate of 50 percent (half of all expected species confirmed breeding) is an elusive goal. Confirming some stealthy species as a breeder in your grid block in the fourth or fifth year of an atlas effort can be more thrilling than discovering a life bird.

For information about how you can participate in a breeding bird census, contact your local or state chapter of the Audubon Society. Summer Christmas counts and study area surveys can be started by any interested amateur, and atlas compilers generally have far more open grid blocks than available census teams and welcome volunteers with open arms.

EXPANSIONS

Most recent expansions of breeding range in North America have been marked by one or both of two dominant themes: *southern birds north* and *eastern birds west.*

Fifty years ago, the cardinal's breeding territory barely extended beyond the Mason-Dixon Line. Today this "southern" species nests regularly in Canada and has bred as far north as Nova Scotia. The mockingbird, tufted titmouse, blue grosbeak, summer tanager, blue-gray gnatcatcher, acadian flycatcher, red-bellied woodpecker, glossy ibis, white ibis, black vulture, turkey vulture, and Louisiana (tricolored) heron have also moved steadily north. The milder climate of the twentieth century is generally cited as the primary cause. The cardinal, mockingbird, and titmouse have also been helped by the proliferation of backyard bird feeders.

Eastern birds heading west include the blue jay, indigo bunting, rose-breasted grosbeak, eastern peewee, and — unfortunately for several western passerines — the brown-headed cowbird, which is a nest parasite.

The group making the steadiest progress west seems to be the eastern warblers, or, as western birders refer to them nowadays, "the so-called eastern warblers." Each summer census takers report first-breeding records for the redstart, ovenbird, parula, and other species farther and farther west, and field guide mappers have been hard-pressed to keep up. Most texts will tell you, for example, that the range of the northern parula reaches its westernmost extension near the hundredth meridian. But parulas have nested at least three times in California, and singing males and apparently mated pairs are being found there with increasing regularity.

The bird that gives field guide mappers the most trouble is the cattle egret. Its mysterious and enormous expansion over the last forty years has been the most spectacular natural range extension ever seen in the history of ornithology. Once limited to Africa and the southern Iberian peninsula, the cattle egret crossed the Atlantic to South America about the turn of the century, colonized North America at Clewiston, Florida, in the early 1940s, and then exploded. By the 1960s, it was already the most numerous egret in North America and was breeding along the East Coast as far north as Canada and west to California. By the early 1970s it was nesting in the interior of the continent into Minnesota and had been seen in Idaho, Alberta, and the Northwest Territories. The bird seems driven by a genetic wanderlust that affects its entire population. Pelagic birders regularly report it at sea, and it has landed on ships hundreds of miles from land in both the Atlantic and Pacific oceans. It has also expanded east from Africa through Asia and has even colonized Australia and New Zealand. Antarctica is the only continent left unconquered.

Some other birds are likely to continue expanding their ranges.

Double-crested cormorant. This species has staged an encouraging comeback in recent years. It has been nesting with increasing success throughout its range and has been expanding northward on the Great Lakes and both coasts. It has recovered most of the territory that it lost in the nineteenth century because of gunning and other forms of persecution. On the Pacific coast it now breeds from Baja to Alaska, and on the Atlantic coast it breeds in two separate populations from Florida to North Carolina and from Massachusetts to Newfoundland.

Kites. Four of our five nesting kites are expanding their ranges. The hook-billed kite, so accidental twenty years ago that it didn't even merit an illustration in the field guides, is now a year-round resident in south Texas and a rare but regular nester. Twenty years ago, the black-shouldered, or white-tailed, kite and the swallow-tailed kite were both considered threatened and declining species. Today their status has moved up from rare to uncommon in much of their breeding ranges. The black-shouldered now nests regularly north to Oregon and east into Mississippi. In 1986 birders working on the Florida Breeding Bird Atlas found three nesting pairs, the first nestings of the species in the state since 1910. Flocks of more than 100 swallow-tails have been reported as far north as South Carolina, and on July 23, 1986, Brian Millsap counted 684 in one hour near Moore Haven, Florida — more swallow-tails in sixty minutes than most birders have seen in their lifetimes. The Mississippi kite is also doing well. Its breeding range is expanding rapidly in several directions, especially westward into Colorado and New Mexico and southward down the Florida peninsula. On the East Coast it may be poised to make a giant step northward from its breeding territory in North Carolina. One pair apparently attempted to nest in Bombay Hook, Delaware, in 1986. The Mississippi kite is now an expected species in late spring at Cape May Point, New Jersey, and it annually wanders north to New England. Raptor experts have predicted that it will soon be found nesting somewhere in the New Jersey Pine Barrens.

Woodcock. Anyone interested in conducting a breeding bird survey for this species will need mittens and a scarf. It's a bird whose summer sometimes begins while there's still snow on the ground. Male displays begin in January in the south and early March in the north. If you can find a courtship site in your area (usually an open field on the edge of deep, wet woods), you'll witness a beautiful aerial display. Starting at dusk, the male flies in an upward spiral hundreds of feet into the air, circles calling, and then zigzags down, singing all the way. The woodcock's breeding range seems to be expanding along the whole length of the western edge of its territory — in Texas, Oklahoma, Kansas, and the Dakotas. The cause of the expansion is unknown, but ornithologists R. W. Smith and J. S. Barclay have speculated that it may be linked to increased rainfall and changing habitat in the fringe areas.

Great-tailed and Boat-tailed grackles. These were once considered two races of a single species. In 1973 the American Ornithologists' Union recognized them as two separate species. Both have been expanding their breeding ranges slowly but steadily throughout this century. The boat-tail colonized Delaware in 1933, New Jersey in 1952, and New York (Long Island) in 1981. The great-tailed grackle was once restricted to dry and open areas in south Texas. With man's clearing of the forests in the late nineteenth and early twentieth centuries, it has expanded north and west. The species first nested in Oklahoma in 1953 and in Kansas in 1964. Now its range extends well into Kansas and west through southern New Mexico and most of southern Arizona. Pairs are now seen regularly in southern California. Stray males have appeared in Oregon and Idaho. In the area of overlap (western Louisiana and the Texas coast), the great-tail's yellow eye stands out at a long distance and is the clue that most quickly differentiates it from a boat-tail. Should a great-tail stray to an eastern state, however, it will have to be identified by someone alert to its slightly longer tail, slanted forehead, and preference for drier habitats. The boat-tailed grackles of the Atlantic coast also have yellow eyes.

CONTRACTIONS

One recurring theme in stories of declining breeders is *ecological specialization.* The ivory-billed woodpecker fed almost entirely on the larvae of certain wood-boring beetles that infested large, newly dead trees in virgin forests in the southern United States. When these forests were logged, the ivory-bill disappeared. The last convincing reports of the species in North America were a calling bird heard and tape-recorded (but not seen) by John V. Dennis on the Village Creek in eastern Texas on February 25, 1968, and a pair photographed at an undescribed location in Louisiana on May 22, 1971. A remnant population survives in Cuba, but most authorities believe that the ivory-bill is now extinct in the United States.

The red-cockaded has inherited the title of our rarest woodpecker. It too is an ecological specialist. It nests almost exclusively in living longleaf pines that have been infected by redheart disease. Logging has eliminated most of the older pine trees in southern forests — the trees most susceptible to redheart — and so red-cockaded populations are critically low. One expert estimated that there may be only 3,000 left. In the last few years nests of red-cockadeds have been found where they have never been seen before — in young, undiseased pines and, once, in a cypress tree. Birders should report active nests of any type to local authorities.

Two other endangered specialists of the Southeast are the limpkin and the snail kite. Both feed on apple snails, the kite almost exclusively, and so both are limited in range and susceptible to population declines in their prey. The kite's numbers have fluctuated radically in the last twenty years — going up and down in synchrony with water levels and with the availability of apple snails in the Everglades — but thanks to careful protection, water level regulation, and the construction of some artificial nest baskets, the species seems to be threatened not quite as critically as it was in the 1960s, when the population apparently dropped below 100 individuals. Recent censuses indicate a population ranging from 300 to 600 individuals. The fact that the snail kite is the most common raptor in Argentina is evidence that ecological specialization is not always a bad thing.

Two warblers that are endangered because of their specialized needs are the Kirtland's and the golden-cheeked. Their situations are especially critical because, unlike the snail kite, they breed only in North America. If we lose them, the world loses them. The Kirtland's nests on the ground exclusively in young jack pine forests, and mated pairs have seldom been found anywhere but in Michigan's lower peninsula. Jack pine has a relatively large range in Canada, but apparently the weather is too cold or the habitats there are not right for the Kirtland's. It has been reported north of the border fewer than half a dozen times. The golden-cheeked warbler breeds only where it can strip bark from the Ashe juniper to build its nest. Other juniper trees will not serve, and so the golden-cheeked's range is limited to the Edwards Plateau in west Texas where the Ashe juniper occurs. As the Ashe juniper declines, so does the golden-cheeked.

Both these warblers are also plagued by *cowbird parasitism,* a secondary theme in the stories of several threatened species.

Snail Kite (above) and Limpkin

The brown-headed cowbird lays its eggs in the nests of various passerines, often after removing one of the parents' eggs. The young cowbird grows faster than the hosts' young, pushes them aside, and in the end is usually the nest's only surviving offspring. Most host species have developed countermoves. Some birds will throw out the cowbird egg; others will add a new layer to their nest, covering the egg (and their own original eggs); others simply abandon the nest. The Kirtland's and the golden-cheeked have not had time to evolve such strategies, however; the brown-headed cowbird has only very recently expanded into their ranges. The cowbird cannot be blamed for the decline of either, but both populations are so low that any losses to parasitism are critical. The painstaking nesting surveys and other research conducted by Harold Mayfield, the world's leading authority on the Kirtland's, led to a brown-headed cowbird control program that has helped *Dendroica kirtlandii* to hang on in its tiny range. A similar program may soon prove necessary for the golden-cheeked and for two southwestern vireos, the gray and the black-capped, which are declining and under extra stress because of the cowbird's recent expansion into their territories.

The greatest problem for most declining species is the simple and obvious one: *habitat loss*. One group that has especially suffered recently is *wetlands breeders*. As housing and industry develop the shorelines of rivers, lakes, bays, and oceans, we lose nesting birds. The short-eared owl, for example, has declined severely through most of its range in the East because appropriate breeding habitat has simply disappeared. The northern harrier (formerly the "marsh hawk"), although still fairly common, also seems to be declining. Both these raptors breed on the ground in wetland areas and have difficulty coexisting with man.

Most terns face the same problem. They need space and relatively undisturbed wetlands. Many have lost significant portions of their breeding areas to residential or industrial development. The inland population of the least tern, which once occupied most of the Mississippi River system, has dwindled enormously. The piping plover's situation is even more critical. It once nested all along the eastern coast from Virginia to Newfoundland and throughout the interior of the country, from Pennsylvania and Ohio north and west. Now its coastal population is limited to small, scattered colonies, and it has disappeared entirely from most of its range in the interior. North Dakota, with a population of about 700 birds, remains the piping plover's last stronghold in the United States. The closely related snowy plover is also declining in its homeland along the Gulf coast. Plovers and terns have difficulty nesting on even undeveloped beaches because they lay their eggs in the open and are prey to off-road vehicles, dogs, and careless beach walkers.

Another group suffering from loss of habitat, especially in the East, is the *open grassland breeders*. Their plight seems less publicized than that of the wetland breeders, but it is at least as bad. The upland sandpiper and the dickcissel, for instance, were once common breeding birds in the eastern interior where they are now rare or nonexistent. The grasshopper, lark, and Henslow's sparrows have also definitely declined or disappeared across much of their eastern ranges. Several other sparrows, including the vesper and the sharp-tailed (a wetlands breeder), seem headed for trouble.

All these stories are sad, and censusing a local breeder as it declines in your area can be a depressing and frustrating experience. One thing to keep in mind is that if it weren't for census takers, the problems confronting these birds would go undocumented and perhaps even unnoticed. Counting birds is the first step toward protecting them.

Something else to keep in mind is that not all declines are irreversible. After DDT was banned in 1969 — largely because census data proved that it was responsible for the disappearance of the peregrine falcon — the peregrine, bald eagle, osprey, brown pelican, and a number of other affected species rebounded strongly. Other birds have recovered from severe population losses. In 1937 the total world population of the whooping crane was down to fifteen birds. Careful management and increased protection on both its wintering and summering ranges have brought about a population increase to more than 100 birds. With the possible exception of the reddish egret, North American egrets and herons seem to have recovered completely from their decimation by hunters in the nineteenth century. And gulls are so numerous nowadays that it's hard to imagine that they too once seemed in danger of being hunted into extinction. Birds are more adaptive and resilient than we sometimes assume.

How about the Eskimo curlew? After the California condor and possibly the Bachman's warbler, the Eskimo curlew is our rarest breeding bird. Birders and ornithologists have been anticipating its extinction throughout this century, but the species somehow, somewhere, keeps hanging on. Between 1932 and 1970 there were fewer than two dozen reputable sightings, most of them from the Texas coast in May. Except for three seen on Galveston Island in 1962 and two seen on Martha's Vineyard, Massachusetts, in 1970, all reports described single birds. In recent years, however, the reports of sightings seem to have increased. On May 7, 1981, David Blankinship and Kirke King, two experts conducting a census of rookery islands in Galveston Bay, spotted what they believed was a flock of *twenty-three* Eskimo curlews! The birds flushed fifty yards from the boat and circled the observers twice. Both saw the short bills and cinnamon-buff underwings that are definitive field marks of our most endangered shorebird. It seems too much to ask, but could the Eskimo curlew be staging a comeback?

CONFRONTATIONS

Another population phenomenon that is a prime subject for amateur censusing is the *niche confrontation*. North America is filled with complexes of closely related species that seem to have divided the continent as carefully as human governments. Take a look in your field guide at the territories of our seven chickadees, for example, and you'll see they lock together like a continent-sized jigsaw puzzle. The fingerlike extension of the southern range of the black-capped chickadee along the Appalachian mountain range fits precisely into the fingerlike gap in the northern end of the range of the Carolina chickadee. The chestnut-back chickadee's breeding range along the Pacific coast is a slice of territory squeezed between the ocean to the west, the range of the mountain chickadee to the east, and the range of the boreal chickadee to the north. The elliptical cutout in the mountain chickadee's range in Arizona and New Mexico is the Mexican chickadee's toehold in North America.

In the chickadees, as in most complexes, the borderlines of these territories seem stable and undisputed and were settled by the ecological principle known as *Gause's rule:* no two species with the same ecological needs can coexist indefinitely in the same territory; one species must eventually replace the other. Most of the confrontations that shaped the jigsaw puzzle occurred long ago, before ornithologists were on hand to observe. In a few intriguing cases, however, we can witness Gause's rule in action. The ebb and flow of evolution can be studied by any birder with a pair of binoculars and a sense of geography. Two of the best-known confrontations have been carefully documented.

Blue-winged and golden-winged warblers. Frank B. Gill and others have established that the blue-winged warbler has been pushing northward throughout this century and has been replacing the golden-wing in all areas where their ranges overlap (see figure 6). The two hybridize regularly, share a recent common ancestor, and probably separated into two distinct populations during the last ice age. Now the ice is gone, the two are meeting again, and the golden-wing is in retreat. The golden-wing seems to require more specialized habitat than the adaptable blue-wing and is disappearing all along the leading edge of the blue-wing's range. From census data gathered throughout the East, Gill estimated that the turnover requires less than half a century, an eyeblink of time on the geological scale. "At present," he noted in 1980, "I know of no localities with breeding golden-wings where blue-wings have been established for fifty years or more." The blue-wing replaced the golden-wing in Charleston, West Virginia, in twenty years. Blue-wings

represented 5 percent of the individuals in the complex in
1960, 30 percent by 1970, and 100 percent by 1978.

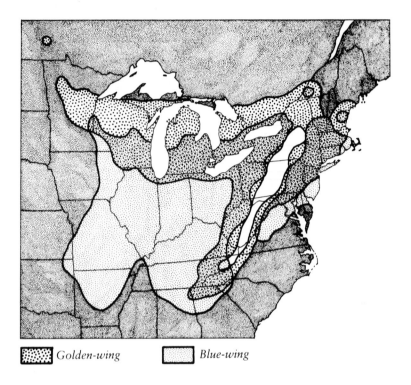

Golden-wing   Blue-wing

FIGURE 6. *Nesting Ranges of the Blue-winged
and Golden-winged Warblers*

Black and mallard ducks. In an article published in 1976,
Paul A. Johnsgard and Rose DiSilvestro analyzed seventy-five
years of census information to establish that the black duck has
been losing ground throughout its range to the mallard since at
least the 1930s. The trend continues today. The black has been
almost totally replaced by the mallard in many areas where it
was once the dominant member of the pair. In counts conducted in Ontario in the period 1900–1939, for example, 97

percent of all *Anas* ducks were blacks. In counts for the period 1970–1974, 22 percent were blacks. Like the golden-winged warbler, the black seems to have more specialized needs than its more adaptable rival. Johnsgard and DiSilvestro cited changing habitat, different game management practices, and different hunting regulations as possible causes for the decline and suggested that the trend might be irreversible; the black may now be destined "to become an increasingly rarer component of the North American bird fauna."

Other confrontations are more recent events and have not yet been studied in detail.

Cattle egret and other herons. Birders who live near heronries can contribute to our understanding of the impact of the cattle egret by counting nests and breeding pairs of the small and midsized herons. Some biologists believe that the cattle egret may be having a negative effect on the breeding success of the little blue heron, the snowy egret, and possibly other species. The cattle egret tends to dominate mixed species heronries because it nests earlier, in denser clusters than its relatives, and takes the best spots. Are the other herons' populations dropping in response? Only time and careful censusing will tell. Birders in those areas just ahead of the leading edge of the cattle egret invasion can contribute to the analysis by establishing baselines for the other herons' numbers. Should the cattle egret move into your area, these data will become very valuable. Birders inside the cattle egret's breeding territory can do comparative censuses each year.

Indigo bunting and lazuli bunting. Here's a confrontation of special interest to birders in Kansas, Nebraska, and Colorado. There is no doubt that the indigo bunting, once limited to the eastern half of the country, is expanding westward into these states. There is also no doubt that it is hybridizing with the lazuli. Hybrid buntings have been seen as far west as Los Angeles. What is not clear is whether the lazuli is retreating. Are the ecological differences between the two species great enough so that they can coexist, or will the indigo push the lazuli into a decline? Are the two forms actually a single species, and will they now behave as one in the overlap area?

Glossy and white-faced ibises. Birders on the Louisiana coast are in place to witness the meeting of two closely related species that have come to North America from Africa in two separate invasions. The white-faced came first, in prehistoric times, perhaps from across the Pacific; the glossy crossed the Atlantic during the nineteenth century. The glossy has been rapidly expanding northward. The white-faced seems to be expanding slowly eastward. Anyone interested in studying the progress of this confrontation will need sharp eyes. The redder legs, redder bill, and white strip on the face of the white-faced are present only during the breeding season. (Even then they are tough to see.) But careful censusing will be crucial to our understanding of the relationship of these two birds.

Table 2 lists some other developing or potential confrontations that birders can help monitor.

TABLE 2. *Confrontations from East to West*

INVADER	DEFENDER	OVERLAP AREA	REMARKS
Chuck-will's-widow	Whip-poor-will	From middle Atlantic states west to Missouri	Whip-poor-will expanding west while declining in South
Antillean nighthawk	Common nighthawk	Southeastern Florida	Newly split species; ecological differences not fully understood
Eastern wood-peewee	Western wood-peewee	Throughout Midwest at about the 105th meridian	Possibly conspecific; will hybrids be recognizable?
Cave swallow	Cliff swallow	Southwestern Texas	Both now nest in culverts; cave rare but increasing
Blue jay	Stellar's jay	Eastern Rockies, esp. Colorado and Wyoming	Hybrids rare but regular
Elegant tern	Royal tern	Southern California	Elegant exploding, royal definitely declining; do these two compete with each other?
Barred owl	Spotted owl	Northern California and Oregon	Spotted declining; barred possibly increasing

7 · WARBLERS

AT THE RIGHT TIMES of the year, glimpsing a warbler is simple enough. In spring and fall flocks can appear wherever trees grow: more than thirty species of warblers have been recorded in New York City's Central Park in a single morning. Furthermore, they live in virtually all North American habitats, including seasides, lakesides, swamps, parks, farms, deciduous forests, coniferous forests, river bottoms, canyons, and mountaintops. Two species, the yellow warbler and the common yellowthroat, nest across the entire continent, from the mangroves of Florida to the alders of Alaska.

Warblers are easy to *find;* it's *identifying* them that's so tough. Hawks, shorebirds, and other challenging groups of birds often allow leisurely observation. You can set up your scope, open the field guide, compare a bird with its associates, and call over an expert for help. Warblers do not stand still for telescopes, field guides, or expert assistance. One glimpse and they're gone: "See us now or see us never."

Some sparrows can be as elusive as warblers, but sparrows seldom travel in mixed flocks. If you can identify one or two species in a flock of sparrows, you've generally identified them all. Warblers usually travel in small bands of several species. While you struggle to identify one or two in a feeding party, four or five others flicker against the light, skip behind the leaves, and slip off into the shadows.

One common sequence of events in warbler watching might be called the warbler four-count. One, a warbler lands on a branch; two, it snatches up an insect; three, it glances around; four, it flies. Stop, snatch, look, *go*. Stop, snatch, look, *go*. From the birder's point of view, the sequence usually translates into "Hey! What? Uh . . . *Damn!*"

"At first I couldn't see it," an exasperated novice once cried, "and then it disappeared."

All warblers except the yellow-rump need insect prey to survive. The majority winter in the Caribbean or in Central America. Since they wait until insects are plentiful in our area, they are generally among the last migrants to arrive. When they come, they come at night, often accompanied by other late passerines in huge waves of birds. Overnight storms sometimes ground tens of thousands of warblers in a single area, and birders who've witnessed such fallouts speak of warblers "filling the trees like Christmas ornaments." The worst storms create grimmer sights. On the night of April 29, 1979, an arctic cold front with winds of sixty miles per hour blew down along the Texas coast and intercepted a wave of warblers and other birds crossing the Gulf. The next morning an observer on San Padre Island estimated that 70,000 to 100,000 dead passerines, most of them warblers, had washed up on the beach.

Warblers are surprisingly strong fliers, however. They usually avoid storms by flying over them (up to altitudes of more than three miles, radar tracking has found). When the weather is good, they frequently cover more than a hundred miles in a single night's flight. A banded yellow-rumped warbler once flew 450 miles in two days.

The family's champion traveler is the blackpoll. It winters in the jungles of South America, and it nests as far north as northwestern Alaska. On their spring migration, blackpolls make landfall on the Gulf coastal states about April 20 and, averaging about thirty miles a day, reach southern Canada about May 20. Then the pace quickens: they fly the next thousand miles in a week and the final thousand miles, from the Yukon Territory across Alaska to the Chuckchi Sea, in five days.

They come back in fall along a different route. They first head east across the continent, then south through New York and New England, reaching Cape Cod and other Atlantic coastal staging areas by mid-September. There they gather and wait for a clear night with the right winds. The conditions must be perfect. The final leg of the blackpoll's annual odyssey is a death-defying marathon: a nonstop overseas flight of 1,400 miles from the northern United States to South America.

Even with good winds, it's an eighty-hour flight from Massachusetts to Venezuela. This means a blackpoll that leaves Cape Cod on, say, Monday evening must fly without food, water, or rest all night Monday, all day and night Tuesday, all day and night Wednesday, and all day and night Thursday to touch land again sometime on Friday morning.

Luckily for land-bound birders, the blackpoll seems to be the only warbler that relies primarily on this overseas route. Warblers are often frustrating, but no devoted birder wants to see fewer of them. A woods without warblers is like a crossword puzzle without trick questions.

WHERE TO LOOK

Good warbler spots tend to have most of the following elements:

- low deciduous trees
- thick, tangled undergrowth
- an open or semiopen canopy
- clear edges
- fresh water

- wind protection
- pathways that are wide (four feet across or wider) and/or elevated.

The first six elements attract the warblers. The last makes it easier to look at them.

Quiet roads around lakes or along rivers are usually excellent warbler spots. The birds frequently feed in the tree limbs closest to the road or reveal themselves by flying across the road and landing in the first tree they reach on the other side. These roads are generally elevated, at least on one side, and the extra height offers an advantage to the birder, since the top of a ten- or twelve-foot tree may be at eye level. Abandoned railroad tracks running alongside wet woods are good for the same reasons. Also usually excellent are hiking trails that wind up hills or mountains. In Acadia National Park (Maine), the Great Smoky Mountain National Park (Tennessee and North Carolina), Mount Lemmon (Arizona), and similar areas, you can loop around a switchback and find yourself eyeball to eyeball with a blackburnian or hermit warbler feeding in the top of a fifty-foot tree.

Ironically, city parks, college campuses, and similar "less natural" habitats are often much better for warbler watching than deep and pretty lowland forests. In artificially landscaped areas, warblers will take refuge in widely separated lines of trees. Unless they are severely disturbed, they tend to move along these lines and so are more easily tracked.

Climax forests are notoriously empty of warblers. The lack of undergrowth means that midlevel and low-level warblers are absent. The closed canopy makes the few high-level species that do appear very hard to see.

At the seashore, warbler chasing is usually an all-or-nothing enterprise. In spring when there's a hard wind blowing offshore, you can sometimes come upon a fallout of exhausted warblers that have settled in the first bushes they came upon. More often, however, incoming migrants will fly inland before dropping into the trees. In the fall, coastal staging areas such as Cape May, New Jersey, and Assateague Island, Virginia, are best when the winds are blowing onshore. You usually won't find many warblers in the vegetation closest to the ocean, but if you search inland in areas with strong windbreaks, you may find flocks of warblers waiting to fly out when the weather changes.

STRATIGRAPHIC SPECIALISTS

Most warblers prefer certain heights (see figure 7). In many cases the preference is so strong that the stratigraphic level occupied by the warbler can be a clue to its identity.

The blackburnian, cerulean, and other *high-level warblers* are most often seen in the top one-third of the tallest trees in the area and rarely appear below eye level unless no higher perches are available.

The magnolia, Canada, and other *midlevel warblers* are seen most often in the middle third of the taller trees in the area, at the tops of shorter trees, or in bushes down to about waist level.

The Kentucky, mourning, and other *low-level warblers* are seen most often at eye level or lower and sometimes on the ground.

Other stratigraphic preferences are more subtle and harder to chart, but may still prove helpful once you become aware of them. In the East, for example, you should look twice at any "female hooded warbler" flycatching over your head: there's a good chance that the bird is a female Wilson's. Hooded warblers will sometimes be seen up in the midlevels (especially singing males), but they are more often seen near waist level and below. The opposite is true for the Wilson's. By the same logic, western birders should take a close at any "female Wilson's" walking on the ground. Hoodeds are rare but regular vagrants west to California.

You may also find that the stratigraphic preferences for particular migrant warblers in your area may differ from those described in the books (including this one). According to a couple of field guides, the bay-breasted is supposed to be a "midlevel"

HIGH
LEVEL

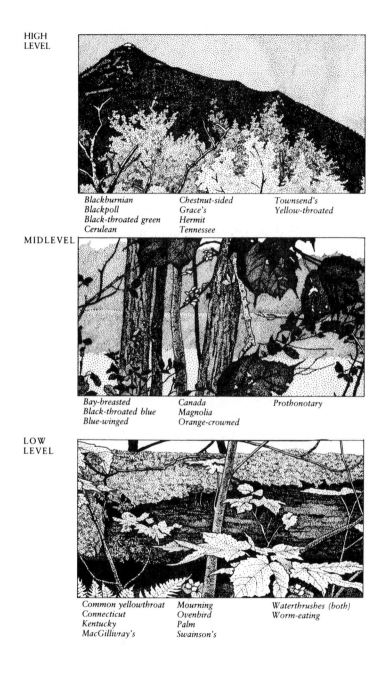

Blackburnian   Chestnut-sided   Townsend's
Blackpoll   Grace's   Yellow-throated
Black-throated green Hermit
Cerulean   Tennessee

MIDLEVEL

Bay-breasted   Canada   Prothonotary
Black-throated blue Magnolia
Blue-winged   Orange-crowned

LOW
LEVEL

Common yellowthroat Mourning   Waterthrushes (both)
Connecticut   Ovenbird   Worm-eating
Kentucky   Palm
MacGillivray's   Swainson's

FIGURE 7. *Stratigraphic Preferences of Warblers*

or "all levels" warbler. I can't remember ever having seen one on a perch lower than ten feet in woods near my house in New Jersey.

SPRING

Spring, as every birder knows, is the best season for warbler watching. The birds are in their finest plumage, and many sing strongly when they are still hundreds of miles south of their nesting grounds. What is not so well known is how brief the spring migration period actually is and how easy it is to miss.

Some warblers move north relatively early — the yellow-rumped, pine, palm, Louisiana waterthrush, black and white, yellow-throated, yellow, prairie, palm, and black-throated green. Three species tend to come late: the blackpoll, mourning, and Connecticut. The rest tend to come together and pass through any given area within a period of three weeks or less. Typical peak periods appear in table 3, and dedicated warbler chasers try to be out in the field at every opportunity during the peak period, since weather patterns will determine the fallouts, and these are almost impossible to predict.

No general guide can list the warblers in the sequence in

TABLE 3. *Peak Periods for the Spring Warbler Migration*

REGION	PEAK PERIOD
SOUTH Florida, Gulf coast, Texas, and so. California	April 10–May 5
MIDLATITUDE Virginia north to New Jersey and west to Colorado and no. California	April 25–May 20
NORTH New York to Maine, west through Dakotas to Idaho and Washington	May 10–June 1

which they will arrive in your area. Different species of warblers migrate at different speeds, so where you live will determine when each reaches you. The parula, for example, is one of the first warbler arrivals in northern Florida, appearing there as early as the first week in March. It moves northward slowly, however, and does not arrive in Maine until mid-May during the main influx of warblers there.

Especially in spring, the morning after a night of hard rain is the best time to look for a fallout of passerine migrants. Birding during days of intermittent rain can also be productive. The birds will continue to feed during light rains. If the showers stop and the sun breaks through, you can find yourself suddenly surrounded by parties of celebrating, hyperactive warblers.

Wind is a more serious problem. Warblers are more sensitive to wind than most birds and tend to stop moving and hide inside the foliage even during moderate gusts. If the wind starts to blow steadily at more than fifteen miles per hour or so, you should search deeper (and lower) in the woods or, better yet, put on your hawk-watching hat and save the warblers for another day.

FALL

So much has been written and said about "the confusing fall warblers" in general and the problems of immature plumages in particular that some birdwatchers believe that if they miss a warbler in the spring, they've missed it for the year — only "warbler fanatics" pursue them in the fall. In some ways, though, warbler chasing is actually better in fall than in spring. The daily stream of migrants is steadier and less weather dependent (there are fewer fallouts, but there are also fewer days with no warblers in sight), and — very important — the period itself is much longer. The fall migration in most areas is more than two months, from late July or early August to mid-October.

Another factor that makes autumn warbler chasing essential

for anyone serious about a year list is the elliptical migration paths followed by many species. Again, consult your regional checklists for information here. In almost every area of the country certain species are far easier to find in fall because the area is not on their regular spring routes.

It's important to note also that not all autumn plumages are puzzling. Many species show virtually no difference from their spring colors. These include the waterthrushes, the ovenbird, the black and white, the yellow-throated, the prothonotary, the blue-winged, the chat, the worm-eating, and several others. Some other warblers — including the redstart, black-throated blue, black-throated green, prairie, cerulean, parula, and blackburnian — are much more numerous in their juvenal or female plumages in fall, but all of these can be identified with a modicum of experience. Furthermore, there are always at least a few males of each species still in their breeding plumages. "The plumages of fall warblers," Pete Dunne has noted, "are like their spring plumages — only less so."

One immature warbler is actually easier to identify than many adult male warblers — the juvenile chestnut-sided. Its lime green back is unique among North American birds.

Two truly difficult fall warblers are the blackpoll and the bay-breasted. During the autumn migration these two species are rarely, if ever, seen in male breeding plumage, and distinguishing immatures and females in areas where both species occur is perhaps the toughest of all warbler puzzles. Some birders refer to both of them as the "baypoll" warbler. One problem is that the blackpoll's legs are sometimes an eye-catching red and sometimes not. A red-legged "baypoll" is definitely a blackpoll, but a dark-legged one is not necessarily a bay-breasted. The converse applies to the streaking on the breast. A clear-breasted "baypoll" is definitely a bay-breasted, but a streaky-breasted one is not necessarily a blackpoll. Some bay-breasts show faint streaking. Another problem is that both species can be surprisingly yellow — much brighter than either appears in most field guides.

Table 4 presents one possible identification sequence. The

TABLE 4. *Blackpoll or Bay-breasted Warbler?*

FIELD MARK		IDENTIFICATION
1. Red legs?	→	blackpoll
2. Dark streaking in breast?	→	blackpoll
3. Definitely no streaks in breast?	→	bay-breasted
4. Rust or bay under wings?	→	bay-breasted
5. None of the above? Or unsure?	→	"baypoll" sp.

fourth field mark would come first in the sequence if it were easier to see. To find it, you must usually work your way into the woods until you are directly below the bird in question, watch for it to raise its wings, and then look quickly under the "wing pits" (the *axillars*). The patch of breast there is frequently still bay colored after the rest of the bird has become buffy and obscure.

One other clue doesn't count as a field mark, but it's useful to remember: these two warblers have different migration schedules. Bay-breasteds ordinarily migrate south two or three weeks earlier than blackpolls. Consult a regional guide for the time in your area.

SUMMER AND WINTER

Summer and winter are definitely the off seasons for warbler watching. From early June, after the last blackpoll, Connecticut, or mourning has moved through, until mid-July, when the first northern waterthrush or redstart returns, warblers are much harder to find. The foliage has grown thick, the birds are more wary, and the only species you can hope to see are the local breeders.

Summer is a time when you can work on your warbler *listening* skills, however. Conducting a nesting survey is good way to learn songs, or you may simply want to wander regularly through the closest woods. You will hear only the warblers that nest in your area, of course, but that can be an advantage; it narrows the possibilities, and you can return again and again to the same warbler's territory. It's best to do this early in the summer, as warblers, like most birds, sing most frequently before the young have hatched.

The yellow-rump is usually considered the "winter warbler," but four others regularly winter in the East as far north as the mid-Atlantic states and occasionally in New England — the pine, the palm, the common yellowthroat, and the orange-crowned. In the west the yellow-rump is joined by the yellow-throat, hermit, Townsend's, orange-crowned, and an occasional Nashville during the winter, at least along the coast.

In the East the orange-crowned warbler ranks with the winter wren and the saw-whet owl as one of the most sought-after prizes of the winter woods. North of the Carolinas, it's a tough bird to find. I know some birders with years of experience who have never seen one. Other birders, however, find it every winter and claim that the species is much more common than is generally believed. If it is overlooked, the reason may be that

Orange-crowned Warbler

it associates with yellow-rumps, which are usually so numerous by mid-November that there's a tendency to ignore them. In some areas, in fact, yellow-rumps are so abundant that any birder trying to examine each one in the hope of discovering an orange-crown could spend the whole day in the field doing nothing else.

The trick is to look casually at the flocks of yellow-rumps for a warbler *hanging head down over the end of a branch like a chickadee.* If it's a dusky gray or gray-green bird, look closely: you've probably just found an orange-crown. Orange-crowns like to climb onto the tips of the smallest branches in the ends of tree limbs and probe for food as the branches bend with their weight. Yellow-rumps, larger and less acrobatic, rarely do this.

BASIC TECHNIQUES

1. *Start slowly.* Here's a paradoxical principle for beginners: *disregard the warblers you can't identify.* When a feeding party appears, look first for the seven species listed in table 5. If your experience is limited, you should study these carefully, and on your first five or ten field trips, forget the rest. Build up your base of experience. When you can tell the easy species at a glance, you will find your eyes moving quickly and efficiently through the flock, and you can advance naturally to the tougher identifications.

Self-restraint and credibility are involved here also. An ornithologist once complained, "The problem with a lot of birdwatchers is they want birds before they deserve them. They add the magnolia warbler to their life list one weekend and the next they're out looking for a Kirtland's. Until someone's seen maybe ten thousand magnolias, ten thousand palms, and ten thousand prairies, I don't think he has the right to even consider the possibility of a Kirtland's." This remark sounds harsh, but it's true that the best birds are the ones you earn. Letting the "might-have-been's" go unidentified hurts at first, but eventually it makes the thrill of a certain sighting all the sweeter.

TABLE 5. *Seven Warblers for the Beginning Birdwatcher*

SPECIES	DESCRIPTION
Black and white	Walks along trunks and tree limbs; the *nuthatch* warbler.
Parula	Tiny and hyperactive; "flickety" wings; the *kinglet* warbler.
Yellow	Frequently found in more open areas than other warblers — e.g., solitary willows and farmside hedgerows; the *canary* warbler.
Ovenbird	Prefers dense undergrowth to open edges and limbs to branches; walks, hops, and teeters; unmistakable song; the *thrush* warbler.
Common yellowthroat	Male is the *raccoon-faced* warbler; both sexes very curious; if you can't pish up a yellowthroat, you can't pish.
Redstart	Fantails and flycatches at all levels; bright and beautiful, the *butterfly* warbler; in Latin America called *candelita* — the little torch.
Yellow-rumped	Widespread and abundant, especially in colder weather; the *ubiquitous* warbler.

Because of its abundance, the yellow-rump is the first difficult warbler that birders should try to learn. There are several clues.

1. It is one of the largest warblers; only the chat is bigger.
2. It's the only warbler that gathers in true flocks. Sometimes as many as thirty or forty can be found in a single line of bushes.
3. It is by far the most likely warbler north of Georgia from November through March.

During spring and early fall the yellow-rump creates problems when it mixes with other warblers and appears in a baffling variety of plumages. In the East, one helpful field mark is always present. In all plumages, yellow-rumps have *a clear white throat over a streaked or smudgy black-and-white breast.* Only one other eastern warbler ever has a similar pattern and then only in the fall: the immature Cape May. And the Cape May's throat is grayer, less sharply outlined, and usually faintly streaked. (Spring-plumaged Cape Mays have yellow breasts and are easily distinguished.)

Unfortunately, the white throat mark doesn't help in the West. Western yellow-rumps (formerly considered a separate species, "Audubon's warbler") have yellow throats (in breeding plumage) or white throats (nonbreeding females), and the picture is further complicated by the presence of "eastern" yellow-rumps, which overwinter regularly in the West. Although Cape Mays and magnolias are very rare west of the hundredth meridian, warbler chasers should be alert to the possibility of mistaking either of those two for a yellow-rump. Take a careful look at the cheekpatches and breasts. Cape Mays and magnolias have lighter, grayer cheeks and usually much more yellow on the breast.

2. *Use the field guide with restraint.* Stopping to consult the field guide is always dangerous when chasing warblers. If the bird is still in sight, you're spending time you could be using to get a better look — and giving the bird a better chance to escape. Try to keep your eyes on the bird as long as possible and use your field guide as your last resort, not your first one. When you do open your book, always try to guess the identity of the bird first, and then look only at the illustration of that particular species. If your guess is wrong, *look back at the bird in the field,* take another guess, and look only at the illustration for that species. This technique requires self-discipline (my binoculars always seem to quadruple in weight at such moments), but it forces you to realize which species give you problems, and it helps you develop your abilities.

Unfortunately, opening the field guide after an unidentified warbler has flown away creates another problem. Each glance at the field guide's pretty closeups interferes with the memory of the real bird. Every flip of a page blurs it further. After a few minutes of page turning, the real vision can evaporate entirely. A notebook and sketchpad are helpful here, but the only real solution is doing your homework — preparing yourself so well you know what field marks to look for *before* the birds appear.

3. *Scan with binoculars.* Search-scanning with binoculars can be an effective technique with warblers, especially in bad light or in thick woods. Search-scanning seems unnatural at first: most people instinctively wait to catch a glimpse of movement, then try to locate the bird with their naked eyes, and *then* lift their binoculars. You'll see more of each warbler, however, if you *go to the binoculars at the first sign of movement.* Doing so saves three or four seconds, and often enough, that's all the time a warbler will give you.

This technique has a bonus: scanning for one bird, you'll stumble on others you've missed with your naked eyes. I owe one of my best life birds to a Townsend's warbler that landed on a branch of a fir tree just long enough for me to focus on it and find the only olive warbler I've ever seen, sitting stock-still on the branch behind.

4. *Aim for the head first.* When you first have a warbler in your binoculars, concentrate on the head and face. Do not shift your gaze until you have studied the bill, eyes, cheeks, cap, and throat. Most of the field guides separate the warblers according to the presence or absence of wing bars, as this is the easiest way to divide them into two groups. The fact is, though, that only four or five species can be identified by their wing patterns alone. If you spend the first precious seconds studying the wings first, the birds will often escape before you've seen anything else — and you'll be left thumbing through your field guide, muttering, "Well, I know it had wing bars."

Ignore the wings until you've examined the head carefully. *Every single spring male, almost all spring females, and even most fall warblers of both sexes can be identified by head pattern alone.*

Once you've seen the head pattern, you can check quickly whether the wings are barred. If you can't decide, don't waste time squinting; it's often hard to tell. Move quickly to the belly markings, which can be easier to see and are at least as useful. Try to determine where the breast color changes: near the throat? under the shoulder? over the legs? Distinctions here will help you separate several of the puzzling immatures — including orange-crowned versus Tennessee, pine versus prairie, and blackpoll versus bay-breasted. Tail and rump patterns are also useful, so you should try to keep your binocs on the bird even as it flies away.

Aiming for the head first solves an identification problem most nineteenth-century ornithologists found impossible — distinguishing between the two waterthrushes. Modern binoculars have made the separation less problematic, but it is still not easy. The two species' habits are identical, the light in the streamside bushes they prefer is usually poor, and both are wary birds, often unwilling to give the birder more than a four- or five-second study. A further complication is the fact that the yellow in the eyelines of some northern waterthrushes is very pale, almost as light as the white in the eyelines of Louisianas. As the field guides note, the Louisiana's eyeline is always longer and wider, but the bill size is an even better field mark.

Louisiana Waterthrush (top)
and Northern Waterthrush

If you can remember that the Louisiana was once known as the "large-billed waterthrush," you'll dazzle your friends with your ability to distinguish between these two species. The distance from the eye to the tip of the bill on the Louisiana appears to be *about two-thirds bill;* on the northern it seems *less than half bill.* The Louisiana's bill is also thicker at the base and more curved.

WARBLER LUCK

Searching for warblers involves spending a lot of time swatting at mosquitoes, wrestling with cat briars, and staring into empty trees. Hours can pass without your seeing a warbler. In fact, even at the peak of migration, whole field days can go by without a single "good" warbler sighting. One way to keep the faith in such moments is to rely on the law of averages. Consider each birdless hour an investment in future luck. The warblers are out there somewhere. If you give them enough chances, they will come — ten minutes from now or tomorrow or next week — and dance over your head.

The simple and ultimately delightful truth about warblers is that you can never identify all you see. No one can. Frank M. Chapman, one of the premier warbler chasers of all time, estimated that only one warbler in a hundred was seen well. Binoculars have improved since Chapman's day, but still, in any encounter between birder and warbler, the odds are with the bird. It's unreasonable to expect to "get" them all — or even half of them.

This is ultimately delightful because it means warblers are always a challenge — warblers will *always* be a challenge — no matter how skilled you become. You can only become faster and more accurate in identifying them; you can never overmaster them. "Warblers are a great leveler," the Rhode Island birder Hugh Willoughby once commented, "and a boon to the cause of humility."

John Hintermister chased his last warbler, the Connecticut, for more than fifteen years without success. Rare and seclusive (and misnamed), the Connecticut is a tough bird to find anywhere outside its breeding range in Wisconsin, northern Michigan, and southern Canada. On migration it keeps out of sight, walking stealthily in brushy tangles. In Florida, John's home state, only a dozen or so are reported each year, and anyone who finds one there is very lucky. But to John, a birder with enormous ability and extraordinary eyesight, this blank on his life list was a source of agony. Long after he'd seen all the rest of Florida's regularly occurring birds he was still missing *Oporonis agilis*.

In Gainesville, where he taught birding classes and led countless field trips, it was a common fantasy among those of us who considered ourselves his protégés to find John his Connecticut. One October afternoon Jim Horner came close. Walking in the woods a hundred yards from home, Jim was startled to discover the white-ringed eye of a Connecticut warbler staring at him from low in an oak tree. He studied the bird just long enough to confirm the identification, then backstepped away and sprinted to his house to phone John at work. John was on the scene, in tie and jacket, within ten minutes, but he was too late. The bird had flown. When Jim began describing the field marks he'd noted, John clapped his hands over his ears. "Oh, don't tell me about it," he said. "That only makes it worse."

The following year in the first week of May ("Connecticut prime time," John called it) I drove with him 300 miles to an area in south Florida where one or two Connecticuts were seen almost every spring. When we stopped at the local expert's house, he told us, "You may be a day too late. I saw *four* Connecticuts at the county park yesterday. I couldn't believe it; I almost got tired of looking at them."

" 'Almost got *tired* of looking at them,' " John repeated as we raced to the park. "I always suspected there was something wrong with that guy."

At the park a full morning's search found us nothing more exciting than a couple of black-whiskered vireos. We were walking back to the car for lunch, dispirited, when John snapped his binoculars to his eyes and pointed into a tangle of bushes. A dark, thrush-sized bird was walking away from us along a drooping branch. I had it in view for perhaps three seconds before it stepped off the branch and disappeared.

"I can't stand this much longer," John whispered. "Come on; we have to go after it."

We tiptoed into the brush and searched, but whatever it was was gone. "Was it a Connecticut?" I asked him.

John nodded. "I think so. It had to be. Just the right size, with a dark gray head, walking the way they're supposed to."

"Did you see well enough to count it?"

"*Hell no!* I want to *absorb* this bird. Let's spread out."

We spent the rest of the day crisscrossing that park. At first, while we still had hope of finding it again, we worked quietly. Then in desperation we tried to flush it out — clapping our hands, shouting, running around. But the bird had flown.

The 300 miles home was a very long trip.

Soon afterward I moved from Florida and heard from John only intermittently — usually just after he'd added some vagrant species to his Florida list. "Hey!" he liked to shout into the phone. "Check off the groove-billed ani!" Or "Hey! Check off the black-capped petrel!" I knew better than to ask in such moments about his nemesis.

Several years passed. Then one October evening when I called him to report some sightings of my own, his end of the conversation was strangely silent. "So," I asked him finally, "what have *you* seen lately?"

"Well, I saw a Connecticut."

"You did! When?"

"Two weeks ago, at Mullet Key."

"Why didn't you call me?"

He waited a long moment, then answered so quietly I could hear voices mumbling on other lines. "I didn't call anybody. Something happened to me looking at that bird. I felt great for a minute or two. Happy, satisfied, relieved. But he wouldn't fly away; he kept walking around right in front of me. And suddenly I felt sad. I mean " — he took a deep breath — "now that I've seen the Connecticut warbler, *what the hell am I going to chase for the rest of my life?*"

8 · HAWKS

PETE DUNNE, then director of the Cape May Bird Observatory, climbed down from his hawk-watching platform one afternoon and approached a couple sitting under a nearby tree. "How are you doing?" he asked.

"Terrific!" said the young man. "We've seen over 1,400 hawks already today."

"That's good," said Dunne. "What's your breakdown?"

The couple looked confused.

"I mean, how many have you seen of each species?"

The couple stared at him blankly.

"Well," said Dunne, "did you catch that peregrine over the bunker about fifteen minutes ago?"

The young man smiled and shrugged. "We don't worry about identifying them. We just count them."

Dunne tells that story frequently. "It shows," he says, "that hawks are enjoyed at every level of knowledge."

I'm not sure he's right. Hawks are beautifully sculpted birds and powerful, dramatic fliers — the kings of the air. Their autumn movements are the most spectacular of all diurnal migrations. Beginners like Dunne's young couple are usually entranced. It seems to me, though, that many *intermediate* birders have a hard time enjoying hawks. Once you move past the "Oh, wow!" stage and want to know what you're looking at, hawks can give you headaches.

One problem is that hawk watching requires a different technique from other forms of birdwatching. Most field and woodland birding is stalk and stab. You walk quietly and, when you come upon a bird, snap your binoculars to your eyes for a quick look. The drama is played out in a few moments, and you either get the bird or you don't. Hawk watching, especially at lookout sites, is more like reeling in a fish. A raptor appears off in the distance, swimming in the sky. You must find the bird in your binocs and then hang onto it — for a long, slow, wrist-trembling, neck-crinking, eyestraining diagnosis. If you keep at it long enough and you're lucky, you may pull the bird in close enough for its field marks to become obvious. More often, the hawk breaks away by dropping below the trees or soaring into the sun.

A second problem is that field guides cannot help with hawks as much as they can with other kinds of birds. Hawk plumages are variable, and the subtle color differences within each group, especially among the accipiters and the buteos, are hard to illustrate and even harder to see. The plumage problem is further complicated because immatures generally outnumber adults at most fall migration sites.

Finally, there is the third and worst problem for intermediate hawk watchers: *expert hawk watchers.* I've been making annual pilgrimages to Cape May, Hawk Mountain, and elsewhere for more than ten years now. It's a rare trip when I don't find myself frustrated and humiliated because I see so much less than the experts do. While I struggle to identify a broad-wing a hundred yards out, they are arguing with each other whether the golden eagle four mountaintops away is a first- or second-year bird.

Even while there are no birds in sight, you can tell who the best hawk watchers are at any lookout. They are the ones in the crowd who, when the skies seem empty, have their eyes to their binocs and their mouths shut. I once asked Clay Sutton why he spends so much time scanning the horizon from the ground below the lookout platform at Cape May Point. Why not climb up with everyone else and get a better view? He laughed. "I just can't concentrate with all that chatter up there."

When the hawks *are* in sight, the best watchers are meticulous observers. "Clay Sutton," says Pete Dunne, "is one of the best hawk watchers I know because he studies each bird for individual characteristics. Most people come out to the Point lookout knowing nineteen species of hawks are possible here —nineteen pegs for nineteen holes — and they study each new bird just long enough to fit the peg to the hole. If in one day a thousand hawks of five species come by, they go home thinking they've seen five different birds. Clay sees a thousand different birds."

Good hawk watchers also seem to tune in quickly to the winds, weather, and local geography. They don't sweep the sky at random; they focus their attention on certain areas, those sections of the sky the birds are using under that day's particular flight conditions. The corridor a hawk is using can be a clue to its identity. Buteos may be passing high on the left in the updrafts off a ridge while the falcons are zipping by on the right, fast and low over the tree line.

The characteristic that most distinguishes expert hawk watchers from us ordinary mortals, however, is their ability to identify hawks at long range. Stand next to an expert at a lookout for an hour on a good fall day and you're sure to have your confidence shaken. He or she will be separating red-tail from rough-leg while you are wondering whether the dots in the distance are birds or dirt specks on your lenses. I used to try to protect my ego in such moments by whimpering about my weak vision, but I've been upstaged too often by too many bespectacled hawk watchers to believe that excuse anymore. The truth is that the best hawk watchers don't really see farther than the rest of us; they see differently. They've learned to identify hawks by their flight style.

HAWKS BY FLIGHT STYLE

Intermediate birders have trouble with hawks because the components we're accustomed to looking for in other birds — color, size, and body shape — are secondary in hawk identification. The most visible field marks in hawks are their motion and rhythm in flight, and this is where experts begin their analysis of distant raptors. While the intermediate birders are straining their eyes to see color or trying to get some sense of the bird's size (very difficult to do at long range in an open sky), the expert relaxes and studies what can be studied: how often the bird is flapping and the silhouette of its wings in gliding position.

Flight styles are difficult to illustrate on the printed page and change with the weather, so figure 8 is only a rough approximation of group tendencies. Still, these tendencies are real and useful. Once you learn to adjust your expectations to the winds and local geography, the differences are very obvious in the field. Experienced observers use the combination of wing silhouette and flap/glide ratio as the first clue to the identity of virtually every distant hawk. Most raptors can be placed in their subgroup from as far away as they can be seen. After that, identification becomes a matter of keeping your eyes on the bird and knowing what differences to look for within each subgroup.

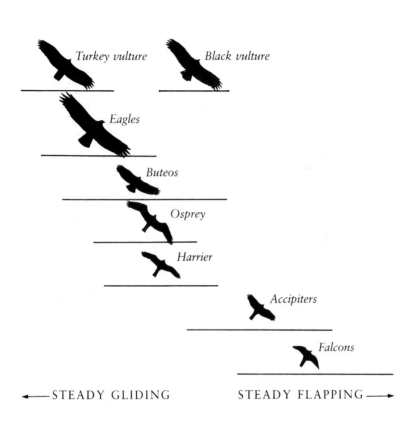

FIGURE 8. *Flight Styles of Hawks*

OSPREY

The osprey's typical flap/sail rhythm is not all that different from that of several other hawks, but its silhouette is very distinctive. It is usually a snap to distinguish the osprey from other raptors. No other hawk except the Swainson's glides as the osprey does, with its wings held in downward kinked position. Head-on, an osprey looks like an elongated **M**.

The one trick with this species is distinguishing it from a gull, especially the similarly colored greater black-back. An excellent hint about the distinction comes from Pete Dunne. "The osprey," he has observed, "is broader winged, particularly broader at the hands. The fuller the soar, the broader the hands appear. Gulls never appear broad-handed."

A hawk with hands? By golly, the man is right! When an osprey strokes, the wide wing tips really *flap*. Gulls' wings are always more pointed, and the stroke is a neater, trimmer movement.

"And," Dunne adds, "ospreys never appear large-headed. Gulls have large heads with very obvious straight bills. There is just about as much head coming out in front of a gull's wing as there is tail coming out behind. Ospreys have a relatively small head, a no-headed appearance. A distant soaring osprey looks like a bird that is all wing and tail."

NORTHERN HARRIER

Another fairly easy raptor is the northern harrier, formerly called the marsh hawk. It is a widespread and well-known bird throughout North America, and, when engaged in its characteristic low-level, zigzagging flight, is usually quickly identified.

The one time this species can present a puzzle is at hawk watches. The harrier's migration flight is very different from its hunting flight. On migration, it soars at great heights and, when seen from directly below, looks like a cross between a falcon and an accipiter and can be mistaken for either. This is the key to identifying it, in fact. *If you see a "peregrine" with the prominent, banded tail of a Cooper's hawk, or a "Cooper's hawk" with the pointed, swept-back wings of a peregrine, you're probably looking at a harrier.* For confirmation, note the flap/sail ratio. Harriers tend to flap less and glide more than either the Cooper's or the peregrine. At close range, you may also be able to note the head profile. The harrier has a flat face and short neck. Its bill and head seem recessed, often trailing behind the leading edge of the wings.

KITES

For simplicity's sake, I haven't included the kites on the flight style chart. All but the Mississippi have limited ranges and are usually easily identified. The kites are not closely related to each other, but they share a characteristic look in the air. They have small torsos in proportion to their aerodynamic surfaces and seem loose and windblown in flight, as if their wings and tails were two or three sizes too big for their bodies.

The best soarer and the most distinctive member of the group is the swallow-tailed kite. If there is one exception on our continent to Ludlow Griscom's famous caveat that "no bird is unmistakable," this is it. The swallow-tailed kite is the most identifiable bird in North America and perhaps the world. Nothing else looks like it, nothing else flies like it, and few thrills in birdwatching will compare with your first sighting of this magnificent animal.

Identifying the snail kite is almost as easy — once you make your way to its very limited territory in south Florida and search it out. (Route 41 between Ochopee and Sweetwater, north of the Everglades National Park, may be the most accessible and reliable spot.) The one identification problem comes in winter, when it's possible to confuse a female or immature northern harrier with a female snail kite. Both course low over the sawgrass and have white patches at their rear ends. Watch for differences in flight style and silhouette that parallel the differences between gull and osprey. The harrier has a more streamlined look, with thinner, more pointed, and slightly swept-back wings; the snail kite has a ragged, floppier look, and its wings have broader, more prominent "hands." The snail kite also flaps more and glides less than the harrier.

The black-shouldered kite is another easy identification if you aren't misled by its new name. In North America the species was long known as the "white-tailed kite." It's a shame the name couldn't have been changed to the "white kite." It is the whitest hawk on the continent and more easily mistaken at first glance for a tern or gull than a raptor. The white-tailed hawk and the ferruginous hawk are light-breasted and light-winged, but neither is the bright unspotted white of the kite (and both are almost twice as big). An adult male harrier is the raptor most likely to be mistaken for a black-shouldered kite. The harrier is most often seen flying in wings-raised, zigzagging glides, and the black-shouldered occasionally courses fields in a similar style. The kite, however, also frequently hovers while it hunts, like a kestrel or a kingfisher and unlike the harrier.

The Mississippi kite is the only problematic member of this group. It has the largest breeding territory, is the kite most likely to stray out of its range, and, with its darkish breast and swept-back wings, can easily be mistaken for a peregrine falcon. Watch for a very different wing stroke: the kite's stroke looks loose and light; the peregrine's is strong and snappy. Also useful is the difference in tail action. The Mississippi kite has a broad and very active tail, which it frequently tilts and twists; the peregrine usually keeps its tail folded in a tight, slightly rounded rectangle.

Raptor enthusiasts might consider a trip to Hancock County, Mississippi, the one place in North America where three kites nest. If you're lucky, it's even possible to see the swallow-tailed, black-shouldered, and Mississippi kites sharing the same airspace. All three have been seen there simultaneously. Another kite watchers' mecca is the Santee River delta in South Carolina, where both the swallow-tailed and the Mississippi nest in good numbers.

VULTURES

Northern birders making their first trip south sometimes misidentify turkey vultures because they overstress the best-known field marks of the black vulture, its black head and white wing tips. Immature turkey vultures have heads just as dark as those of black vultures, and against a bright sky even the red head of the adult turkey vulture can appear black. Turkey vulture wing tips also sometimes seem to flash white in the distance. The trick is to forget about the differences in head and wing tip color and concentrate on aerial behavior. The differences in flight style between the two species are usually very evident, even when the bird in question is a pinpoint in the distance.

The TV is a *glider*; the BV is a *flapper*.

Turkey vultures seem to labor in flight only while they are close to the ground, at tree level or lower, and while they are working their way upward. Once they've gained altitude, they flap their wings slowly and infrequently. Riding thermals, they seem to hang in the air effortlessly, rocking back and forth in the wind, their wings almost constantly held in a V-shaped dihedral. In good flying conditions they can glide for several minutes without flapping their wings.

Black vultures, in contrast, are more often seen working hard to stay airborne. Only on strong, high thermals does the black hold its wings for long intervals in gliding position. More often it's seen flapping quickly and frequently and gliding in short, tight circles. It never holds its wings in a sharp dihedral. In wing-extended silhouette it resembles a short-necked, stumpy-tailed eagle or a big owl more than a turkey vulture.

When you come upon a vulture in a tree or on the ground, remember not to be fooled by a black head. Look instead at the amount of tail and wing extending past the legs. The long wings and long tail give a standing TV an *unbalanced* look, as if its rear end is weighing it down. A walking TV looks particularly awkward; the tail drags. BVs have shorter tails and shorter wings and so appear better balanced while perched and more comfortable when walking.

One intriguing puzzle associated with the vultures involves distinguishing the turkey vulture from its southwestern mimic, the zone-tailed hawk. The zone-tail copies the vulture's flight style, apparently so that it can sneak up on the birds, lizards, and other animals it preys on. Experienced hawk watchers of the Southwest can distinguish between these two by subtle differences in their flight styles. The zone-tail is said to hold its head differently and to flap its wings more frequently. Birders on their first trip to the zone-tail's territory in Arizona and New Mexico, however, would be wise to check for tailbands on *every* "turkey vulture" they come upon. No matter how much you've read about the zone-tail's mimicry, it's a good bet the imitation will stun you when you first see it — or, if your first experience is like mine, when you don't see it. I spent several afternoons searching for a zone-tail until three fellow birders pointed one out to me, a hundred feet over my head. I had seen the bird approach, had dismissed it as an obvious turkey vulture, and had gone back to searching the horizon.

THE EAGLES

Flight style is the best way to separate an eagle from a distant turkey vulture. Both eagles soar on flatter, wider wings than the turkey vulture. Because they do not rock back and forth as the turkey vulture does, they look much more powerful in the air — as if they've been chiseled into the wind.

Separating the two eagles from each other is another question — for several reasons. First, immature eagles outnumber adults in most midlatitude areas. The adult golden eagle is not difficult to identify, and the adult bald is easy, but at most hawk lookouts you are far more likely to encounter an immature in one of the confusing intermediate plumages. Second, first-year bald eagles are very dark on top and in certain lighting conditions seem as brown above as adult goldens. Also, the cleanly demarcated white undertail of the immature golden is not as definitive as some field guides suggest. Subadult bald eagles go through a transitional stage when their undertails can show the crisp white wedge usually associated with immature goldens, and goldens' tails are variable. The single field mark that differentiates the two species at any age is subtle and hard to confirm: the bald eagle's bill and head project farther out from the wings than the golden's.

According to some experts, flight style is a good way to distinguish the two eagles: the golden eagle is supposed to fly with its wings held in a slight, upward-curving dihedral (like a moustache); the bald eagle is supposed to fly with wings held either horizontally or in a very slight downcurve. Recently, however, Bill Clark and other raptor specialists have questioned the dependability of this field mark. Clark has seen and photographed both species in both flight postures and has suggested that the distinction might hold true only at certain inland ridge sites. He believes the head and tail ratios are the best mark. The bald eagle's head protrudes more than half the length of the tail; the golden's projects only about a third of the length of the tail.

My sense is that Clark is right about the wing attitudes but that the head/tail proportions may be useful only to birders with considerable experience with eagles. There's something about seeing an eagle that renders me incapable of the cool mathematics required to measure head versus tail. A different field mark noted by Clark seems to me to be the real key. Clark divides the bald eagle's immature and subadult plumages into four stages: dark immature, white belly, mottled, and transitional. *In all plumages before the adult, the bald eagle has white triangles in the wing pits.* The golden eagle's wing pits are always dark. If you can remember this one field mark and the sequence of questions shown in table 6, you should be able to identify most of the eagles you encounter.

TABLE 6. *Eagle Identification Sequence*

FIELD MARK		IDENTIFICATION
1. White head?	→	adult bald eagle
2. White wing pits? Or mottled upper surface?	→	immature bald eagle
3. White underneath restricted to tail and crook of wings?	→	immature golden eagle
4. Entirely dark above and below?	→	adult golden eagle
5. None of the above? Or unsure?	→	eagle sp.

One other underemphasized field mark helps with perched birds. Unlike the bald eagle, which doesn't acquire its adult head until its fourth or fifth year, the golden eagle nape is golden *in all plumages*. Bad lighting can conceal this color, but when you do see it, the mark is definitive.

FALCONS

With their streamlined tails, boxers' torsos, and jet fighter wings, falcons are built for speed and live by it. The prairie falcon has been observed overtaking and capturing white-throated swifts on the wing, and estimates for the top speed of a peregrine in full stoop exceed 200 miles an hour.

No other hawks fly as falcons do — with steady, lashing strokes on swept-back wings. In fact, the only birds whose flight style bears any real resemblance are the jaegers, the falcons of the sea. All falcons will soar occasionally, especially as they come over water on migration, but if you keep your eye on any possible falcon for more than a minute, you should see it break out of the glide with a series of quick, strong whip strokes. If it doesn't, it's probably not a falcon.

In the East, the key piece in the falcon puzzle is the merlin. Once you learn the merlin, you should have few problems identifying the kestrel or peregrine.

First-time hawk watchers should be careful not to be deceived about the merlin's size. Since its illustration appears between the kestrel's and the peregrine's in all field guides, there's a tendency to think of it as the middle-sized of the three. The merlin is actually a *small* falcon — much smaller than the peregrine and only slightly bigger than the kestrel. You should not attempt to distinguish between the kestrel and merlin by size alone.

The merlin is best identified by its flight, which is the quintessence of the falcon style. Watch for a kestrel-sized, streaky-dark falcon flying with deep, quick, and *continuous* strokes. Pumping, pumping, pumping, it zooms by you, straight and swift. Remember: *the merlin is the bullet hawk.*

The kestrel flies with a more flickety stroke interspersed with short, weak glides. At hawk lookouts it is the falcon most likely to be seen circling overhead, soaring. For these birds Frank Haas has noted a useful field mark: "The base of the kestrel's wing is very narrow compared to the wings of both the merlin and the peregrine, which are broader-based. In between the point where the trailing edge of the kestrel's wing meets the body and where the tail starts, invariably a short section of body shows. This space is generally lacking in the merlin and the peregrine. So even when they're at great height, you can separate out the kestrel quite easily."

Kestrel (left) and Merlin

In the West, the falcon puzzle is complicated (deliciously complicated) by the presence of the prairie falcon. Distinguishing the peregrine from the prairie falcon by silhouette or flight style is a game for experts. "Look for a shallower wingbeat and a chunkier bird," says Steve Hoffman. "The prairie has a larger head and a stiffer wingbeat — without the peregrine's liquid ripple," says Clay Sutton. Less experienced birders might want to concentrate on plumage differences, however. These are visible at ranges of up to several hundred yards. The prairie is a much paler bird. Its back, tail, and upperwings are a sandy pale, more washed out than those of even the lightest female kestrel, and close (in my mind's eye) to the color of the back and upperwings of a meadowlark. The dark triangles that begin in the wing pits and extend about halfway out the underwings are the best field mark. Once you know to look for them, they're surprisingly obvious, even easier to see than the similar but less extensive markings on the underwings of the black-bellied plover.

It's interesting that the prairie falcon has been reported so seldom in the East — less often than either of the other two western hawks that breed in the northern U.S. and Canadian prairies, the Swainson's and the ferruginous. The Swainson's seemed to find its place on the eastern hawk watchers' possibilities list for the first time sometime in the mid-1970s and, since then, has moved up in status to "rare but regular vagrant." In the last few years the ferruginous has also been reported with increasing frequency in the mideastern interior and on the coast. There are about four records of individuals in Florida. Both of these apparent changes in status probably owe more to heightened awareness and increased confidence among observers than to sudden new developments in the birds' migration behavior. Could our understanding of the prairie falcon's status in the East change with a similar conceptual breakthrough? Have eastern birders been dismissing as shadows any dark areas seen on the underwings of passing "peregrines"?

ACCIPITERS

The accipiter flight style is usually described as "flap, flap, glide" or "flap, flap, flap, sail." But other hawks will flap, flap, glide to a certain extent — the kestrel especially.

What makes the accipiters' style distinctive is a peculiar, herky-jerky hesitancy. *Flap, flap, hitch, glide* might be a better description, or *flap, flap, hitch, glide, hitch*. Watching an accipiter laboring past a hawk lookout leads you to wonder how it will reach its destination. Raptor enthusiasts often confess they'd like to come back in their next life as a falcon, eagle, or rough-legged hawk. I've never heard one talk about being reincarnated as an accipiter; it looks like too much work.

Although the three accipiter species do not actually overlap in size, the differences can be so slight between female sharpie and male Cooper's and between female Cooper's and male goshawk that identification by size and silhouette is only certain at the ends of the spectrum — for the dainty male sharpie and the imposing female gos. Between the extremes, accipiters must be identified with care.

1. *Take your time.* The distinction between the female sharpie and the male Cooper's is probably the most difficult of all hawk-watching puzzles. It's not something you should attempt at a glance or within a few moments after arriving at a hawk-watching site. One of the important differences between the two species is rhythmic. The sharp-shin shows a quicker wingbeat with shorter glides. "The sharpie is a clipper," Jack Padalino has pointed out. "The Cooper's is a clopper." But before applying this subjective standard, give yourself a chance to tune up on other birds and to adjust to the weather and wind conditions of the day.

2. *Know the ratios.* Except in the Far West, sharp-shins outnumber Cooper's hawks in most migration sites by five or ten to one up to a couple of hundred to one. Except in Canada and the northern states, Cooper's usually outnumber goshawks by similar percentages. Your luck with all three will depend on the status of each in your area, but generally speaking, weekend birders recording more than one or two Cooper's hawks in an outing or more than one or two goshawks in a season should take another look at their field guides.

3. *The rounded tail of the Cooper's is not a reliable mark for inexperienced hawk watchers.* This well-known field mark may do beginning birders more than harm than good. A

squared and notched tail is reliable mark for a sharp-shin, but to identify a Cooper's it's best to look first for a *longer* tail and then check for roundedness. And wait until the tail is folded; the tails of all accipiters (and virtually all hawks) look rounded when they are fanned.

4. *Watch for white in the tail of the Cooper's.* When closed, the sharp-shin's tail shows a thin white line at the tip or no white at all. Since the feathers in the Cooper's tail are of all different lengths, the tips do not overlap, and together they form a wide white rectangle visible to a hundred yards or more.

5. *Watch for the Cooper's neck.* Allen Fish and others have pointed out that the sharpie's head projects less than the Cooper's. The sharpie's no-neck look also accentuates the length of its wings. The Cooper's longer neck and longer tail make its wingspan appear proportionately shorter.

6. *The goshawk has the least accipiterlike flight.* By flight style, size, and silhouette it's very easy to mistake a gos for a buteo, especially the red-shouldered hawk. In fact, one of the best ways to find a goshawk is to check any "buteo" you see for a streaky-gray breast and underwings. The female goshawk is an especially large and powerful-looking bird, even bigger than the red-shouldered and close in size to the red-tail.

7. *Be grateful for high winds.* Good, strong winds often make for better hawk watching. In the case of the accipiters they're especially helpful because they accentuate the differences in the flight styles of the three species. The sharpie's weaker flight is most noticeable on a gusty day, when the bird will be blown up and down, left and right, and even backward. The Cooper's can usually hold its own in a strong wind — and watch for its longer tail ruddering back and forth to become much more obvious. The goshawk is an even stronger flier, able to plow into the wind, Bill Clark has pointed out, like "a flying log."

8. *Don't call them all.* Birders who never see an accipiter they can't identify are probably fooling themselves. This is especially true for birds seen away from hawk watch sites. When

not migrating, accipiters are most often seen zipping through bushes and trees and a quick glance is all you get. Serious hawk watchers restrain their imaginations in such situations and write down *Accipiter* sp. for those birds.

BUTEOS

If all twelve species were equally possible anywhere in North America, the buteos would present an impenetrable puzzle. All have similar silhouettes and flight styles, and most take their colors from a muted palette of black, brown, gray, and white. Worse, the plumage variations within each species are more complex in the buteos than in any other subfamily of birds except the gulls. All buteos have at least two distinct plumages, adult and immature; two have four distinct plumages, adult and immature for two different phases; and three have more than eight different plumages. The red-tailed hawk, which *is* equally possible just about anywhere in North America, has more than a dozen different plumages.

The hard truth about this group is: *no single, readily visible field mark is diagnostic for all members of any species of buteo.*

The red in the tail of the red-tailed hawk, for example, is what a logician would call a "sufficient but not necessary" field mark. All buteos with bright red tails are red-tailed hawks, but not all red-tailed hawks have bright red tails. Young birds have grayish tails; melanistic birds have brownish tails; "Krider's" red-tails have pink or white tails; and "Harlan's" red-tails have gray or white tails streaked or spotted with brown or black.

The chestnut (or rusty bay) in the upperwings of the Harris' hawk is a mark a logician would call "necessary but not sufficient." All Harris' hawks have chestnut in their wings, but not all buteos with chestnut in their wings are Harris' hawks. The adult red-shouldered has similar coloration and can be mistaken for an immature Harris'.

And these are two of the most useful field marks. Most buteo marks are like the pale chin on the Swainson's hawk or the whitish underwings of the ferruginous, neither of which is sufficient *or* necessary!

Immature buteos are more variable than adults, and field guides ordinarily have only enough space to illustrate one of the possible variations. One of the most puzzling hawks I've ever seen was a small buteo that soared over my head at Flamingo, Florida, for five minutes one afternoon in December 1975. It had all the field marks of a dark-phase short-tailed hawk except one. The tail had faintly speckled vertical streaks rather than the clear horizontal bands shown in all the books. I have yet to find this plumage illustrated in any text and the short-tailed hawk hangs on my life list by a thread: a sentence in Howell's *Florida Bird Life* mentions that immatures sometimes lack the banded tail.

All the buteo color phases are another problem for field guide artists. Phases in some birds are an either/or situation. A snow goose is blue or white. A reddish egret is red or white. Ornithologists call these species *dichromatic*: there are two possible color phases with no intergrades. Two buteos are apparently dichromatic, the short-tailed and the ferruginous.

But the three widest-ranging buteos — the red-tail, Swainson's, and the rough-legged — are *polychromatic*. Each appears in a multitude of phases with many intergrades. Their colors vary across a spectrum of possibilities too diverse to be fully represented in any general field guide.

When an immature or oddly plumaged buteo passes overhead, identification must be a multistep process. You must resist the natural urge to lock onto one field mark and force yourself to scan quickly from one feature to another. Try to remember the acronym BUTEO:

B = breast (or breast, belly, and bib)
U = underwings
T = tail
E = extras (what else can you see? head color? feather color on legs? upperwings? upper tail? wings in a dihedral?)
O = odds (what are the chances of seeing the species at this season in this locale?)

If you can train your eyes to move quickly from one component to another and if you know which species are possible in your area, you will identify most of the buteos you encounter.

There are a couple of shortcuts. Six of the North American buteos are nonmigratory or short-distance migrants and are unlikely to appear outside their limited ranges: the short-tailed hawk (restricted to Florida) and the five southwestern specialties — Harris', black, gray, zone-tailed, and white-tailed.

Elsewhere we have two midsized hawks, the broad-wing and the red-shoulder, and four large ones, the red-tail, the rough-leg, Swainson's, and the ferruginous.

Although the broad-wing is the smallest of these six, its silhouette is often inseparable from the red-tail's at a distance. To distinguish a broad-wing from a red-tail (or a red-shoulder), study the underwings. *The underwings of a broad-wing seem very light at long range and sharply contrast with the feather edges, which are tipped with black.* The broad-wing is also the

Broad-winged Hawk

only eastern buteo to migrate in large flocks (thirty or more individuals). East of Baton Rouge a large, single-species kettle of buteos must be broad-wings. West of San Antonio a large, single-species kettle of buteos is probably Swainson's hawks.

The red-shoulder can sometimes be differentiated from the other buteos by its longer-tailed, slimmer-winged, *accipiterlike* look. Most field guides also mention the windows in the red-shoulder's primaries, but as Roger Tory Peterson notes in his guide, these are "not infallible." Don't depend on them, and be careful. Any buteo can show translucent areas in the underwings. Call it a red-shoulder only when the windows are *crisp, clear crescents.* In the Northeast the red-shoulder is generally a later migrant than the broad-wing, and you can see in tables 8–14 that the odds for broad-wing or red-shoulder reverse in early October. In the West the few migrating red-shoulders stay close to the coast, and so the species is seldom seen outside California and Oregon.

Four buteos remain, and now things become really complicated. One of the four, the ferruginous, has a seldom discussed though not so rare dark phase; another, the rough-leg, has long been thought to have just two phases but is now believed by many experts to be polychromatic. Finally, the other two large buteos, the red-tail and Swainson's, are as variable as any birds in North America. Hawk watchers everywhere should be prepared for any of these four buteos. The red-tail and rough-leg have continentwide ranges; the Swainson's and ferruginous are widespread in the West and occur rarely (the Swainson's annually) in the East.

Table 7 compiles the most important field marks of the more common light-phase forms of these four large buteos and is intended as a quick guide, not a complete summary. Only the points in all capitals are sufficient by themselves (and none is "necessary"). The best thing to do is study as well as you can the breast, underwings, tail, and extras (the B-U-T-E of the acronym) on any puzzling buteo you see, write down your notes, and *then* consult your field guide. Good luck. May you be the first on your block to find a ferruginous hawk at the local refuge.

TABLE 7. *Typical Field Marks for Large, Light-Phase Buteos*

POINT	RED-TAIL	ROUGH-LEG	SWAINSON'S	FERRUGINOUS
Breast	Dark band (most plumages)	Dark lower belly	DARK BIB OVER LIGHT BREAST	All whitish (imm.) or WHITE OVER DARK LEGS
Under-wings	Dark leading edge from shoulder to crook of wings	Thick, dark "wrist" patches	Flight feathers darker than coverts	Whitish with some flecking
Tail	ORANGE-RED	WIDE, DARK TAIL BAND	Many bands (most of four species)	Whitish; bands absent or slight
Extras	Vociferous; steam-whistle call	LEG FEATHERS LIGHTER THAN BELLY	Long, pointed wings; glides in dihedral; migrates in large flocks	FLASHY WHITE PATCHES IN UPPERWINGS
Other	Probable to unmissable throughout United States in any season	A widespread "cold weather" bird, seen in United States in late fall and winter	Western "warm weather" bird seen in United States in spring, summer, and early fall	Usually restricted to open lands west of 100th meridian

AUTUMN MIGRATION TABLES

Thanks to permission from the Hawk Migration Association of North America (and thanks to the efforts of the dozens of observers who counted the birds), I'm able to include in tables 8–13 the daily summaries from six of the premier hawk-watching spots in North America for autumn 1985. For directions to the spots and an explanation of table 14, see page 160.

TABLE 8. *Holiday Beach, Ontario: Daily Totals for Selected Species, Fall 1985*

Month and Day	Turkey Vulture	Northern Harrier	Sharp-shin	Cooper's	Red-shoulder	Broad-wing	Red-tail	American Kestrel	Total
AUGUST									
31		18	17			46	14	67	170
SEPTEMBER									
1		6	61					39	107
2	1	53	132			38	6	243	479
3		1	63					29	93
5		1	30					9	41
7		6	263					251	521
8		4	150					56	212
10	1	39	1,049			32	4	386	1,519
11		27	522			71	7	55	586
12	12	44	1,394	2	1	30,404	19	234	32,121
13	25	56	1,094	3		598	53	59	7,284
14	11	30	1,280	8	3	2,033	7	71	3,444
15		6	520	1		48	7	23	606
16		1	274					3	279
17		1	96					3	101
18		2	113	2				4	122
19		4	207	1				12	227
20		1	120	3				31	156
21	16	19	449	8		54	8	725	1,280
22		9	262					14	287
23		11	239	7		1		14	273
24	17	20	404	4		5	1	119	570
25	22	4	190	16		254	6	19	511
26	22	2	92	1			1	5	123
27	89	14	734	13		3,582	23	230	4,691
28	129	14	576	12		5	5	195	889
29		3	175	1			1	12	194
30	8	3	58	1					70
OCTOBER									
1	97	3	166	4				13	284
2	49	15	331	22	4	4	16	96	590
3	69	19	237	10	2	17	6	34	396
4	6	6	134	2				7	158
6	79	9	298	2	1	2	12	43	452
7	110	9	291	11			6	18	447
8	90	2	153	2				2	250
9		2	145	1				2	151
10			39	1				2	42
11	777	7	269	12	1		97	57	1,233
12		13	35	3				4	56
13	789	50	936	53	31	17	168	77	2,154
14	65	29	271	12	4	1	4	15	393
15	164	6	282	16	3		9	23	506
16	1,097	24	267	47	7	13	171	20	1,661
17	54	16	47	5	1		4	10	140
18	99	3	74	1			3	5	177
19		13	101	4		1	3	23	146
20	586	142	260	50	364	1	238	41	1,699
21	246	25	26	39	76		177		621
25	146	10	29	9	27		144	2	399
26	35	5	4				15	1	61
27	227	20	18	11	138		223	7	660
28	141	13	18	38	135		705	5	1,065
29	5	15	11	19	97		630	3	788
30	2	7	9	5	65		279	1	373
31	11	10	6	6	40		533		612
NOVEMBER									
15	7	4	19	4	22		830		1,075

TABLE 9. *Hawk Mountain, Pennsylvania: Daily Totals for Selected Species, Fall 1985*

Month and Day	Osprey	Bald Eagle	Northern Harrier	Sharp-shin	Cooper's	Goshawk	Red-shoulder	Broad-wing	Red-tail	Golden Eagle	American Kestrel	Total
AUGUST												
23	2		2					31	13		3	52
28	7	1	1	9				24	11		7	64
SEPTEMBER												
1	18		7					7	8			41
4	12	4	6	9				22	10		17	80
5	3		2	12				33	6		7	63
6	4	1		28				43	7		6	89
7		1	1	30	4			48	3		7	95
8	3		5	46	1			85	1		13	454
9	10		6	61				72	1		10	160
11	19		4	42	2			425	6		14	526
12	8		2	25	2			165	8		4	214
13	15	1	1	35	3			73	11		4	157
14	9	1	2	26	2			93	17		4	157
15	6		4	10	4			63	2		1	90
16	8	1		21	3			104	4		3	151
17	12		9	52	4			926	8		13	1,028
18	1	1		58	1			344	1		6	418
19	1			24	1			18	2		5	52
20	4		3	69	1			47	3		7	137
21	8		2	57	9			100	1		9	187
22	7		12	67	10			98	8		8	213
23	4		7	14				7	5			40
24	8		3	65	1			4	2		8	91
25	7		3	103	12			130	5		18	281
26	24		11	126	1			256	3	1	3	437
28	23	1		380	17			32	8		37	503
29	11		6	167	7		1	7	2		3	210
30	5		13	94	5			20	8		7	160
OCTOBER												
1	6		5	124	1		3	4	10		2	157
5	17		3	322	11		1	2	3		4	366
6	11		8	1,330	66		8	4	12		63	1,512
7	10		3	379	17			5	18	1	8	442
8	26		23	312	22			1	28		5	423
9	17		10	161	3			1	11		2	215
10	2		3	139	3	1			3	1	8	164
11	2			79			8		60		2	144
12	7		17	85	12		20		95		1	252
16	10		9	494	23				30	4	25	607
17	3	2	4	21	1		5		15			58
18	2		14	47	1		1		7	1	1	66
19	1		8	60	1				3	1	3	76
20	5		11	141	9	1	28		95	1		301
21	2	1	4	31	6		19		91	2		174
22			5	13		2	7		41	1		82
23	1			13	1	2	3		48			75
25		3	6	95	3	1	11		131	3	1	261
26			5	66	3	1	12		176	3		269
27	1		7	12			3		138			164
28	1	1	4	14	2	5	13		344	6		401
29			8	13	1	4	11		148	1		196
31				15	1		3		107			130
NOVEMBER												
1			3	3			12		35			61
2				3		1	3		36			47
6		1	11	4			7		74	8		109
7			2	15					23	4		53
8			3	19	1	4	2		83			120

TABLE 10. *Cape May Point, New Jersey: Daily Totals for Selected Species, Fall 1985*

Month and Day	Turkey Vulture	Osprey	Northern Harrier	Sharp-shin	Cooper's	Red-shoulder	Broad-wing	Red-tail	American Kestrel	Merlin	Peregrine Falcon	Total
AUGUST												
28	1	13	14	1			3		284			318
29	3	32	30				15	3	252			337
SEPTEMBER												
4		12	7	5	1		1		266	2		294
5		24	40	11					185	4	1	266
6	14		33	3				1	172	4	1	228
7		51	40	82	2		15		229	6		426
11	5	48	62	429	1		34	3	458	35	1	1,077
12	11	11	34	711	6		52	8	306	50	1	1,191
13	4	34	78	2,046	19		68	9	397	33		2,688
14	6	14	24	487	8		25	4	108	34		710
15		34	32	1,356	19		10	3	146	29		1,632
16	5	20	12	446	9		2	2	78	30	2	606
17	3	3	16	328	5		4	1	85	16		461
18		9	5	511	20		5	1	94	30	2	677
19		19	10	1,331	17		11	1	469	26	2	1,886
20		30	15	946	24		18	1	597	49	1	1,681
21		7	9	757	12		6	1	235	25	6	1,058
22			8	312	3		12		103	29		467
23	5		3	187	1				190	80	6	472
24		120	3	169	10				144	192	7	645
25	2	96	54	2,125	24		180	3	913	80	3	3,480
26		33	23	692	9		2		256	77	5	1,107
28	2	151	118	739	32		12	2	388	227	13	2,685
29	6	227	155	1,785	70	1	322	4	336	165	11	3,082
30	10	90	29	475	28				69	41	13	755
OCTOBER												
1		18	15	234	22				15	15	9	328
2	62		15	211	11				6	36	12	353
3		12	11	124	5				1	15	7	175
4		142	50	390	34		10	2	85	81	46	840
5		97	14	212	11		1	1	122	135	21	614
6	9	308	179	2,367	210	2	31	7	1,321	127	24	4,588
7	10	142	80	979	132	2	172	8	299	80	26	1,931
8		57	28	469	111		113	2	144	99	11	1,036
9	12	132	18	647	291		324	10	82	81	24	1,622
10		187	21	998	167		33	3	262	115	31	1,817
11	12	247	124	2,295	421	13	323	13	975	273	28	4,727
12	20	94	83	1,075	116	4	75	13	121	59	5	1,669
14		12	13	116	21	1	12	1	28	14	14	232
15	5	22	15	981	16				16	17	15	199
16		40	46	779	44	15	25	6	163	51	6	1,175
17	34	63	58	1,111	175	40	34	30	66	6	1	1,619
20	2	27	34	153	18	3		6	31	57		331
21		13	25	79	6				26	42	1	192
22	15	9	36	639	18			1	5	27	2	755
23	8	11	33	509	38	15		20	53	11	4	704
25	10	23	21	742	66	109		23	280	125	1	1,291
26	66	20	121	864	111	2	3	264	45	16	1	1,629
27	7	7	18	180	13	49		5	27	4	1	266
28	75	16	39	645	83	53		162	15	5	2	1,103
29	43	5	51	316	28			200	9	2		721
NOVEMBER												
7	12	15	28	401	38	84		107	17		2	718
8	34	2	44	491	39	28		124	17	1		783
11	6	1	12	202	5	8		14	14	1		265
14		2	6	99	2	32	1	74	16			236
15	49	1	22	385	16	158	1	395	17		1	1,054
17	7	1	15	151	8	14	1	85	4			288

TABLE 11. *Kiptopeke Beach, Virginia: Daily Totals for Selected Species, Fall 1985*

Month and Day	Black Vulture	Turkey Vulture	Osprey	Northern Harrier	Sharp-shin	Cooper's	Broad-wing	Red-tail	American Kestrel	Merlin	Peregrine Falcon	Total
AUGUST												
31			10	1					35		1	47
SEPTEMBER												
1			5	1			1		33			40
7			20	24	1				66	1		112
13	11	9	13	3	70	1	2	4	48			170
14			11	12	268	5	3		74	1		377
15			4	3	119		4		9	1	2	143
17		3	4	4	16		1	2	32		1	69
19		1	6	4	142	1	22	3	60	4	2	269
20			3		31				7	3		45
21			9	3	84	1			42	8		148
23		1	10	4	292		3	1	109		2	431
24			2		72				77	11	2	165
25		9	85	85	307	2	7	2	1,090	6	3	1,612
26			38	33	2,168	3	4		463	2	2	2,715
28			31	9	121	4	2	2	275	7		460
29			31	12	245	2	250	11	160	3	7	832
30			6ó	4	283	1	34	1	27	5	13	443
OCTOBER												
1			12	9	344	12		1	26	12	2	418
2			5	3	143	3	3		16	7	6	187
3			5	2	59	3			5	10	1	85
4			5		25	2			3	16	1	52
5			14		74	2			20	23	18	153
6			22	5	148	1		1	53	4		237
7	4		20	3	273	13	7	1	52	3	5	384
8		1	13	17	855	27	16	8	98	39	8	1,090
9		11	98	2	422	10	186	4	99	9	21	877
10			16	2	290	5			59	5	4	371
11	26	86	98	4	579	29	137	10	153	117	25	1,331
12			87	56	999	19	57		195	36	2	1,452
13			6	9	347	2	2		17	4		387
14		56	16	27	517	17		1	151	18	8	815
15			18	14	219	16		2	48	6	5	328
16	17	59	40	55	446	12		8	184	2	6	840
17	2	133	57	61	1,519	30	39	29	188	8		2,066
18		62	18	40	243	23	2	29	15	3	1	441
19			19	4	59	5			4	4		95
23	7	106	79	49	254	13	21	24	117	5	5	680
24	25	27	22	4	56	3		1	4			142
25		6	5		17	2		1				31
26	15	104	9	19	1,472	14	21	18	18		1	368
27		6	8	10	43				2		1	70
28	37	85	8	7	36	3	3	26	5	1		215
NOVEMBER												
15	18	14	1	2	5			2	1			43
23	4	71		2	5			10				95
24		18		1	5			8			1	34

TABLE 12. *Goshute Mountains, Nevada: Daily Totals for Selected Species, Fall 1985*

Month and Day	Turkey Vulture	Osprey	Northern Harrier	Sharp-shin	Cooper's	Swainson's	Golden Eagle	Red-tail	American Kestrel	Total
AUGUST										
28			6	10	4		2	15	27	76
30			1	11	6	1	6	13	31	74
31	1	1	4	4	4	1	5	18	11	56
SEPTEMBER										
1	1	1	2	11	3			29	36	86
3			1	15	11		3	12	5	49
4	7		1	15	9	1	3	19	14	75
5	5	2		27	16	1	1	34	14	106
6	2			41	16	3	2	30	21	123
7	2	1	2	32	11	1	1	11	10	75
9			3	65	32	2	3	9	11	133
10		1	2	36	16	3	3	7	7	81
12	14	3		47	18		2	23	4	135
13		4	1	117	82	1		22	25	258
14	51	2	1	239	111	25	8	86	75	658
15	14	7	6	108	87	3	5	89	15	365
16	31	5	5	331	310	13	2	274	132	1,159
17	7	5	1	126	143		4	52	45	387
19	2	1	2	74	75		2	39	5	207
20	34	7	2	65	106	6	5	113	11	367
21			2	22	21	1	1	23	7	93
22			4	16	16			18	7	68
23	13	1	1	37	83	4		129	25	345
24	1	1	6	89	46	1	3	32	24	218
25	9	1	3	54	58			49	24	218
26			1	256	164	1	4	57	98	592
27	2	1	5	85	57		1	21	60	243
28	3		3	78	70			57	12	262
29				49	21	1	3	33	8	117
30	1			43	33		4	24	6	117
OCTOBER										
1	4		6	153	25	2	5	95	20	326
2				25	6		3	5	2	49
3			2	21	3		2	10	2	45
4				11	7		1	29	4	52
5		1	9	162	16		4	49	28	272
6			2	93	8	1		24	6	137
11				34	1		2	19	4	77
14				10			4	15	1	42
15				51	1		13	30	2	106
16				42				6		54
18				16	1		3	24		47
19			6	33	2		8	5	2	57
20			4	51			4	22	2	95
21			1	3			3	42		61
24			2	77	1		5	17	1	106
25			5	53			9	36	1	120
26			4	40	5		9	26		92
27			3	24	5		8	14	1	65
28			3	12	4		3	20	1	47
29			5	42			4	99	1	164
30			3	13			4	24	2	53

TABLE 13. *Golden Gate, California: Daily Totals for Selected Species, Fall 1985*

Month and Day	Turkey Vulture	Osprey	Northern Harrier	Sharp-shin	Cooper's	Red-shoulder	Broad-wing	Red-tail	American Kestrel	Total
AUGUST										
21	3	3						14	6	27
22	3	2		3				15	2	25
27	2				4			21	6	33
31	7	1		1	4			14	14	42
SEPTEMBER										
10	14	4	1	10	14			19	2	69
11	10	1	3	16	31		1	40	8	114
12	12		1	15	32			22	2	88
13	6			11	15			9	3	48
14	5	7	1	38	33			25	13	140
15	3	1	2	39	53			15	4	124
16	4		1	11	17			11	6	56
18	12	3	2	126	105	3		63	2	334
19	5		2	247	318			136	2	730
20	6	3		117	151		4	88	1	392
21	3	1		235	172			40	2	502
22	2	2		143	94	2		33	5	294
23	7	2	1	21	27		1	43	2	120
24	3		2	212	75		5	45	3	364
25	15		4	102	77	1	3	29	3	255
27	7			34	26			9	1	86
28	4		1	126	62	7	12	35	2	311
29	23	1		64	34	1		40	1	182
30	7	1	3	70	36	6		56	2	194
OCTOBER										
1	4		3	42	43	2	1	9	4	113
2	7	3	11	153	104	16	1	51	12	400
3	3		4	92	99	9	12	45	5	286
4	6		5	130	85	3	2	36	3	321
5	20	2	1	91	54	2	1	25	4	217
7	4		3	17	35	1	1	17	2	89
8	5		1	35	27	3		26	3	104
9	6	1	4	124	94	4		38	4	287
10	7			11	15	5		34	2	79
12	5		1	30	17	2		11	4	80
13	3	2	2	46	34	7		34	6	142
14	2		3	23	23			38	3	96
15	9		8	17	20	4		34	2	102
21			2	7	5	1		13		30
25	2		2	19	15	2		14	2	66
26	2		4	43	29	1		68	3	175
27	2		2	47	17	2		47	4	136
28	2		3	38	21	2	1	50	8	136
29	2		5	9				25	3	53
30	3	1	8	18	6			57	12	115
31	2	1	3	60	28			103	4	217
NOVEMBER										
1			4	39	18	1		68	2	141
2			5	43	28	3		81		180
3			6	14	12			45	1	83
6		1	3	10	3			50	4	73
7			3	6	7			144		165
8	1		3	14				139	6	165
9			3	7	6	1		36	4	61
13			14	4	7			126	2	159
14			1	1	2			37		42
19			2	1	2			22		27
DECEMBER										
12					1			31		32

TABLE 14. *Eastern Hawks' Typical
Migration Periods and Peaks
(approximately 40 degrees latitude)*

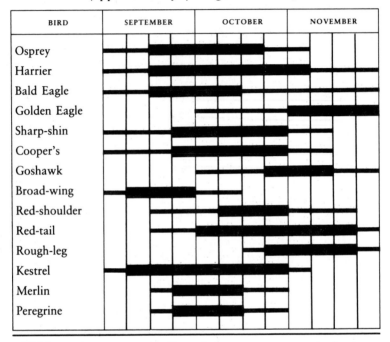

BIRD	SEPTEMBER	OCTOBER	NOVEMBER
Osprey			
Harrier			
Bald Eagle			
Golden Eagle			
Sharp-shin			
Cooper's			
Goshawk			
Broad-wing			
Red-shoulder			
Red-tail			
Rough-leg			
Kestrel			
Merlin			
Peregrine			

Table 14 is a composite intended to represent typical migration periods and peaks for the most widespread species at mid-latitude lookouts. Adjust it by a week or two, depending on how far north or south you live of 40 degrees latitude. Also important is the altitude and habitat of your local site. Buteos tend to be more common on the inland ridges, falcons along the coasts.

Holiday Beach, Ontario

Directions: Take Highway 18 south from Windsor to Essex County Route 50. Go south about three miles to the entrance of Holiday Beach Provincial Park. The best spot is generally the western end of the parking lot, between the beach and the fish pond.

Hawk Mountain, Pennsylvania

Directions: From U.S. 78 take Exit 29 at Hamburg and go north on Route 61 through Port Clinton to Route 895 East for about 2.5 miles to the sign for Hawk Mountain Sanctuary. Turn right, cross the railroad tracks, bear left at the fork, and proceed uphill to the headquarters.

Cape May Point, New Jersey

Directions: From Cape May, follow Sunset Boulevard west for approximately two miles to Lighthouse Avenue. Turn left there. (The lighthouse is visible in the distance.) Continue to the end of Lighthouse Avenue. The entrance to the park is on the left. The hawk-watch platform is in the southeastern corner of the parking lot.

Kiptopeke Beach, Virginia

Directions: Go north from the north toll bridge plaza of the Chesapeake Bay Bridge Tunnel on Route 13 for 3.3 miles. Turn left on Road 704. Proceed about two blocks, then move to strip *left* of the median strip (the right side is no longer in use) to the unpaved drive on the left. Turn there and follow the track to the edge of the cultivated fields. Park and walk north to the wood's edge. The site is open from Labor Day to mid-October.

Goshute Mountains, Nevada

Directions: This newly discovered lookout is on a 9,000-foot peak at the western edge of the Great Salt Lake Desert and is inaccessible by car. Birders interested in participating in observations here should contact Steve Hoffman, P.O. Box 1382, Albuquerque, New Mexico 87103, for details.

Golden Gate, California

Directions: From the Golden Gate Bridge head north on Highway 101; take Alexander Avenue Exit toward Sausalito. Make the first left, then go right onto Conzelman Road. Follow it 1.8 miles above the Gate, then park next to the old concrete tunnels, known as Battery 129. Walk to the top of Hawk Hill on the ocean side of the hill.

9 · SHOREBIRDS

WARBLERS AND HAWKS can be exasperating; shorebirds can be ego crushing.

Warblers and hawks generally escape us by dropping into the bushes or flying over the horizon, so there's always bad luck to blame: "At first I couldn't see it, and then it disappeared." Too often in shorebirding, the unident stands right there, thirty yards away, waiting patiently while we first flip quickly through our field guide, then backward more slowly, checking all the plumages, then forward again, this time being sure to look at the pages with the Eurasian vagrants, and it's *still* standing there when at last — meekly and painfully, hoping no one is watching — we close down the scope and walk on.

I once asked John Hintermister how long it had taken him to learn the shorebirds.

"A couple of eons," he said. "Not counting the time I spent on the peeps."

The inscrutability of this group of birds is made even more painful by their enormous aesthetic appeal.

"The restlessness of shorebirds, their kinship with the distance and swift seasons, the wistful signal of their voices down the long coastlines of the world make them, for me, the most affecting of wild creatures," Peter Matthiessen has written. "To the traveler confounded by exotic birds ... the voice of the wind birds may be the lone familiar note in a strange land, and I have many times been glad to find them; meeting a whimbrel one fine summer day of February in Tierra del Fuego, I wondered if I had seen this very bird a half year earlier, at home."

The long-distance charm works in reverse too. To nontravelers surrounded by the birds of home, the shorebirds represent the ends of the earth — visitors from lands we may never see. The golden plovers found each September on the local sod farm have nested on the Alaskan tundra and will winter on the Argentinian plains. Hudsonian godwits nest on the coast of James Bay and winter on the Falkland Islands. The little white-rumped sandpiper that nests across the top of the world, from Alaska to Baffin Island, has been seen on South Georgia Island, just north of Antarctica. And recent banding studies suggest that some sanderlings, two and a half ounces of feathers and bones, circle the American continents each year, migrating up the Pacific coast from Peru to California to the Canadian arctic, then coming back the other way, down through Nova Scotia and Virginia on their way back to South America.

The allure is of course easier to appreciate at home in an armchair than out in the field. Out in the field, the sun is shining in your eyes, the sandfleas are nipping your ankles, the deerflies are biting your neck, and that mysterious gray and brown bird over there just refuses to fly away!

BASIC PRINCIPLES

Five principles are especially important in shorebird identification.

1. *Learn the habitat preferences.* Like the "song" in "songbird," the "shore" in "shorebird" is something of a misnomer. Most shorebirds prefer marshes and wetlands to coastal shores, and inland areas (habitats D, E, and F in table 15) attract nearly as many species as saltwater areas (habitats A, B, and C). In fact, several species — upland and buff-breasted sandpipers, mountain and golden plovers, and others — are actu-

---

TABLE 15. *Habitat Preferences of Migrating and Wintering Shorebirds*

Birds are listed by areas in which they are most likely to be found. The species shown in italics have a strong preference for the area listed and are hard to find elsewhere.

A. SANDY BEACHES

snowy plover
Wilson's plover
semipalmated plover (prefers C)
piping plover
American oystercatcher (prefers C)
marbled godwit
ruddy turnstone
black turnstone
red knot
whimbrel (prefers C, D, and F)

long-billed curlew (also C, D, or F)
sanderling
semipalmated sandpiper (prefers C, D)
western sandpiper (prefers C, D)
least sandpiper (prefers C, D)
white-rumped sandpiper (prefers C,D,F)
dunlin

B. ROCKY SHORES AND JETTIES

black oystercatcher
wandering tattler
spotted sandpiper (occasionally)
ruddy turnstone

black turnstone
surfbird
purple sandpiper
rock sandpiper

C. COASTAL MARSHES AND MUD FLATS

black-bellied plover
lesser golden plover (prefers F)
semipalmated plover
killdeer (prefers D and F)
American oystercatcher

ruddy turnstone
black turnstone
red knot
semipalmated sandpiper
western sandpiper

black-necked stilt
American avocet
greater yellowlegs
lesser yellowlegs
solitary sandpiper
willet (strong preference in East)
spotted sandpiper
whimbrel
long-billed curlew
Hudsonian godwit
marbled godwit

least sandpiper
white-rumped sandpiper
pectoral sandpiper
dunlin
stilt sandpiper
short-billed dowitcher
long-billed dowitcher (prefers D)
common snipe
Wilson's phalarope (prefers D)
red-necked phalarope (after storms)
red phalarope (after storms)

D. INLAND, FRESHWATER MARSHES, WET FIELDS, AND RAIN POOLS

black-bellied plover (prefers C)
lesser golden plover
semipalmated plover (prefers C)
killdeer
black-necked stilt
American avocet
greater yellowlegs
lesser yellowlegs
solitary sandpiper
spotted sandpiper
upland sandpiper
whimbrel
long-billed curlew
Hudsonian godwit

semipalmated sandpiper
western sandpiper
least sandpiper
white-rumped sandpiper
Baird's sandpiper
pectoral sandpiper
dunlin (prefers A and C)
stilt sandpiper
buff-breasted sandpiper (prefers F)
short-billed dowitcher (prefers C)
long-billed dowitcher
common snipe
Wilson's phalarope

E. EDGES OF FRESHWATER RIVERS, LARGE PONDS, AND DEEPER LAKES

killdeer
greater yellowlegs
lesser yellowlegs

solitary sandpiper
spotted sandpiper
common snipe (prefers D)

F. INLAND AREAS WITHOUT WATER: Prairies, Meadows, Sod Farms, Plowed Fields, Airports

black-bellied plover (prefers C)
lesser golden plover
semipalmated plover (prefers C)
killdeer
mountain plover

upland sandpiper
white-rumped sandpiper
Baird's sandpiper
buff-breasted sandpiper

G. DEEP, WET WOODLANDS
woodcock

H. OPEN OCEAN, OCCASIONALLY IN LARGE LAKES
red phalarope   *red-necked phalarope*

ally easier to find thousands of miles inland than near the ocean. Shoreless shorebirders can't expect the totals seen by coastal birders, but some inland areas make for better birding than coastal wetlands because they are smaller and more accessible by car and foot and the birds can be approached more closely. Especially during spring migration — when white-rumped, Baird's, and stilt sandpipers, golden plovers, and lesser yellowlegs prefer the interior flyways to the ocean shorelines — the variety inland is excellent. Birders on either coast have a total shorebird possibility list of about forty regular migrants; inland birders can find as many as thirty.

Something else to note as you examine table 15 is that certain species have very specific habitat needs. This statement holds even in the best coastal wetlands. Thirty-five species of shorebirds are regularly recorded from the dikes of Brigantine Refuge in coastal New Jersey, but not the purple sandpiper; the refuge has no rock jetties, and so purple sandpipers are simply not found there, though they are common elsewhere on the Jersey shore. Similarly, the sanderling — one of the most numerous of all coastal birds — can be a tough bird to spot at Brigantine. It occurs only along the hundred-yard stretch of sandy beach at Turtle Cove. Similar situations occur wherever shorebirds are found, and the first step to mastering the shorebirds is making your way to a variety of habitats.

2. *Slow down and specialize.* Shorebirding requires a radical change of pace from other forms of birdwatching. Since only a handful of shorebirds are identifiable at a glance, it's seldom possible to reel off a string of identifications without hesitation. Ordinarily, a lot of work is involved, and there is much time for doubt. Urgency and impatience are the mortal sins, dogged persistence the cardinal virtue.

Changing the pace involves abandoning the scanning technique most of us use instinctively and semiconsciously with ducks, swallows, sparrows, and other flocking birds. This tactic doesn't work with shorebirds. Some of the most sought-after species are eminently overlookable. You can't find a long-billed dowitcher or a Baird's sandpiper by scanning randomly and waiting for something different to leap out of the crowd. Finding a long-bill requires looking at and listening carefully to hundreds of dowitchers; finding a Baird's means studying thousands, even tens of thousands, of peeps, a bird at a time, one after another. "Today I'm going to separate the two dowitchers," you have to tell yourself, or, "I'm going to spend the next hour looking only at the peeps."

A different way to focus is to declare July "Shorebirding Month." There is generally little else happening then in the bird world. The flycatchers, thrushes, and warblers have stopped singing; the ducks and hawks have not yet begun migrating. The shorebirds are moving, though — on their way from one end of the world to the other. Giving yourself four weeks to concentrate on them will do wonders for your identification skills. You may even find yourself declaring August "Shorebirding Month II."

3. *Concentrate on standing birds.* Shorebirds fly fast; several species can cruise at seventy miles per hour. They also tend to fly erratically and evasively, twisting and twirling against the sun, into shadow, back against the sun. A few species (willet, black-bellied plover, and a couple of others) are best identified on the wing, and shorebird experts can identify almost all species in flight. As a rule of thumb, however, less experienced shorebirders need not concern themselves with flying birds. Shorebirds spend the majority of their time with their feet on the ground. For most of us one shorebird on the ground is worth ten in the air.

4. *Study the silhouettes. Postpone the plumages.* Most shorebirds are better identified by their shapes than by their colors. Their light browns, creamy buffs, and subtle grays tend to wash out in the harsh light of the open areas they prefer. Even more important, the seasonal changes of shorebird feathering are complex and variable. All species have at least three visibly distinct plumages:

- the *juvenal* plumage, acquired on the nesting grounds when a newborn bird fledges and loses its natal down;

- the *adult winter* (or "basic") plumage, usually acquired sometime between August and December;
- the *adult breeding* (or "alternate") plumage, usually acquired sometime between March and June.

Many species add two other visibly distinct plumages to this array; a "first winter" plumage (following the juvenal stage and different from adult winter plumage) and a "first summer" plumage (actually acquired in the bird's first spring and worn through the bird's second summer of life).

Most field guides illustrate only one or two of these plumages, and no general guide has room to illustrate all the intermediate stages — though many species molt during migration and are often seen in transitional steps between plumages.

The result is that few plumage-based field marks are consistently reliable, and some are misleading. If you rely on the chestnut cheek patches to identify a stilt sandpiper, for example, your chances of finding the species will be 10–20 percent as good as they could be. The chestnut is hard to see at any distance and is not present at all in juvenal and winter-plumaged birds. Other well-known but unreliable field marks include the gold in the upper parts of the golden plover, the black in the belly of the black-bellied plover, the red in the breast of the red knot, and the spots on the spotted sandpiper. Since these marks are absent in some or all individuals for much of each year, it is a mistake to depend on any of them.

The good news is that learning shorebird plumages is less essential to identification than learning the plumages of hawks, warblers, and gulls. Almost all North American shorebirds can be identified by their size and shape — if you remember principle 5.

5. *Divide and conquer.* Identifying shorebirds is a *sorting operation.* Here more than with any other group of birds, the process of elimination is the key technique.

Sorting the shorebirds into identifiable groups and subgroups is easier than it seems at first. There are three problems — two developing from nomenclature and one from the logistical limitations of field guides — but all are solvable.

The first problem is the species names. Only eight of the forty-seven North American shorebirds have names that are clearly and consistently linked with their field identification: snowy plover, black-necked stilt, black oystercatcher, long-billed curlew, greater yellowlegs, lesser yellowlegs, black turnstone, and least sandpiper. Half a dozen others have names that are moderately helpful because they suggest the species' preferred habitat: woodcock, sanderling, American oystercatcher, surfbird, rock sandpiper, and upland sandpiper. Another half dozen are named for their voices, though only the willet ("pee-wee-*willet*, pee-wee-*willet*") and the killdeer ("kill-dee, kill-dee," or "kill-dee-ah," "kill-dee-ah") have calls that are distinctive enough to jog the beginning shorebirder's memory. There remain approximately thirty species and thirty puzzling names to learn.

Some are puzzling because the etymology is unfamiliar or the referent is unclear: avocet, whimbrel, snipe, semipalmated sandpiper, semipalmated plover, Hudsonian godwit, wandering tattler, solitary sandpiper, Eskimo curlew. Other names are accurate for only part of the year: dunlin, ruddy turnstone, spotted sandpiper, and so on. In several of these cases the nominal plumage is the one the species is *least* likely to be wearing when it is seen in the continental United States: the purple sandpiper, golden and black-bellied plovers, red and red-necked phalaropes. Finally, some names are simply enigmatic. The short-billed dowitcher has a very long bill. The western sandpiper is a common bird in the East. The marbled godwit is no more marbled and the stilt sandpiper no more stiltlike than several other sandpipers. The mountain plover should not be sought in mountains. Birders are by and large adaptable folks, however — able to shout out names like "yellow-bellied sapsucker!" and "northern beardless tyrannulet!" without even flinching — so this first problem is usually solved with time and a little homework.

The more troublesome nomenclature problem develops at the level *above* species. Other large groups of birds can be divided quickly and conveniently along taxonomic lines. Even when a hawk is not immediately identifiable, it's generally possible to tell whether it's a falcon or a buteo and so to turn to the appropriate pages in the field guide. We usually know, too, whether a songbird is a thrush, wren, or junco. Even very closely related groups, crows and jays, titmice and chickadees, vireos and warblers, have readily perceptible group characteristics that lead us to the appropriate pages in the field guide to start browsing. This is not the case with shorebirds; the taxonomy is too unbalanced.

There are only four families of North American shorebirds, but one of them contains three-quarters of all the species. Two of the families have just two species each: our two oystercatchers belong to the family *Haematopodidae*; the avocet and black-necked stilt belong to the family *Recurvirostridae*. All four of these shorebirds are so easily identified that knowing

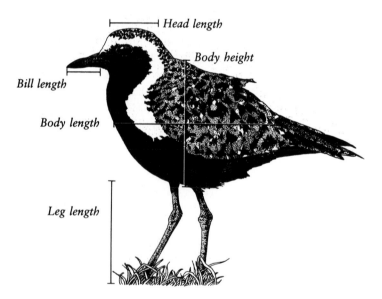

FIGURE 9. *Plover,*
Showing Five Dimensions to Study in All Shorebirds

the family characteristics is irrelevant. The one shorebird family worth learning to recognize as a subset is the plovers, or *Charadriidae*. Eight species of plover occur regularly in the United States, and they appear in a convenient, bite-sized cluster in all field guides.

The remaining thirty-eight shorebird species belong to a single family, the sandpipers, or *Scolopacidae*. The variations within the family are so great — from whimbrel to phalarope to woodcock — that "sandpiper," unlike "falcon," "buteo," "wren," and "junco," is virtually indefinable and certainly too inclusive to be a useful key to identification. Worse, the size of the family and the space limitations in a general field guide make clustering all sandpipers with all their lookalikes impossible. The stilt sandpiper can be confused with a dowitcher by behavior, with a dunlin by bill shape, and with a lesser yellowlegs by posture, but a dowitcher can be confused with a snipe, a dunlin with a knot, and a lesser yellowlegs with a greater yellowlegs. And the complexities multiply: a snipe can be confused with a woodcock, a knot with a surfbird, and so on. Field guide authors are forced to arrange the sandpipers in rough taxonomic order, add a few warning notes about similar species, and trust that birders will flip back and forth through the fifteen or twenty pages of illustrations when necessary.

THE PLOVERS

The first question to consider when identifying a shorebird is: is it one of the instantly identifiable shorebirds — an oystercatcher, avocet, or black-necked stilt? If not, the next question is: is it a plover?

The key components of plover silhouettes (figure 9) are:

· rounded, relatively thickish bills that are *shorter* than head lengths;
· short necks;
· body lengths (excluding wings) not much longer than body heights;
· legs that appear roughly equal to body heights.

The plover silhouette is made of circles and soft curves. The British pronunciation of the name — "plover" rhymes with "lover" — might help you remember that plovers are shaped like doves. "Don't you love plovers and doves?"

Three plovers are usually easy identifications. The killdeer is widely distributed and well known. The mountain plover is limited to the Southwest and may be distinguished from its closest lookalike, the lesser golden, by its brighter underwings and, in winter, from all other plovers by its preferences for very dry, sometimes desertlike habitats. Wilson's plover is a bird with a reputation for being overreported by desperate listers, but people who've seen a genuine Wilson's — with a bill so heavy and rounded that it seems to belong on a gull — should have little trouble with the species. If shorebirds were better named, the Wilson's would be known by its alternate name, "the thick-billed plover."

The identification problems within the plover family involve the remaining five species, three small plovers and two large ones.

Piping, Snowy, and Semipalmated Plovers

The primary problem with the smaller plovers may be bad lighting. In those few areas where the piping and snowy overlap (especially along the Gulf coast) leg color must be studied carefully. The snowy's legs are darker. Good lighting is also important for distinguishing the semipalmated from both piping and snowy. The semipal is by far the most numerous of these three, and a bright sun combined with the "lure of the list" can play tricks with the eyes. The time to be especially careful is in the fall, when the juvenile semipals are migrating through. If you see a possible piping/snowy, try to get the sun at your back. Juvenile semipals are slightly lighter than adults, but in good light they're two or three shades darker than the darkest members of either of the other two species. The piping and snowy are the color of sun-bleached driftwood. As they scurry around they can almost disappear against a sandy background.

Habitat is another cue. If your plover isn't scurrying around against a sandy background in a type A habitat, it's probably not a piping or a snowy. On migration both are most often found on sandy beaches beyond the wrack line. They nest in sandy, barren places — on beaches just above the high tide line, on alkali flats, on dry lake beds, and so on. Semipalmateds, on the other hand, are birds of mud and marshes, as their back color indicates. When they do come to beaches, they tend to stay close to the water on the dark, wet sand. They'll seldom be found standing side by side with either of their rarer relatives.

Lesser Golden and Black-bellied Plovers

A flying *Pluvialis* plover is easy. The black-belly's dark wing pits and white rump are visible several hundred yards away. The golden plover in flight seems uniformly dark; to my eye, a flying golden plover (in nonbreeding plumage) is the most monocolored of all shorebirds.

The challenge is separating the two species when they are resting or walking, without throwing stones to force them to take wing. Beware the plumage variations within both species, and remember a seldom-mentioned fact: *the lesser golden plover can be less golden than the black-bellied.* Winter-plumaged golden plovers are grayish, and juvenile black-bellies often have yellowish golden flecking in their backs and wings. The black-bellied has a white rump in all plumages, but this is only occasionally visible on a standing or walking bird.

On standing birds, the bill/eye/head proportions are the most visible *Pluvialis* field mark. The golden has a gentle, "babyish" look because its shorter, more pointed bill makes its head look large and its eyes huge. The black-bellied has a big bill for a plover (only the Wilson's is proportionately larger), and the bill is especially thick and and *clearly longer than half the length of the head.* The golden's bill is about half the length of its head, but in the field it seems even smaller. Mnemonic: *the black-bellied has the big bill.*

SORTING THE SANDPIPERS

The first two shorebird-sorting questions separate all other shorebirds from the sandpipers. 1. "Is it one of the instantly identifiable shorebirds?" leads to four species. 2. "Is it a plover?" leads to eight species. If the answer to both these questions is no and the bird in question is a shorebird, it must be a sandpiper, one of the thirty-eight species that nest in North America. A third question must then be considered.

3. *Is it one of the odd sandpipers?* Five sandpipers are identified by their weird, eye-catching bills. The three *curl*ews have long, *curling* bills and the two godwits — *God, what* bills they have — upswung, huge, and two-toned. These two groups are also clustered together in all field guides, and sorting them out is seldom a problem.

Three other odd sandpipers are made easy by their exclusive habitat preferences. The woodcock is the only shorebird to be found under a closed canopy in deep woods. Two phalaropes, the red and the red-necked, are the only shorebirds regularly found far offshore. (The red-necked sometimes also flies overland and can be found, for example, in North Dakota during autumn migration, but it is generally easily identified.)

From this point onward, the questions become tougher, and the distinctions blur. The next question most birders ask is:

4. *Is it a peep?* And most of the time most of us hope the answer is no. The term "peep" is correctly applied to only six species, the sanderling and the five *Calidris* sandpipers that are smaller than the sanderling. They are clustered together in all field guides, but the fine distinctions required within the group make identifying the peeps one of the toughest problems in all birding. We'll return to this group at the end of the chapter and imagine for now that the bird in question is not a peep.

It is possible to continue sorting by size. Twelve of the remaining sandpipers are as big as or bigger than the ruddy turnstone, and nine are smaller. But size can be hard to judge, especially in the middle of the spectrum. Quick (without consulting your field guide): is a Wilson's phalarope bigger or

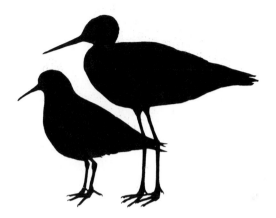

Plump and Longlegs:
Purple Sandpiper (left) and Lesser Yellowlegs

smaller than a turnstone? And how about the dunlin — bigger or smaller?

A much better way to divide them is by *thematic silhouette.* We then have another sorting question.

5. *Is is a longlegs?* Eleven sandpipers fit this description. They have

- legs that are noticeably longer than their body heights;
- body lengths noticeably longer than their body heights;
- relatively straight bills that are at least as long as their head lengths and in most cases obviously longer.

Most members of this group also have long necks and a *lanky* look. The lesser yellowlegs is typical.

The last sorting question can be "Is it none of the above?" Or:

6. *Is it a plump?* Ten midsized sandpipers have short necks

and a *chunky* look. In specific contrast to the longlegs the plumps have

- legs that seem not noticeably longer and in many cases much shorter than body heights;
- body heights nearly equal to body lengths (excluding the wings);
- bills of various shapes but most obviously curved or noticeably shorter than head length.

TABLE 16. *Six Convenient Questions for Sorting the Shorebirds*

---

1. *Is it one of the instantly identifiable shorebirds?*

American oystercatcher	avocet	black-necked stilt
black oystercatcher		

2. *Is it a plover?*

killdeer	semipalmated	black-bellied
mountain	piping	lesser golden
Wilson's	snowy	

3. *Is it one of the odd sandpipers?*

long-billed curlew	Hudsonian godwit	red phalarope
whimbrel	marbled godwit	red-necked phalarope
Eskimo curlew	woodcock	

4. *Is it a peep?*

sanderling	Baird's	western
white-rumped	semipalmated	least

5. *Is it a longlegs?*

willet	wandering tattler	Wilson's phalarope
upland sandpiper	snipe	solitary sandpiper
gtr yellowlegs	lb dowitcher	stilt sandpiper
lsr yellowlegs	sb dowitcher	

6. *Is it a plump?*

knot	purple sandpiper	pectoral
ruddy turnstone	surfbird	spotted sandpiper
black turnstone	buff-breasted	
rock sandpiper	dunlin	

The ruddy turnstone and purple sandpiper are typical plumps.

Since apparent leg length and body width can change with posture, "Longlegs or plump?" is sometimes a close judgment call, and a couple of species barely fit into one group or the other. All in all, however, distinguishing the two thematic shapes is much easier than sorting by size. Quickly (without consulting your field guide): is a Wilson's phalarope a longlegs or a plump? How about the dunlin — longlegs or plump? Table 16 presents six questions that group the shorebirds conveniently for identification.

THE LONGLEGS

The eleven longlegs are all relatively tall and long. All but the three smallest — Wilson's phalarope, the solitary sandpiper, and the stilt sandpiper — are both taller and longer than the knot, the tallest and longest plump. In approximate order of descending size, they are as follows.

Willet

In flight the willet's flashy white wings and loud call are definitive and hard to miss. A standing willet, however, is remarkably nondescript. Size is the key. *The willet is the tallest of the straight-billed sandpipers* — and its typical elongated posture accentuates this feature.

Eastern birders traveling west may be surprised to come upon a willet inland. The eastern race of the willet is very rarely found away from type C habitat, coastal marshes, and mud flats, but the western race nests from Nevada northeast to the Dakotas.

Upland Sandpiper

The uppie's unique proportions combine the body length of a dowitcher with a bill the size of a spotted sandpiper. No other longlegs — in fact, no other shorebird in any category — has such a long body and such a short bill. The small bill also accentuates the length of the neck. Together these features give the bird such an odd shape that one birder I know claims to have identified upland sandpipers at night by telescope as they flew across the face of the moon.

The upland sandpiper is more easily found in type F habitat — meadows, sod farms, and so on. It nests farther south than most shorebirds and as one of the earliest southward migrants is often on the move by the Fourth of July.

Greater and Lesser Yellowlegs

The identification problem with the two yellowlegs is an interesting optical illusion. As anyone who has ever seen them together can testify, they are very different in size. The greater is nearly 40 percent bigger. Every time I see them side by side I wonder how I could ever confuse the two. Fifteen minutes later I come upon a solo yellowlegs, and I'm struggling again. Their plumages and body shapes are virtually identical, and their leg colors are absolutely identical.

The distinction on which most birders seem to depend is the greater's tendency to have a very slightly upswung bill, a feature that is hard to see at a distance and is a "sufficient but not necessary" field mark in any case. It seems present and visible in perhaps half of all greater yellowlegs, so its absence should not be used to confirm a lesser yellowlegs.

Claudia Wilds solved my problem with these two when she pointed out a much better distinction for solo yellowlegs and single-species flocks. The greater's bill is *proportionately* much longer, *almost one and half times the length of the head.* The lesser's is just slightly longer than the length of the head. This is a terrific field mark! The first time I used it I felt like I'd balanced a checkbook that had been out of order for the last ten years.

Wandering Tattler

The tattler is somewhat similar to the lesser yellowlegs in overall proportions, but its neck is shorter (so that it has a hunched, less lanky look), it occurs only on the Pacific coast, and — most important — it has a strong preference for rocky surfside areas (type B habitat), where no self-respecting yellow-legs should be found. Since it bobs frequently and has a gray back, the tattler most resembles a giant winter-plumaged spotted sandpiper, but confusion is likely only at extreme distances.

Common Snipe

To identify the snipe by nonvariable field marks, note its huge, woodcocklike eyes, its sometimes visible orange tail, and the always visible stripes on the head and back. Mnemonic: *the snipe has stripes.*

Those big eyes also give the snipe a wary expression that reflects its habits. It is a solitary bird, most active at dawn and dusk, and nearly as shy as a rail. It seldom occurs in flocks and does not venture out onto the open mud flats that the dowitchers prefer.

Long-billed and Short-billed Dowitchers

To separate the dowitchers from other shorebirds by behavior, remember: *dowitchers are down stitchers.* They feed by pumping their long bills up and down in the mud like walking sewing machines. The only other shorebird that feeds in this style is the smaller and much shorter-billed stilt sandpiper, and its stitching is a quicker up and down movement that is less persistent.

Until 1950 there was no problem telling the dowitchers apart. All were simply dowitchers. Then Frank Pitelka published his exhaustive study of the four races and argued that one — slightly longer billed, slightly shorter winged, with a preference for fresh water, and nesting further north and west than the others — was a separate species. The American Ornithologists' Union agreed and declared the long-billed dowitcher a full species soon after. If there's one "split" birders would gladly trade in for one of the "lumps" we've lost in recent years, this is it. The long-bill is a pain in the neck to identify, and most birders would be much happier counting Bullock's orioles, Ipswich sparrows, or great white herons.

For those determined to identify the long-bill, three tips:

1. Forget about bill length. The overlap between long-billed short-billed dowitchers and short-billed long-billed dowitchers is only one problem. Worse is the problem of proportions. The bills of both species are so long that estimating length by ratio — for example, bill versus head length — is extremely difficult and rarely satisfying.
2. Listen for their calls. *The short has the longer and lower call*: "phew-phew-phew" or "do-witch-cher." *The long has the shorter and squeakier call*: "keek."
3. In areas where the short-bill is the dominant species, wait until mid-September to search for the long-bill. The long-bill migrates later and, more important, molts later. A few long-bills will still have red bellies and sometimes other traces of their breeding plumage after all short-bills are well into their transition to gray winter plumage.

Wilson's Phalarope

Because it is so distinctive in its adult plumages and because the field guides usually illustrate it in comparison with the two pelagic phalaropes, this bird seems easier to identify than it is. Most field guides also picture the Wilson's sitting in water with its legs hidden. Note that the Wilson's frequently forages on land, and *beware the juvenal plumage*. Juveniles are browner and much drabber than adults and they have *yellow* legs.

I finally learned my lesson with this bird when twice within one week I found an immature Wilson's while trying to decide whether I was looking at a greater or lesser yellowlegs! Yes, the Wilson's is much smaller, and the bill is needle thin, but I missed these marks both times. I'm certain now that I must have missed dozens of subadult Wilson's over the years. The time to be especially wary is in late summer, when the juveniles are migrating and most adults are long gone.

Solitary Sandpiper

This species and the stilt sandpiper are the two shortest longlegs and are the two most likely to be mistaken for one of the plumps.

The solitary is not as much of a loner as the snipe, but it does tend to live up to its name by separating itself from other members of its species. Also, because it prefers type E habitat, it's seldom seen with other shorebirds except an occasional spotted sandpiper. Its silhouette combines the very slightly downcurved bill of a spotted with the torso lines of a lesser yellowlegs, but the solitary should probably not be identified by shape alone. The best mark seems to be the white eyering, which is present (though very variable) in all plumages.

Stilt Sandpiper

If "longlegs" and "plump" were taxonomic categories (which they aren't, of course), we could call the stilt sandpiper the missing link. It is either the plumpest and droopiest billed of the longlegs or the leanest and leggiest of the plumps. In any case, it's the most overlookable of all common shorebirds and a nemesis species for countless birders. Elliot Coues discovered the first he ever saw in his hand after he shot what he thought was a dowitcher; Arthur Cleveland Bent, author of the classic *Life Histories of North American Birds*, never once in his life identified a stilt sandpiper in the field.

In its nonbreeding plumages the stilt sandpiper can be mistaken for a dowitcher, yellowlegs, or dunlin. The late shorebird grandmaster Tom Davis once noted that in size, posture, and wing and rump colors it actually most closely resembles a winter-plumaged curlew sandpiper, our most common Eurasian vagrant.

The stilt sandpiper is one species seldom found by random scanning. You must look consciously for something a little too thin to be a dowitcher, a little too tall to be a dunlin, and a little too short to be a yellowlegs. And you can't count too heavily on the supposedly "greenish" legs; they are sometimes more yellow than green. The slightly (and variably) drooping bill seems the best means of confirmation, but — like all other features on this quintessential shorebird — it won't leap out at you. Since stilts have a preference for slightly deeper water than dowitchers, the deepwater side of a dowitcher flock is a good place to start your search. Look for a bird stitching more quickly and less persistently than the rest of the crowd.

THE PLUMPS

The ten species in this silhouette group present fewer problems than the eleven longlegs or the six peeps. They are ranked below in approximate order of increasing difficulty.

Spotted Sandpiper

With the possible exception of the killdeer, the spotted sandpiper is our most widespread and familiar "shorebird" and generally presents few problems. Its unspotted juvenal and winter plumages can surprise beginners, but its size (it is smaller than a sanderling) and teeter-tottering walk generally give it away. Its odd flight style — quick and shallow flaps, bowed wings held below the body — is another cue. The least sandpiper occasionally flies in a similar style, but the least is not as noisy in flight and has darker wings.

Knot

The knot's silhouette is distinctive in several ways. This bird is the longest and the heaviest plump and the only one with a straight bill that seems longer than its head length. *All other chunky, midsized sandpipers have drooping bills or bills that are clearly shorter than their head length.* Linnaeus named the species for King Knut of Denmark, who was interested in trying to hold back the tide. This story might help you remember it is a heavy, round bird; if you had to build a seawall out of shorebirds, knots would be your best choice. They are *knots of fat.*

The Five "Rockpipers"

Five midsized sandpipers separate themselves from most other shorebirds by their strong preference for type B habitat, the rocks and jetties of coastal shores: the surfbird, the rock and purple sandpipers, and the black and ruddy turnstones. The first three are seldom found in any other habitat, and none of the five occurs regularly inland south of Alaska. The size overlap and very similar plumages of the rock and purple sandpipers are never a problem. To separate these two from each other, face the ocean at dawn and determine whether the sun is in your eyes or at your back. In the United States the purple sandpiper occurs only on the Atlantic coast, the rock only on the Pacific.

If the ocean sun is in your face at dawn, you won't have trouble identifying a turnstone either. The ruddy is the Atlantic form.

On the West Coast identifying a turnstone is little trickier — and a lot more fun. The ruddy must be separated from the black turnstone and both must be told apart from the surfbird. Since their habitat choice sometimes makes the western trio hard to approach, this is one group of shorebirds whose in-flight patterns reward careful study. All three have white in their tails, which — together with their much shorter bills — differentiate them from their most frequent flying companions, the rock sandpiper and the wandering tattler. To find a surfbird in a flock of turnstones on the wing, look for a bird with a *gray, unmarked* back. And remember: *not all ruddies are ruddy.* In winter and juvenal plumage ruddies in flight can be so hard to separate from winter and juvenal blacks that West Coast veterans listen for the black's shriller call. Visitors to the coast may find they have to depend on the black's somewhat darker, less mottled back feathering, its darker head, and, best, its more extensive, more square-cut breast marking; *the black has the block.*

Buff-breasted Sandpiper
The biggest problem in identifying a buff-breasted sandpiper is finding one to look at! Except at a few midcontinental areas, this is a rare bird, and it is everywhere a master of camouflage, able to vanish before your eyes as it walks in an open field.

Its jizz is an odd combination of features from the three birds whose type F habitat it shares. It has the short, thin bill of the upland sandpiper, the dovelike torso of the golden plover, and the back color of the juvenile Baird's sandpiper. The last is its closest lookalike. According to legend, the buff-breast sometimes stands in grass that is low enough and in light that is good enough to make its yellow legs visible. (The Baird's legs are black.) In the real world of tall grass and bad light, bill length versus head length might be the best clue. The Baird's bill appears slightly longer than its head length; the buff-breast's is definitely shorter. Neck and leg length are also sometimes useful. In certain postures the buffy's neck and legs seem disproportionately long for such a chunky bird.

Dunlin

This is the Dr. Jekyll and Mr. Hyde of the shorebird clan. Somehow the shorebirder's spring does not seem fully under way until the first breeding-plumaged "red-backed sandpiper" arrives, as unmistakable and beautifully painted as an avocet. In fall, in its alter ego, the dunlin is the last shorebird migrant and it seems always to appear on a day as dull and dismal as its winter colors. The shorebirder's year is now in its last weeks.

Side by side, a dunlin and a peep are clearly different sizes and easy to tell apart. To distinguish the dunlin in other situations, notice that its weight seems unbalanced toward the front end. Its bull neck, puffy chest, and rounded shoulders make the legs appear to be slightly behind the fulcrum of the body — an effect you won't see in any of the peeps. Though variably curved, the dunlin's bill is always tellingly longer and thicker than any peep's — a scimitar to the sabers, swords, and daggers in the peep group.

Pectoral Sandpiper

The pectoral sandpiper is another deceptive bird. A breeding-plumaged male with its neck outstretched is distinctive enough, but be careful to study that "peep" standing next to it. There's a good chance that's a pectoral too! Females are much smaller, and with their necks hunkered down, they are easily mistaken.

A solo spring-plumaged least sandpiper is the bird most likely to be mistaken for a pectoral. Like the pectoral it feeds in the grasses of wetland edges, and it too has yellow legs and a brownish, clear-cut breast above a white belly. It's just as close in size to the pectoral as a lesser yellowlegs is to a greater yellowlegs. If no other birds are present to help you estimate size, look at the black marks *inside* the brown of the chest. The least's blotchier spots seem to have been tapped onto its breast with a crayon stub; the pectoral's are drawn with a fine-tipped pen.

THE PEEPS

Okay, here they are — and there they are, little brown and gray puzzles swarming in the hundreds or the thousands at every good shorebird site in the country, probably the most-often-seen/least-often-identified birds in North America.

Dividing and conquering the peeps requires stepping up the intensity another notch, but it can be done.

1. *Eliminate the sanderling.* The sanderling is a peep only by default. In size and body shape it's close to the five smaller members of *Calidris.* In all other ways it's really a subset of one. It has that telltale wing stripe, that white winter plumage, and that thick naillike bill. It winters along both coasts much farther north and in much greater numbers than any of the other peeps. Finally, its foraging behavior is unique.

No other sandpiper likes sandy beaches as much as sanderlings do, and none will be seen feeding in the same style, sprinting to the surf edge to dabble at tiny crustaceans washed up by the waves. A peep-sized bird running in and out of the surf is almost certainly a sanderling. A peep-sized bird more than a quarter mile from waves is probably something else. Even sanderlings that come inland generally find their way to the beaches of lakes and large rivers. Mnemonic: *sanderlings linger only on sand.*

2. *Expect single-species flocks.* The five problematic peeps — least, semipalmated, western, white-rumped, and Baird's — sometimes feed near one another, and an individual of one species will often scurry through a flock of another. But if you watch long enough, you'll see that each usually clusters with its own kind — ten of one species over here, three or four of another over there — and they do not ordinarily stand and rest in close association. This statement holds true even for the most problematic pair, the semipalmated and the western. "My impression," Allan Phillips has noted, "is that most 'mixed flocks' are cases of misidentification; [the western and semipalmated] associate only to the usual shorebird extent, i.e. when safe and food-rich areas are limited. When good habitat is extensive, each tends to keep to itself."

Expecting uniform flocks is important because otherwise, after studying thirty or forty or a hundred peeps and finding them all apparent semipals, it's easy to lose faith. "There *has* to be western in here," you tell yourself. "I must be misidentifying them." Resist this doubt, and move on to the next spot. What happens often enough is that you come upon another thirty peeps, and these are all westerns!

3. *Learn the limitations of the best-known field marks.*

- The yellow in the least's legs is not always apparent.
- The white-rump's rump is readily visible only in flight.
- Not all Baird's are buffy and scaly backed, and not all buffy, scaly-backed peeps are Baird's.
- Not all semipalmateds have short, stubby bills.
- Not all westerns have long, drooping bills.

The least is the most distinctive of the five problematic peeps, and when they are perceptible, its yellow legs are a dead giveaway. The dark shadows and black mud in the least's favorite haunts, however, make its bill a more reliable mark. Look for the *thinnest, sharpest, and daintiest of peep bills* (see figure 10). Richard Veit and Lars Jonsson have noted, "From a distance least sandpipers' bills are so tiny as to be almost invisible,

FIGURE 10. *Bill Shapes of North America's Five Problematic Peeps*

which is not the case with semipalmated or western sand-pipers."

The white-rumped sandpiper's most definitive feature gives field guide artists a real problem. Since the patch on the rump is hidden from sight in the bird's natural standing posture, the bird is usually drawn with its wings held below its back, a pose not often seen in life and one that suggests the white is much more obvious than it is. Peep aficionados find this bird by searching flocks for a more subtle cue — its "wing flag." The white-rump's wings are longer than those on any of the three more common peeps. In the bird's natural posture (wings folded, rump obscured) the wings project well past the body. This feature is especially evident when the tail curls and blows in the wind. Once you have spotted the "wing flag," you can train your scope on the bird's back and (with patience) get a confirming glimpse of the white patch underneath.

The only peep with as extensive and flexible a "wing flag" is the Baird's. Separating the Baird's from the white-rump by silhouette is tricky, and I know of only two good cues. One comes from Larry Balch: the Baird's upper mandible is dead straight from tip to forehead. The white-rump's bill droops ever so slightly near the tip, and the upper mandible tends to curve upward as it connects with the forehead. The other silhouette cue comes from Frank Nicoletti. "The Baird's is the peep with the most ternlike torso. It's much slimmer and more streamlined than the white-rump."

Identifying a Baird's by plumage is tough. The Baird's rump is dark (not white), but a couple of seldom mentioned complexities sometimes make trouble here: (1) adult Baird's are buffy *only in breeding plumage*, and their winter plumage may be inseparable from the semipalmated's; (2) all *five* of the problematic peeps show scaliness on their backs in their juvenal plumages.

In summary, the Baird's can be confused by wing flag with the white-rump, by its winter plumage with the semipal, and by its scaly back with any subadult peep.

Separating the semipalmated and the western sandpiper is probably the most common peep problem, and it's not easy. Pessimism about the two species' field marks goes back at least to 1946, when Richard Pough noted in his field guide, "[The western] is so much like the semipalmated that the two species were not separated until 1864. Audubon, Wilson, and other early ornithologists failed to distinguish them, and it takes an expert to separate them in the field, except for particularly long-billed or very strongly marked individuals."

In 1975 Allan Phillips's article in *American Birds* (see chapter 3) made the situation sound even more dismal. After noting that female semipalmateds and male westerns often overlap in bill size and that the two species' winter plumages are virtually identical, Phillips asked, "Of what value, then, are the usual field guide characters of bill lengths and colors? It would be just as easy to identify by sight the two races of willet, which no one attempts."

Phillips's solution is the voices, but there's another answer to this question and to the Baird's problem.

4. *Search for "textbook" individuals, and always use double-checks.* One key with the peeps is not to be intimidated. The warnings from Pough, Phillips, and the other experts should be

TABLE 17. *Peep Identification Sequence*

FEATURE	PROBABLE IDENTIFICATION	DOUBLE-CHECKS
1. Yellow legs? Or thin, *pointed*, slightly decurved bill?	→ least sandpiper	→ Small? warm brown back?
2. Stubby bill, esp. thick at base?	→ semipalmated sandpiper	→ Grayish head and back? little or no rufous? bill shorter than head?
3. Long, attenuated, and drooping bill?	→ western sandpiper	→ Rufous on cap and shoulder?
4. Prominent wing flag?	⟨ white-rumped sandpiper	→ Larger than semipal? white rump? bill slightly drooped? streaky flanks?
	Baird's sandpiper	→ Larger than semipal? upper mandible very straight? buffy breast and cheeks? thinner than white-rump?

taken only as they are given — as cautions against carelessness and overconfidence. Figure 10 shows the heads and the classic bill shapes of the five problematic peeps. Out in the field you will find some peeps whose bills match none of these shapes precisely, but with patience you will also find birds who could have posed for this picture. In fact, you can find birds that are "ultratypical" — leasts with bills even thinner than shown, westerns with bills even droopier, and semipals with bills even shorter. ("Ultratypical" semipals don't look like leasts; the bill is stubby, almost ploverlike.)

If you begin with the silhouettes (bill shapes for the smaller three and "wing flags" for the white-rump and Baird's) and follow the identification sequence shown in table 17, you will find peeps you can identify. Despite the problems of molt and overlap, plumage makes a good double-check. On average, the least is the brownest of the three smallest peeps; the western is the reddest, especially on the shoulders; and the semipal is the grayest. The white-rump has the streakiest sides. In at least two of its primary plumages Baird's *is* the buffiest. The single-species nature of most flocks is a help here, since you can search for a classical or ultratypical bird in the group and then use that individual to compare to the others with it.

The final trick with the peeps is a matter of attitude. It makes a good trick to end the chapter, since it's a key component in every shorebirder's repertoire.

5. *Glue your eye to your scope, and don't let them beat you!*

10 · TERNS

BIRDERS TRYING TO DESCRIBE the rigors of the sport to nonbirders tend to focus on the physical demands. "You think birding is easy?" we say to our running, golfing, or tennis-playing friends. "Try waking up at 5:00 A.M. in the dead of winter, driving a hundred miles, then walking around in an arctic wind for three or four hours. Or try hiking through a swamp all day in the middle of June with ticks in your hair and chiggers in your socks." What we ought to brag about more often is the *mental* demands of our game. A golfer, lost in analysis of the lay of the green while lining up a putt, is never required to snatch for the bag, yank out a tennis racket, and return a serve, but birding requires such changes of pace all the time.

You are hunched over your scope, scrutinizing a cluster of peeps, lost in your analysis of the nearly invisible bends in their bills, when a tern zigzags through the field of view. If you want to get it, you must step away from the scope, grab your binocs, and put an entirely different mindset into gear — instantly. Flipping the pages of your mental field guide from peep marks (length and curve of bill, color of legs, pattern of rump, and so on) to tern marks (color of bill, length of tail, pattern of underwings, and so on) is only part of the challenge. You must also change your whole emotional attitude. Shorebirds are won with patient, dogged persistence; terns demand sharp, speedy efficiency.

Terns are as aerial as shorebirds are terrestrial. They are shyer, too, and less willing to linger for close, careful study. Typically they fly past us once or twice, and then they're on their way. The birder who wants to return their serve must be on his toes.

SORTING THE TERNS

Tern identification begins with a series of questions that experienced birders answer unconsciously:

Is it a tern or a gull?
How big is it?
What's the basic color of its wings and mantle?
Does it have an eye-catching bill?

Few other groups of birds as closely related as terns and gulls are so easily distinguished. Taxonomists consider terns and gulls members of the same family, the Laridae, and believe that the two groups descended from a single species of ancestral seabird. In the field, however, they are separable as far as the eye can see. Terns differ from gulls by silhouette; by flying, feeding, and resting behavior; and by seasonal distribution and habitat preferences. (See table 18.)

TABLE 18. *Features Distinguishing Terns from Gulls*

FEATURE	TERNS	GULLS
Shape	Lean and long; sharper, swept-back wings; elongated, sometimes crested heads	Stocky and thick; wider wings; rounded, never crested heads
Tail	Prominently forked (roseate, Forster's, and others) to slightly forked (gull-bill and Caspian)	Short, rounded except Sabine's and kittiwake (very slightly forked)
Bill	Most thin and pointed at tip; usually held angled downward in flight (the "terned"-down bill)	Most thick and hooked at tip; usually held straight ahead in flight
Color	Most are brighter white than gulls; little difference between plumages, so all members of a single species flock look similar	Often browner, grayer, "dirtier" than terns; much variation between plumages, so members of single species flock look very motley
Feeding behavior	Dive or swoop for food; never scavenge on land; feed only on live prey— fish, crustaceans, and (some species) insects	Do not dive (except kittiwake); frequently scavenge on land; omnivorous and often piratical
Flight style	Snappier wing flap, little gliding, only soarers are gull-bill, sooty, and bridled	Slower wing flap, much gliding and soaring, esp. larger species
Resting behavior	Swim very rarely and briefly (usually only to bathe); weak paddlers	Swim regularly; strong paddlers; often sleep on water
	Usually rest very close to water; stand on flotsam at sea	Often rest far from water (parking lots, house tops, grassy fields, etc.); rarely stand on flotsam
	Flock in small groups (usually a dozen or fewer birds) except at nesting colonies	Often in large to enormous flocks (hundreds to thousands of birds)

TABLE 18, *continued.*

FEATURE	TERNS	GULLS
	Shuffling walk; usually fly, not run, to escape disturbance	Ambling walk; sometimes run from disturbance or to pursue prey
Distribution	Much more numerous April to October; no species common north of 40 degrees latitude in winter	Many species common November to March; several species common year-round; in many areas (esp. near cities) more numerous in winter than any other birds

With practice, terns are also fairly easy to size. Twelve of the thirteen regular species fall into three distinct classes.

SMALL	MEDIUM		LARGE
least	arctic	gull-billed	royal
black	common	sandwich	Caspian
	Forster's	bridled	[elegant]
	roseate	sooty	

The two smallest species, the least tern and the black tern, are perceptibly shorter than the Bonaparte's gull and 30–40 percent smaller than the medium-sized terns. The two biggest, the Caspian and the royal, are perceptibly longer than the laughing gull and 20–30 percent bigger than the medium-sized terns.

The one tern whose size places it in between classes is the elegant. It is equal in length to the laughing gull, which makes it perceptibly smaller than a royal and perceptibly larger than the eight midsized terns. Because of its long yellow or orange bill, however, and its limited range (it is restricted to the California coast), it is generally quickly distinguished from all others but the royal.

Birders with good eyes for size can sort the remaining eight terns into two subclasses, medium large and medium small.

This subdivision can be made easier if you remember that all four of the medium-large birds have distinctively colored wings and mantles. The two darkest winged, the darkest winged of all terns, are the sooty and the bridled, also identifiable by their very strong preferences for offshore waters. The two lightest winged, the lightest winged of all terns, are the gull-billed and the sandwich. These two are also identifiable by their eye-catching bills and limited ranges.

The remaining four terns, the medium small-species, are the "problem terns": Forster's, common, arctic, and roseate. All are approximately the same size, slightly smaller than the gull-billed and the sandwich — roughly equal to the Franklin's gull in body length and about half as heavy. All have mostly gray and white wings tipped with black and very similar bills and caps. Separating them is the toughest of tern tests.

THE SMALL TERNS: BLACK AND LEAST

Possible to probable throughout the interior, along both coasts, and even offshore, the black may be the most widespread of all our regular terns and is certainly the most distinctive. It is the only one that is not a member of the genus *Sterna*, and it can be regarded as the *black sheep* of the group. It has a unique silhouette and flight style. Flapping its slightly rounded, vaguely gull-like wings sometimes like a butterfly (especially in strong winds) and sometimes like a nighthawk, coursing and swooping here and there, it seems less interested in making forward progress than the other terns. It is also by far the most variably feathered, showing colors that range from a glossy all-black breeding plumage through a motley molt to a wholly white-bellied winter plumage. In all seasons, however, the black has the darkest wings and mantle of any tern found inland or onshore. In its winter plumage it sometimes also has "earpatches," which recall the Bonaparte's gull and are seen on no other North American tern.

The least is the second most distinctive of all North American terns. In flight, its petite torso, white forehead, almost buzzing-quick strokes, and crisply cut, very dark wing tips make identification simple and certain. The one occasional difficulty occurs with standing birds. It is embarrassing but not impossible to mis-size a perched least — especially in bad light — and to call it a Forster's or a common. Look for a seldom mentioned field mark: *the least's bill is much longer proportionately than the bills of any of the medium-sized terns*, so that its head and bill have a silhouette matched only by that of the royal tern, which is twice as big.

THE BIG TERNS: CASPIAN, ROYAL, AND ELEGANT

Any large tern more than thirty or forty miles from the ocean may safely be called a Caspian. The royal and elegant are so loyal to salt water that neither should be expected inland except after hurricanes. Mnemonic: *the Caspian Sea is inland, and inland you see the Caspian.*

Royal Tern (left) and Caspian Tern

The Caspian/royal distinction so conspicuous on the page of the field guides, the difference in bill color, may be the most overrated field mark in North American birding. Sunlight plays tricks with red and orange, and both species' bills are variable, so the difference is surprisingly difficult to see on flying birds and less reliable than at least five other marks. Better characters are the following five.

- *Wing tip color.* As soon as you know you're looking at a big tern, aim your binocs at the underside of the wings. Royals' underwings show only a smudgy line of darkness. Caspians' underwings are much darker tipped, showing a black area that is almost triangular. Both species fly with less upstroke than the medium-sized terns, so the undersides can usually be glimpsed only for an instant at the top of the stroke, but if you concentrate your attention on the nearer wing, the difference in darkness is visible almost as far as the bird can be seen and is so reliable that the remaining field marks are really only double-checks.
- *Forehead color.* Royals' foreheads are dark to the bill for only a short time during the breeding season. For most of the year, they are distinctly white. Caspians' foreheads are dark or splotchy to the bill all year long. If you have the impression of a black cap over a white face, it can't be a Caspian: *the royal wears the crown.*
- *Size.* The Caspian, the largest tern in the world, dwarfs even the ring-billed gull and approaches the herring gull in size. The royal does not give such an impression of bulk and strength and is only about equal to the ring-billed gull in size.
- *Tail shape.* The royal's tail has a ternlike sharp fork. The Caspian's tail is almost gull-like; the "fork" is a softer indentation and sometimes disappears entirely.
- *Bill thickness.* Bill thickness as a distinguishing mark is also better than bill color. The Caspian's bill matches the rest of its jizz: it is bulky and imposing, giving the Caspian an expression somewhere between a herring gull's and a snapping turtle's. The royal's bill is thinner and seems longer.

In California, from Monterey County south, elegant versus royal is a problem. Again, bill color is unreliable. Better is the difference in size (the elegant is perceptibly smaller, equal in size to the laughing gull), and best is the difference in the *shape* of the bill. Look for a tern that combines the colors of the royal with the overall leanness and *thin, droopier bill* of the sandwich tern.

Western birders have been complaining for years that most field guides show an eastern prejudice, and Rich Stallcup has pointed out that the illustrations in at least one major field guide have the elegant's and royal's head patterns exactly reversed. The elegant should show more black on the face, so that the eye is entirely within the cap. West Coast royals have very "bald" (that is, white) heads, and their eyes are well forward of the black. Now eastern birders have cause for complaint; in a new field guide, the California head pattern is presented as if it were universal for the royal. It isn't. Atlantic royal terns have their eyes well within the black. Perhaps partly for this reason the elegant has seldom been reported away from the Pacific, a couple of times in Texas and once — amazingly — in Ireland. "If they can find one in Ireland," Rick Mellon said while presenting some slides on the elegant at a 1985 meeting of the Delaware Valley Ornithological Club, "we ought to have our eyes open here." Six weeks later an elegant tern appeared at Chincoteague National Wildlife Refuge in Virginia, the first record for the species on the Atlantic coast of North America.

Whatever your chances for an elegant tern on the East Coast, they're excellent on the West. Since it first nested in the United States at San Diego Bay in 1959, the elegant's numbers have steadily increased. Flocks of as many as a thousand birds have been reported, and individuals wander regularly as far north as San Francisco Bay.

THE DARK-WINGED TERNS:
BRIDLED AND SOOTY

The enormous increase in deep-sea birdwatching expeditions in the last twenty years has demonstrated that both the bridled and sooty terns are far more common off our southeastern coasts than was once believed. The thrill of a life sighting was almost ruined for me when a hotshot birder nearby muttered, "Relax, everybody — it's only a sooty."

Both sooty and bridled are now considered regular to mundane offshore in the Gulf of Mexico and north up the Atlantic coast to the Outer Banks of North Carolina. Individual bridleds may wander annually north to Delaware and New Jersey, even without hurricanes. The sooty has nested in Texas, Louisiana, and North Carolina, has a spectacular colony at Dry Tortugas, Florida, and is generally considered the most abundant tern in the world; Claudia Wilds and others have suggested that it may be one of the most abundant *birds* in the world. It certainly seems the most reliable exotic after hurricanes, when it has reached Nova Scotia, Maine, Vermont, and upstate New York.

Distinguishing the sooty from the bridled can be troublesome, since neither follows ships and both are most often seen at long distance from a rolling deck in the blasting light of the summer sea. One underemphasized distinction is the difference in white on the face. The sooty's white is an *open patch*, giving it a expression that seems happy or relaxed. The bridled's white is a *slash*, so that the bird seems to be frowning or squinting — bristling under its bridle? Both these facial marks can be visible when the back and nape colors are uncertain.

The black tern is much smaller than either the sooty or the bridled and flies very differently, but birders in the Gulf of Mexico and southern Atlantic should note that it is more pelagic than is generally realized, and a dark-backed tern offshore is not automatically sooty or bridled.

THE SILVER-BACKED TERNS: GULL-BILLED AND SANDWICH

The gull-billed tern should have been named the gull-*winged* or the gull-*tailed* tern. The broad wings and forkless, straight-cut tail are the easiest features to spot. These combined with the very evenly colored, silver-gray upper parts make *Sterna nilotica* identifiable at distances that will astound your friends. Only the Caspian can be identified at such long range.

The bill is a good mark at closer range, within a hundred yards or so. If you don't like "gull-tailed," how about "*alcid*-billed"? The gull-bill's triangular head and bill resemble a murre's or murrelet's much more than a gull's.

Three other points about this odd species are helpful.

- No other tern shows as bald a head as a winter-plumaged gull-bill. Only the Forster's comes close, and on the Forster's the black patches flaring backward from the eyes are always visible. The heads of some gull-bills appear entirely white.
- Insects are a favored prey, so the gull-bill is most often seen circling and swooping like a swallow. Unlike the typical terns, it rarely, if ever, dives into water.
- It is the most inland oriented of the coastal terns, probably because of its dietary preferences. It is hard to find over ocean beaches (where winds make insect hunting difficult) and is rare to nonexistent offshore. It prefers protected marshes away from open water and can be found thirty or forty miles inland, coursing over freshwater lakes and bogs and even muck farms, places where you might expect a Forster's or a black but not a royal, sandwich, or any of the other saltwater terns.

The sandwich tern is like the gull-bill in that it appears silver-backed in flight, is on the large side of medium, and occurs only along our southeastern coasts. Distinguishing these two species from each other should never be a problem, however. In all other ways the sandwich and gull-bill are at opposite ends of the tern spectrum. The sandwich is the ultratypical tern and bears no resemblance to a gull. The silhouette is all angles and points: prominent crest, sharply forked tail, rakish, swept-back wings, and a thin, drooped, and pointed bill. It often flies far offshore, will not be found inland, and feeds almost entirely on fish, which it catches with ferocious, distinctively swift dives.

TABLE 19. *Tern Identification Sequence*

1. Bigger than laughing gull?	Inland? dark underwing wedge? blunt bill?	→	Caspian
	White forehead? sharply forked tail? lightly smudged underwings?	→	royal or elegant
2. Smaller than Bonaparte's?	Yellow bill? buzzing flight? dark strip on upper wing tips?	→	least
	Dark gray wings? fanning or indirect flight? "ear patches"?	→	black
3. Medium sized with dark wings?	Coal black upper parts? dark nape? white *block* on forehead?	→	sooty
	Wings brown or dark gray? white *slash* on forehead?	→	bridled
4. Medium sized with silver wings and odd bill?	Alcidlike face? forkless tail? fresh water? bald head in winter plumage?	→	gull-billed
	White/yellow billtip or "invisi-bill"? offshore? crested head?	→	sandwich
5. None of the above	See text on problem terns	→	Forster's common arctic roseate

The trick with the sandwich is differentiating it from the four slightly smaller "problem" terns, especially the roseate, the whitest member of that group. The best mark here is the bill color: *mustard makes the sandwich*, and the mustard yellow (or white) tip of the sandwich's bill is visible at fairly long range. To identify a sandwich at more impressive distances, look for a tern that seems to be missing its bill tip. At long range (or in harsh light), the sandwich's bill tip looks like it's been snapped off. *Mustard makes the sandwich invisi-bill?*

One small cautionary note: winter Forster's terns occasionally show a very small white tip in their bills. As far as I know, this feature has been illustrated only by Peter Harrison in his *Seabirds*, but it occurs often enough and can give an inland birder a real start.

The identification sequence shown in table 19 separates all terns but the four most problematic.

THE PROBLEM TERNS: FORSTER'S, COMMON, ARCTIC, AND ROSEATE

The trouble with these four very tough birds is that no easily seen feature separates any one species from the other three at all seasons. The Forster's and common have similar underwings; the arctic and roseate have similar upperwings; a tern with a short red bill might be common or arctic; a tern with a long black bill might be a winter-plumaged Forster's or a spring-plumaged roseate; and so forth. Resting birds can be identified by a careful sorting operation, but like all members of their group, the problem terns are most often seen in flight. A medium-sized, gray-and-black tern comes winging along, the birder's eye flits unhappily from upperwing to underwing to cap to bill to tail, and then the bird is gone.

The trick is memorizing what to look at *and what to ignore* before a tern flies by. This is easier than it seems at first. The puzzle can be subdivided neatly and helpfully into three simpler pieces.

Common Tern (top) and Forster's Tern

1. *Inland and Onshore: Forster's versus Common*

By frequency of occurrence, this is far and away the number one problem in tern identification in the United States. Nothing else comes close. Roseate terns are seen only along the East Coast, and inland or onshore south of Alaska and New England, arctic terns are as rare as jaegers. For most birders in most areas of the country, "Forster's versus common" is all ye know of the problem terns and all ye need to know. The best distinctions are wing colors, bill shape and color, and Forster's winter eye patches.

Wing colors. Every field guide highlights this difference, but you have to know exactly where and when to look for it. Concentrate your attention on the *middle three-fifths* of the upperwing and *ignore the wing tips.* Either species can show dark outer primaries; it's the inner primaries and secondaries where the difference always shows — Forster's light, common dark. The difference is best seen when the bird has finished a downstroke and has its wings fully extended in a banking turn. Next best (and important for birds passing at an angle overhead) is at the peak of the upstroke; look past the body to the far wing, and ignore everything else for at least half a dozen wing strokes.

Bill shape and color. This is another difference that seems impossible at first and soon becomes striking. The Forster's bill is noticeably thicker and longer, giving its head a jizz vaguely like that of a scaled-down royal or a scaled-up least. The common's head never gives this impression. In their breeding plumage the bill colors on the two species vary and overlap in the orange-red range, but individuals at the ends of the spectrum may be clearly differentiated. One with a black-tipped pale orange bill is a Forster's; one with a black-tipped scarlet red bill is a common.

The Forster's winter eye patches. This would be the number one distinction if it applied all year. A Forster's/common with two black eyes must be Forster's. Some individuals will be showing this feature by the end of July; others, however, molt later, and so a fully capped Forster's/common can't be identified by head pattern alone.

Also helpful by late summer is a feature that Will Russell once noted in a "Photo Quiz" in *Birding* magazine: Forster's terns show more "powder bloom" than any other species. Powder bloom is the disintegrating fluff from old feathers. On the Forster's this material can give the wings a very dusty look, sometimes covering the whole upperwing so that the outer primaries look as gray-white as the inner primaries. The Forster's flashy wings, "bald" winter head, and powder bloom can all be remembered in a mnemonic: *The Forster's tern is a frosted tern.*

One last point about these two: don't get discouraged and start doubting your eyes if all the terns you see seem to belong to one species and never to the other. It is very likely that all the problem terns in your area *are* one species and not the other. The ecological differences between the two are still being worked out by biologists, but it seems the two species mix together only accidentally. Most flocks are single species, and in many localities one species is abundant, the other rare or absent.

2. *Offshore on Both Coasts: Common versus Arctic*

British birders solve the problem of distinguishing between the two species by dubbing unidentifiable individuals "comic" terns. American birders have less of a problem because the arctic is generally encountered only on pelagic trips. When arctic terns finish nesting early in August, they head straight for deep water. Wallace Bailey has reported that, even on Cape Cod, their southernmost nesting area in the United States, migrants are rarely seen from land.

Birders who've spent time on the arctic's breeding grounds can distinguish between these two by remembering the arctic's short-necked, short-billed, bull-headed look, its darker gray breast, the slightly more contrasting white and gray on its face, or its more translucent wings, but for most of us the distinguishing characteristic reduces to a single, challenging feature: *the pattern of dark markings on the primaries.*

Again, it's important to know where and when to look. In this case the difference is clearest on the underwings. The arctic's thinner, longer line of darkness can be seen on the upperwing also, but it stands out in sharpest contrast on the underside, when the wing is fully extended. Wait for the upstroke, and look at the nearer wing on passing birds. It's the same spot that you should study on Caspians and royals, but in this case there's much more wing lift and a slight hesitation at the top and one day you'll find yourself shouting "Arctic tern!" with that special thrill of certainty.

To remember which wing pattern is which, think of the darkness as representing the two species' migration patterns. The arctic has a longer migration, limited to the edges of our continent, and its wings show a longer line of darkness, limited to the edges of the feathers. The common has a shorter, less restricted migration, and its wings show a shorter, smudgier darkness.

A length-of-the-planet migrant, the arctic has a very compressed nesting season. Since it comes and goes so much farther than the common, it arrives on the breeding grounds later and leaves earlier. In spring, birders on pelagic trips as far south as northern California and the midatlantic states can still hope to spot one in late May or even early June. In fall, your best chances come in mid- to late August and decline rapidly in September (see chapter 5).

3. East Coast, Onshore and Off: The Roseate Tern

Here's a real mystery bird. The roseate tern is found easily only in and around its two disjunct breeding areas in the Florida Keys and New England. It must pass up and down the Atlantic coast in fair numbers every year, but it is seldom reported on migration and seems harder to spot from New Jersey to Georgia than the lesser black-backed gull, a Eurasian vagrant.

None of the four best-known field marks is helpful for flying birds on migration. The more extensive tail feathers, the sometimes rosy breast, and the longer, black bill are all hard to verify. The call (described by Edgar Reilly as "a ripping, rasping *aaark* and a distinctive *chee-wee* whistle") will seldom be heard.

In flight away from its nesting grounds, the roseate can probably be found only by birders who consciously and deliberately search for it or for an arctic. If you see a tern with a particularly long tail, aim your binocs as you would at a possible arctic — at the undersides of the primaries at the peak of the upstroke. The roseate's underwing differs from all others in showing a thin line of darkness *only on the leading edge* or *no darkness at all*. (The roseate can be found only on one coast or not at all.) For quick confirmation, try comparing the breast color with the underwing color. Like the Forster's (not seen offshore), the roseate has a body and underwing that show no contrast. Both are overall light below. The arctic, whose underwings most closely resemble the roseate's, has a much darker breast. You may also look for a frost like that on Forster's or even whiteness on the upperwings much like that on the sandwich tern, though sunlight often makes upperwings harder to judge than underwings.

BEYOND THE TERNS

One day you are studying a tern as it flies over your head, descends to the ground, wiggles its wings a couple of times to settle down, and then shuffles out of sight behind a dozen gulls. You wait a few moments, but the tern stays hidden. Now what do you do? Should you check out the gulls?

If you drop your binocs from your eyes, turn your back, and walk away, there's nothing to be ashamed of. Gulls are a group of birds disdained by many birders.

But should you decide, what the heck, let's take a look, congratulations are in order. You are moving on to the most intricate and time-consuming of all birding challenges.

11 · GULLS

MY WIFE ONCE TRIED to convert a friend to birdwatching by taking her to a local marsh. For a few minutes all went well. "There's a pintail duck," Jesse pointed out.

"Beautiful!" said her friend.

"There's a great blue heron."

"Majestic!"

"And here's a snowy egret."

"Oh, so elegant!"

"And that's a herring gull," Jesse said.

Her friend put down her borrowed binoculars. Her nose was

wrinkled in distress. "Do you mean to tell me," she said, "that a dirty old seagull is a bird, too?"

Yes, gulls are birds too, but even some diehard birdwatchers wish they weren't. For many people, gulls are "trash birds" in both senses of the term: too attracted to garbage dumps and parking lots to be appealing and too numerous to be intriguing. Nature lovers tend to love best the ecological underdogs — golden eagles, blue whales, Kirtland's warblers, mountain lions — animals that in their rarity and dwindling numbers symbolize a virgin world we have lost. Gulls in their omnipresence and exploding populations have somehow come to symbolize the world we have gained.

The routine abundance of gulls makes a convenient excuse for ignoring them. No other group of birds presents so many subtle identification problems or such an array of overlapping plumages. Sweeping your scope through a flock of a hundred gulls and honestly trying to identify each individual can make you dizzy. There are more plumage variations *within* most gull species than there are *between* species. The first-winter herring, for instance, looks more like the first-winter versions of western, lesser black-backed, California, Thayer's, and several others than it does an adult herring.

Gull sizes and silhouettes, unlike shorebird sizes and silhouettes, are only moderately useful as guides to identification. Sorting out the plumages is essential, and this is one part of birding that seems to get *harder* with experience. The more you know about gulls, the more carefully you have to look at them. Even the experts often find themselves confounded.

In November 1974 a gull appeared on Brigantine Island near Atlantic City, New Jersey. It was first thought to be a Franklin's gull in an abnormal molt. Then, after observers realized that the field marks of the Franklin's didn't quite fit, it was identified as a mew gull from Europe. When the mew's field marks didn't seem to match either, some observers speculated that it might be a brown-headed gull from India. Others thought that it was a hybrid form of the Andean gull from South America. The bird remained on the beach for three weeks, walking within yards of the dozens of birders who had arrived on the scene to debate with each other and to photograph it from every conceivable angle. Adding insult to injury, it returned to the same beach the following October and for several years thereafter until observers simply abandoned hope of identifying it. Photographs were circulated to various experts and were eventually published, but to this day the identity of the "Brigantine Mystery Gull" remains undetermined.

The story of another mystery gull, "Old One-Foot," has been twisting and turning like a serial adventure for the last decade. A dark-backed gull missing its right foot was discovered in October 1977 at Fort Morgan, Alabama, by a group of veteran birders who identified it as a lesser black-back, making it the first of the species to be reported in Alabama. For the next month other birders came to the site, photographed the bird, and added it to their lists. It returned to Mobile Bay the following September, however, and was photographed by Charles Duncan. Examining his slides back home, Duncan was struck by a thought: how could he be sure "One-Foot" wasn't a western gull? Although westerns rarely stray from the Pacific coast, they are also dark backed and close in size to the lesser black-back. Duncan borrowed slides from those who'd photographed the bird the previous year, enclosed his slides, and began circulating the file to various gull experts around the country. Their analysis confirmed his doubts: all agreed "One-Foot" was definitely not a lesser black-back, and most thought it was probably a western.

The gull had disappeared in the meantime and did not return to the bay in 1979 or 1980. In April 1981, an observer in Fort Pickens, Florida, about fifty miles east of Mobile Bay, reported seeing a dark-backed, one-footed gull. It disappeared before others could see it, but then in September 1981 "Old One-Foot" was found again back at Mobile Bay. Duncan and others studied the bird for the next few weeks, photographed it in all possible lights, and concluded that the bird was a western gull, one of the very few ever reported east of California. Other expert observers weren't convinced, however, and deemed both "lesser black-back" and "western" unsatisfactory identifications. The field marks of neither species fit exactly.

Some observers began to think the bird was a hybrid, perhaps the result of cross-breeding between the greater black-back and the lesser or between the lesser black-back and the herring gull. The gull has returned every year since, but by winter 1986 local birders were no longer attempting to name its species. It had become just plain "Old One-Foot." European gull expert K. H. Voous once responded to the description of another mystery gull with a comment that all birders might want to copy into their field guides: "A gull like yours should not exist; indeed, it does not exist. Bird watchers should congratulate themselves when never seeing a gull like this; it would give them nightmares, for it is not identifiable."

SORTING THE PLUMAGES

The first thing to realize about gull plumages is that no general field guide illustrates them all. All gulls have five to nine distinct plumages, not counting periods of transition or racial and individual variations. General field guides are designed for portability and ease of use and simply lack the space for a comprehensive presentation of all possibilities. Of the specialized guides, Peter Grant's *Gulls: A Guide to Identification* (Buteo Books, 1986) seems the most detailed, and Peter Harrison's *Seabirds* (Boston: Houghton Mifflin, 1983) the most impressively illustrated. Harrison illustrates far more gull plumages than are shown in any general field guide and describes all plumages for every gull in the world, but he says Grant's book "is an absolute necessity, [and] no progressive birder should be without a copy."

The second thing to realize about gull plumages is that there's no avoiding the lingo. Anyone interested in mastering the gulls must adjust to the gull specialists' categories: "two-year gulls," "three-year gulls," "first-winter plumage," "second-summer plumage," and so on. To the expert gull watcher, "I saw an immature herring gull" is as useless a description as "I saw a sparrow" would be to the average birder.

Sorting gull plumages begins with a straightforward principle: *the number of plumages increases with the size of the bird.*

Small gulls, for example Bonaparte's and Franklin's, are two-year gulls and have five plumages. Midsized gulls, for example laughing and ring-billed, are three-year gulls and have seven plumages. Large gulls, for example herring and glaucous, are four-year gulls and have nine plumages. (See table 20.) There are no "one-year" gulls or "five-year" gulls, and the only species whose plumage sequence seems not to match its size is the newly recognized yellow-footed gull, which is the size of a herring gull but apparently reaches adult plumage after only three years of life.

TABLE 20. *Gull Plumages and Terminology*

After the last stage shown below, birds alternate between adult winter and adult breeding plumages.

TWO-YEAR GULLS (FIVE PLUMAGES)	THREE-YEAR GULLS (SEVEN PLUMAGES)	FOUR-YEAR GULLS (NINE PLUMAGES)
little[a]	laughing[a]	California[b]
Bonaparte's[a]	mew	Iceland[b]
Sabine's[a]	ring-billed	Thayer's[b]
Franklin's[a]	Heermann's	lesser black-back[b]
black-headed[a]	yellow-footed[b]	herring[b]
Ross'		western[b]
red-legged kittiwake		glaucous-winged[b]
black-legged kittiwake		glaucous[b]
ivory		greater black-back[b]
1. juvenal	1. juvenal	1. juvenal
2. first winter	2. first winter	2. first winter
3. first summer	3. first summer	3. first summer
4. adult winter	4. second winter	4. second winter
5. adult breeding	5. second summer	5. second summer
	6. adult winter	6. third winter
	7. adult breeding	7. third summer
		8. adult winter
		9. adult breeding

[a]Hooded gull.
[b]Member of herring gull complex.

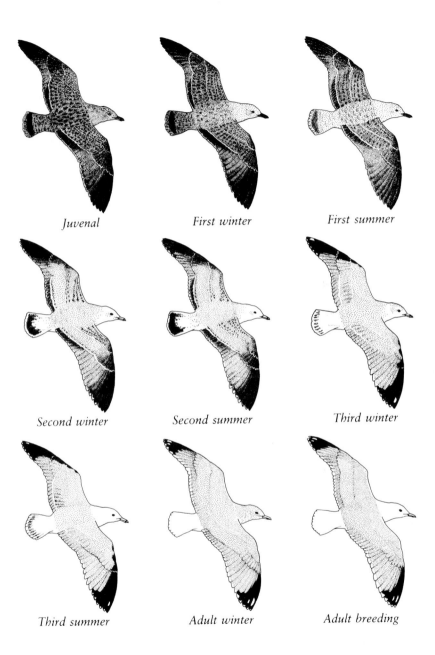

Juvenal · First winter · First summer

Second winter · Second summer · Third winter

Third summer · Adult winter · Adult breeding

FIGURE 11. *The Nine Plumages of the Herring Gull*

The general progression (figure 11) is from a muted (often brown) juvenal plumage through a series of increasingly less motley intermediate plumages to the cleaner, crisper colors of the adult plumages.

The head and body feathers and sometimes the tail feathers change in both the spring and the fall molts. Most gulls molt their wing feathers only in the fall, when all feathers are molted. Late summer is thus the toughest season for gull identification, since wing feathers are then nearly a year old and appear faded and scruffy.

Juvenal

The juvenal plumage is worn by all gulls from the time they leave their nest until late summer or early fall. Generally, it is the least important plumage to study, since most gulls, unlike shorebirds, molt their juvenal plumage before migrating. You will see juvenal-plumaged gulls regularly only if the species nests in your area.

The Sabine's gull is one exception to this rule. Birds of the year fly south before molting and are regularly seen off the West Coast, especially Washington, in their juvenal plumage. The *triple triangle* on each wing (black, white, and scaly copper) makes them easy identifications.

First Winter

The first-winter plumage is very important to learn and is the subadult plumage most often illustrated in the field guides. It is acquired in late summer or early fall of the gull's year of birth and worn until the following spring.

First-winter gulls are almost always more numerous than gulls in other nonadult plumages and frequently outnumber adults. In fact, if a gull occurs only as an autumn or winter stray in your area, knowing the first-winter plumage is more important than knowing the adult's. Vagrant gulls are most likely to be "lost" first-winter wanderers. Glaucous and Iceland gulls seen south of the Great Lakes, for example, are usually first-winter birds; adults of either species are extremely rare outside their normal ranges.

First Summer

The term "first summer" may seem confusing, since the plumage of a gull's (or any bird's) initial summer of life is its juvenal plumage. A gull in first-summer plumage is in its *second* year of life.

In most three-year and four-year gulls, first-summer plumage is hard to distinguish from first-winter plumage. Generally the head and breast are whiter, but distinctions are so fine that even gull fanatics seldom bother with the separation and lump "first winter" and "first summer" under the term "first year."

Second Winter and Second Summer

Since two-year gulls achieve their adult-winter plumage in their second winter and breeding plumage in their second summer, the terms "second winter," "second summer," and "second year" are used only with reference to three- and four-year gulls.

As three-year gulls move into their second-winter plumage, they gain more adultlike wings. At their next molt, into second-summer plumage, three-year gulls become very adultlike. The most visible differences from adult plumage appear at the two ends of the bird — the bill and the tail. The tails are banded or smudgy, and the bill has (generally) not yet achieved its adult color.

Four-year gulls in second-summer plumages often show a telltale mark. Most of the bird is obviously subadult: the wings are smudgy or spotted; the tail is banded; the bill lacks the adult's red spot. But the back (or "saddle") is the color of the adult's back. One gull that shows this pattern very clearly at this age is the greater black-back. The bird's tail and wings are rather ill defined and nondescript, but there in the "saddle" is a beautiful glossy square of black, leaving no doubt about the bird's identity.

Third Winter and Third Summer

These terms are used with reference only to four-year gulls. All smaller gulls have reached adult plumage by their third year.

Anyone who's tried to complete an "all forms" checklist (see table 21) knows that the toughest gull form to find is a four-year bird in its third-year plumage. This problem is a conse-

TABLE 21. *All Forms Checklist for Ring-billed Gull and Herring Gull*

BIRD	DATE	SITE
Ring-billed gull		
— Juvenal		
— First winter		
— First summer		
— Second winter		
— Second summer		
— Adult winter		
— Adult breeding		
Herring gull		
— Juvenal		
— First winter		
— First summer		
— Second winter		
— Second summer		
— Third winter		
— Third summer		
— Adult winter		
— Adult breeding		

Date list begun:

Date list completed:

quence of the same population dynamics that make first-year birds easier to find than second-year birds. The cohort for any given year declines each season as its members die off. Each year the cohort's population grows smaller, and by the third year only a minority survives. The population in adult plumage outnumbers birds in third-year plumages only because it includes birds of many ages — a third-year herring gull seen in spring 1987 must have been born in the summer of 1984; any adult seen could have been born in 1983, 1982, 1981, or any of the previous ten or fifteen years.

Four-year gulls in their third-year plumages resemble adults except at each end — the tail and the tip of the bill. The tails generally still show bands or smudges of darkness, and the bills often retain some dark color and lack the adult's red spot. The wings also tend to be less cleanly marked (for example, there are fewer white windows and more black) than the wings of full adults.

Adult Winter

To separate adult-winter plumage from breeding plumage, study the heads. The hooded gulls and the kittiwakes have ear patches or partial hoods in adult winter plumage. Most other gulls in adult-winter plumage have streaky or spotted heads.

Adult Breeding

This plumage is achieved by two-year gulls in their fifth plumage, as they are nearing two years of age; by three-year gulls in their seventh plumage, as they are nearing three years of age; and by four-year gulls in their ninth plumage, as they near four years of age.

All gulls have easily recognized breeding plumages. All hooded gulls have beautiful *black or chocolate brown hoods* in breeding plumage. All other regularly occurring North American gulls have *white, unspotted heads* in breeding plumage. One simple and excellent double-check for adult gulls at all seasons is the tail. Except for the Heermann's gull, all North American gulls have bright white tails in both adult plumages.

Once a gull has reached full adulthood, its plumage alternates between adult winter and breeding adult for the rest of its life. All feathers are renewed at least once annually, and plumage cannot be used to estimate age. Twenty-year-old gulls are indistinguishable from five-year-olds.

THE HOODED GULLS

These six gulls — laughing, Franklin's, Bonaparte's, black-headed, little, and Sabine's — are by far the easiest gull group to learn. In their breeding plumages, they are unmistakable. No other North American gulls show the slightest suggestions of hoods. In nonbreeding plumages, you can separate members of this group from other gulls by a number of features. (See table 22.) The identification problems with the hooded gulls occur *within* the group.

1. *Franklin's versus Laughing*

For most localities in the United States, how you make this separation depends on which is the dominant species in your area. The only place in North America where both are common is along the Texas coast in May and October. In the Far West, along the Pacific coast, and in the Northeast interior both are so rare that an individual of either species usually draws a close look. Almost everywhere else, one of the two is common to abundant, the other an occasional needle in a taken-for-granted haystack.

Breeding-plumaged adults can be separated by the patterns of black and white in their wing tips, but a stray from either species is more likely to be in one of the other plumages. More often useful is a different distinction. *In first-winter and all later winter plumages, the laughing gull is the least hooded of the hooded gulls; the Franklin's is the most.*

All other hooded gulls in winter plumages (and some summer plumages) have dark and sharply etched ear patches, so that they have more black on their heads than the laughing gull and less than the Franklin's.

TABLE 22. *Features Distinguishing Hooded Gulls from Other Gulls*

The six hooded gulls — laughing, Franklin's, Bonaparte's, black-headed, little, and Sabine's — can be distinguished from other gulls by a number of traits.

FEATURE	REMARKS
Jizz	The hooded gulls are the most ternlike of North American gulls. Bills are more pointed, less bulky, and more subtly curved than those of larger gulls; bodies are leaner; at most ages plumage has more bright white and more clean-cut contrast with dark areas.
Size	The hooded gulls are noticeably smaller than all other gulls except the pelagic kittiwakes and the two very rare arctic gulls, the ivory and Ross'.
Flight	More flapping, less gliding than larger gulls.
Plumage	All but the laughing gull reach adult plumage in two years (and so have just five plumages), and flocks appear more uniform than flocks of larger gulls (all of which have seven to nine plumages).
Rump and tail	Subadults have bright rumps and upper tails often with sharply etched black bands. Subadults of other gulls tend to have speckled or dark brown rumps and tail bands often speckled, brown, or mottled black.
Bill color	For most of the year most hooded gulls have bills of one color, black or red, with no spots. Most of the larger gulls show bicolored bills at most ages and a prominent red spot on lower mandible in breeding plumage.
Neck	White in all plumages after juvenal (only the laughing gull shows faint streaking). Most larger gulls have streaked or spotted necks in all plumages except breeding adult.

Birders in the Franklin's territory can also be alert to bill size and shape. The laugher has the least ternlike bill of any hooded gull. It's longer and has a perceptible bend along the upper mandible and a clear hook at the tip.

Identifying a Franklin's in laughing gull territory is tougher than the reverse. There are two clues.

A gull with a half hood and a tail band can't be a laughing gull. Any laughing gull with a half hood must be of adult age and will have the adult's white tail. The same is true of the wings. No laughing gull with a half hood will have the mottled wings of the subadult. Stray Franklin's gulls, on the other hand, are often first-winter birds — showing half hoods, dark-banded tails, and subadult upperwings.

The smaller size of Franklin's gull is especially evident when it's sitting on water. It floats as high as a bathtub toy and its small head and bill, short tail, and ball-like shape suggest a Bonaparte's more than they do a laughing gull.

2. *Black-headed and Little Gulls versus Bonaparte's*

Here's another needle-and-haystack problem, with the Bonaparte's gull playing the haystack for two recent Eurasian invaders.

Thirty years ago, both the little and the black-headed gulls were considered accidental in North America. Today the black-headed has been reported in double-digit flocks in New England, has strayed south as far as Florida, is regularly reported on the Pacific coast, and has been found nesting in Newfoundland, Quebec, and Massachusetts. The little gull, the world's smallest gull, was first found nesting on our continent in Ontario in 1962 and in the United States in 1975 in Green Bay, Wisconsin. It is now especially likely around the Great Lakes and off the coast of British Columbia, seems to appear annually in most states on the East Coast, and has wandered a number of times south to California and inland to Colorado.

The birder who wants to find either of these rare gulls needs to cultivate the habit of studying the underwings of every Bonaparte's encountered. Separating black-headed from Bonaparte's is an identification problem of the first magnitude, and separating the little can be tougher than it looks in the books. *The Bony's underwings, however, are light in all plumages.*

The black-headed's underwings range from dusky tipped in the juvenal and first-winter plumages to darkly wedged in the adult plumages. You'll need to confirm a black-headed by its red or yellowish bill, but the underwings are the field marks (the only field marks) that stand out at any distance.

Studying Bony underwings may also win you a little gull. In both its adult plumages, the little gull's underwings are shockingly dark. Wanderers are more likely to be younger birds, though, and here you need to be on the alert for the little's head pattern and tail shape. In its subadult plumages the little has more darkness on the peak of its head than any hooded gull but the Franklin's. Its sometimes dusky, sometimes black cap might remind you of the cap on the Wilson's warbler. "The tail shape is a good field mark for all plumages," Lyn Atherton has noted. "The Bonaparte's has a rounded tail. The little's tail is notched."

THE "EASY" GULLS: KITTIWAKES, IVORY, ROSS', AND HEERMANN'S

The remaining two-year gulls and one three-year gull, Heermann's, pose few identification problems except general scarcity.

The only one in this cluster common and widespread enough to be a species of concern to most birders is the black-legged kittiwake. It is primarily a pelagic bird, but wanderers are found inland every fall and winter, especially around the Great Lakes. On both coasts it's a "feast or famine" species, unmissable one year and unfindable the next. Although it's the size of the laughing gull, its more rounded wings, dark ear patches, and winter habits make it more likely to be mistaken for Bonaparte's. Adults are easy; their wing tips, as Roger Tory Peterson has observed, look as if they had been *dipped in ink*. To distinguish first-year birds from the similarly patterned first-year Bonaparte's, think of this species as the "black-*naped*" kittiwake. The thick, inky black stripe on the back of the neck is visible at long range.

The Heermann's gull, a Mexican nester and limited in the

United States to the beaches, channel islands, and offshore waters of the Pacific coast, is the easiest to identify of all North American gulls. The adult's flashy red bill and breeding-plumaged white head are hard to mistake. The dark banded tail is a dead giveaway. *All other American gulls have white tails in their adult plumages, and none has such a crisply banded tail in any plumage.* To identify Heermann's in its subadult plumages, let "Heermann's" remind you of "Hershey's" and watch for a bird that looks as if it had been dropped in a vat of melted chocolate. Especially in its first-year plumages, the Heermann's is an overall deep black/brown.

The remaining three easy gulls — ivory, red-legged kittiwake, and Ross' — are species of the Far North and are so rare in the Lower Forty-eight that the primary value of their inclusion in North American field guides is to fuel birders' fantasies.

The most "reliable" wanderer of the three is the ivory, and no more than half a dozen individuals are seen annually on either coast. Identification is made even simpler because the vagrants are inevitably first-year birds with an eye-catching black face and white wings speckled with black.

The red-legged kittiwake is the rarest of all North American gulls in the Lower Forty-eight and is generally a species of concern only to birders visiting its nesting grounds in the Alaskan islands of the Bering Sea. It has been recorded occasionally off the Oregon coast and once in Nevada (!), but gull chasers should be aware that black-legged kittiwakes sometimes show red legs. Peter Harrison has suggested that the red-leg's darker wings in adult plumages and paler neckband in subadult plumages may be more useful distinctions.

The Ross' is the most famous of rare gulls. On March 2, 1975, when Walter Ellison, a young birder from White River Junction, Vermont, and Paul Miliotis from Newburyport, Massachusetts, spotted a pinkish, wedge-tailed bird on the Merrimac River in Newburyport and identified it as a Ross' gull, the whole North American birding community reverberated. Here was a bird that was believed to nest only in Siberia and that had been seen only by birders lucky enough to be standing at

Point Barrow, Alaska, and other Arctic Ocean lookouts when one flew by.

Miliotis called Dr. P. A. Buckley of the National Park Service in Boston who, before grabbing his binoculars and sprinting out the door, called a friend in New York City and thereby set off a geometrically progressing wave of phone calls. Buckley later estimated that within twenty-four hours of the identification at least one person in every state in the Union and every province in Canada had been notified. Dozens of birders were on the scene by the following morning and 2,000 by the following weekend. While the gull lingered in the area for several weeks, an estimated 10,000 birders added it to their life lists.

It was called "The Sighting of the Century" and was believed by most who traveled to Newburyport to be a once-in-a-lifetime chance to see the species. Christopher Leahy wrote in the *New York Times,* "As I watched it, I felt that it might easily come over to where I was standing and speak to me, after which I would die and be carried on its back down the Merrimac, out to sea, and after a short flight, to a mountain peak of ice at the North Pole. Something like that. The perfect end to a birdwatcher's life. A Ross' gull and then the cold beyond."

But it was not the last Ross' gull of the century — not even the last of the decade. In June 1978, one was spotted perched on an ice floe on the Churchill River in Manitoba, Canada, where it remained for three days. Later that year, in November 1978, one appeared at Wilmette Harbor near Chicago. This one, too, remained for several days, and differences in the plumage made clear that it was not the Newburyport bird. Now the question was: why did we suddenly have three Ross' gulls in four years after having none in the previous 200 years?

The answer came from Manitoba. On June 10, 1980, Yves Aubry of Montreal found a breeding-plumage Ross' gull in the midst of an arctic tern colony near Churchill. Another adult was seen in the area two days later, and within a few days searchers combing the area had found four more bright pink adults. On June 29 outside Churchill the searchers made one of the most exciting discoveries in the history of North American ornithology — a Ross' gull nest with two eggs. Within a week two other nests were found close by, and the word went out: the Siberian gull had defected. Ross' gulls were colonizing the Western Hemisphere.

A handful of nesting pairs have been returning to Churchill annually, other nesting sites have been found at Bathurst Island (Northwest Territories) and in Greenland, and stray Ross' gulls have been appearing at widely separated spots across the continent. In April 1983 a Ross' gull appeared near a dam in Julesberg, Colorado, and remained for more than a week. In April 1984 two Ross' gulls were present simultaneously in the United States — one in the Agassiz National Wildlife Refuge in northwestern Minnesota (just south of Manitoba) and the other in West Haven, Connecticut. Gull watchers everywhere can scan the horizon with a new gleam in their eyes. Says Paul Buckley, one of the first on the scene at Newburyport, "Now I'd like to be the first person to find a Ross' gull in New York City."

TWO YOU HAVE TO LOVE

If identifying Ross' gulls and red-legged kittiwakes were what gull watching was about, all birders would be out there doing it. There'd be no more jokes about gull enthusiasts being the lunatic fringe of a lunatic fringe.

But there aren't enough Ross' gulls or red-legged kittiwakes around to keep anyone going, and gull watching is a minority sport because it seems at first glance downright boring. What gull watchers do most of the time is study two of the most common birds in North America, the ring-billed gull and the herring gull, over and over and over again. Both are extremely successful, unmissable birds that occur in the thousands in urbanized areas. On the 1982 Christmas count, for example, more than one of every two birds seen in Brooklyn, New York, was a herring gull (59,501 of 97,283). Cleveland, Ohio, had the same percentage for the ring-billed gull (23,526 of 52,096), and in Elyria-Lorain, Ohio, more than four of every five birds seen (88,984 of 106,765) were ring-billed gulls.

The ring-bill's name sometimes misleads beginners, since the ring doesn't become a true band until the second summer or third winter. First-year ring-bills are not ring-billed at all; the bill is tipped with black, like a first-year herring gull's. Also, some second-year and third-year herring gulls' bills can suggest a smudgy ring. But *the herring's bill is always much stouter and longer, never truly ringed, and the bird itself is 20 percent to 30 percent larger.* With a little experience, most of us can identify these two without thinking about it. Which means most of us can identify nine of every ten gulls we encounter without thinking about it.

What separates the ordinary birder from the passionate gull chaser is the commitment to that tenth gull — and to the one hundredth, one thousandth, and ten thousandth gull. Knowing all plumages of the ring-billed and herring and scrutinizing gull after gull after gull is the key to identifying the ring-bill's near twin, the mew gull, and each of the herring's nine sibling species.

A quick fix to ring-billed/herring ennui is the "all forms" checklist. (See table 21.) Give the ring-bill seven slots on your list and the herring gull nine, and suddenly these "trash birds" will challenge your skills all over again. February and March are a good time to begin. This is generally the winter doldrums of the birding year, but it's the time when both the ring-bill and the herring are molting. With luck and persistence, you can find individuals in almost all plumages, from first-winter to breeding adult. Even better, one of the goodies — mew gull, California, lesser black-back, etc. — may turn up when you least expect it.

Something else to work on with our two most abundant gulls is the "snap identification." Learning to separate herring from ring-bill by flight style or general impression trains your eye for the more subtle analysis required to identify the less common species.

The ring-bill is not a true member of the herring gull complex. It and the mew gull are a separate subcluster of midsized three-year gulls not given to hybridizing with their larger relatives. In areas where the ring-bill is king, however, it can be an excellent reference point for all herring lookalikes. All larger gulls *are* members of the herring gull complex, and the ring-bill's adult mantle is very close to the shade of the herring gull's mantle. If there's no herring gull around to compare to some odd gull, the ring-bill is the best substitute.

The herring gull is the centerpiece of its complex, a cluster of closely related large gulls whose numbers vary between three species and eleven, depending on who is doing the taxonomy. At the moment ten species are recognized, and a cheater's crib sheet to the complex would look something like figure 12.

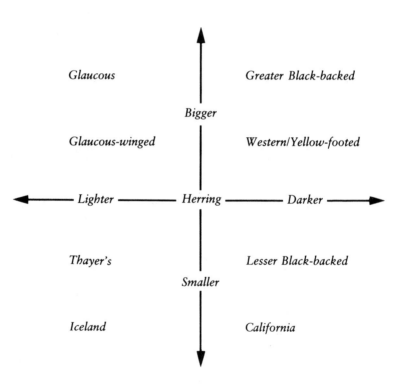

FIGURE 12. *A Key to the Herring Gull Complex*

Figure 12 ignores some complexities (for example, greater black-backs are usually bigger than glaucous gulls, and lesser black-backs can be slightly smaller than Iceland), but it's a useful, simplified key. Three members of the complex are darker and generally larger than the herring, two are darker and smaller, two are lighter and larger, and two are lighter and smaller.

TWO OVERLOOKABLES: MEW AND CALIFORNIA

The mew gull and the California gull are two western species that probably wander eastward more often than we know. Reports of each have been increasing steadily, apparently as more and more birders learn to search for them. Both are easily missed, however, by any birder not interested in scrutinizing ring-bill and herring flocks.

Their field marks draw an odd parallel. The mew is a down-sized and darker version of the ring-bill; the California is a down-sized and darker version of the herring. Each is separable from its more widespread lookalike by the same series of field marks:

- a smaller bill;
- a smaller, more rounded head and a "gentler" expression;
- a leaner torso;
- darker plumage overall in juvenal/first-year plumage;
- darker wings and mantle in adult plumages;
- wings proportionately longer, extending farther past the tail and giving the bird a more "leaned back" stance than its lookalike.

In subadult plumages neither mew nor California has a single definitive field mark, and identification east of the Dakotas must be done with extreme caution and clear references to the field marks of its lookalike at the same age.

In adult plumages, both are relatively easier identifications.

The mew has a yellow, unspotted bill something like a kitti-wake's. The California, which is halfway in size between a her-ring and a ring-bill, has a bill that is half herring gull and half ring-bill. It combines the herring's red spot and overall yellow with a black marking that suggests the ring-bill's band. Be aware, however, that some herring gulls may have similarly colored bills — so that the California's dark eye is an essential double-check. Note, too, that "California gull" is a somewhat deceptive name. *Larus californicus* is the state bird of Utah and breeds in inland areas from the Great Salt Lake north and east to Canada and North Dakota. It is most numerous in Califor-nia during the winter.

DARK-WINGED LARGE GULLS

The four members of this group fall into two pairs, one pair for each coast.

1. *Greater Black-Back and Lesser Black-Back*

The greater black-backed gull could be named "the great*est*, black*est*-backed gull." It is the biggest larid in the world and has the darkest wings and mantle of all North American gulls.

It has been expanding steadily southward down the East Coast throughout this century, but it's still very much a coastal gull, less given to wandering westward than the lesser black-back (or any other eastern gull). Inland birders generally need to visit salt water or the shores of the Great Lakes if they want to add it to their lists.

In its adult and third-year plumages, the wings make identi-fication a snap. The only large gull with wings nearly as dark is the yellow-footed, which is separated in range from the greater by the diagonal width of the continent.

To the practiced eye, greater black-backs in their mottled-winged first- and second-year plumages are also very distinc-tive. The two keys here are the huge bill and the white head, which contrasts strikingly at all ages with the wings and man-tle. You can remember both these keys if you think of the greater black-back as the *bald eagle* of gulls. It harasses and dominates all smaller species, including the ordinarily unshakable herring gull, as eagles dominate ospreys.

Until the early 1970s, the lesser black-backed gull was considered accidental in North America. The first North American specimen was not collected until 1948 (at Assateague Island, Virginia). For the next twenty-five years of so, birds on our side of the Atlantic were few and were assumed to be strays from the colonies in Iceland or Great Britain. But in the last fifteen years the lesser black-back has become so common in North America — it is now an expected species in winter in most northeastern and midatlantic states — that many ornithologists believe it must be nesting on this continent in some yet-to-be-discovered location. *Inland away from the Great Lakes, from Pennsylvania west to Nevada, a large dark-backed gull is now as likely to be a lesser black-back as any other species.*

Confusion between the lesser and greater black-backs has more to do with their names than with any physical resemblance. The lesser black-back is lesser in two senses. It's perceptibly smaller than the herring gull, which is perceptibly smaller than the greater black-back. And the birds we see in the United States are less dark: the mantle and inner two-thirds of the wings on adults and third-year birds are slate, not black. Only the primaries are black, so that the wings have a *two-toned* shading not seen on greater black-backs. Beware the field guide illustrations of the Scandinavian race of the lesser black-back *(Larus fuscus fuscus),* which has a very dark, single-toned back like the great. Reports of individuals of that race in North America are usually disputed. We see the grayer, double-shaded "British" race, *Larus fuscus graellsii,* birds that are more likely to be mistaken for dark herring gulls than for small greater black-backs.

The increase of the lesser black-back has probably been even more explosive than it seems. If you study *American Birds* or your regional birding magazine, you'll note that first-year birds, which should be more numerous than other subadults, are rarely reported. Separating first-year lessers from first-year herring gulls is an identification problem still largely unsolved by American birders. Even in Europe, where the lesser black-back is abundant, good birders struggle with this distinction. The keys seem to be the lesser's smaller size; smaller bill; longer, slightly more pointed wings (extending farther past the tail in standing position); and winter belly with distinct chocolate spots.

2. Yellow-foot and Western

These two large, dark-backed gulls of the Pacific coast are hard to tell apart and harder to understand. One is North America's most recent split; the other may be our next lump.

Separation in the field is simplified by the yellow-foot's extremely limited range in North America. Once considered the least numerous, darkest-winged, and southernmost race of the western gull, the yellow-foot has recently been granted full species status because of its disjunct breeding population (in Mexico), different plumage sequence (three years as against the western's four), different call, and other distinctive features. No one seems to have told the birds about the change in taxonomic status, however, and the upgrading has had no apparent effect on their numbers. The yellow-footed gull is still a rare bird in North America. If you want to see one, you need to visit the Salton Sea in southern California during postbreeding wandering (late summer and fall) and have luck on your side.

You may also want to have a veteran gull watcher from the West Coast at your side. "Yellow-footed" applies only to adult birds. Subadults ordinarily have the same pinkish feet worn by westerns and most other members of the herring gull complex. Juvenal/first-winter birds are best identified by their pale bellies and heads. Birds in the intermediate plumages are allegedly separable by their more bulbous bills, deeper call, and a couple of other "for-experts-only" features.

North of the Salton Sea, up the coast to the Canadian border, any gull larger and darker than a herring may be assumed to be a western gull until proven otherwise, but birders taking this trip can watch a taxonomic puzzle unfold. The western gulls of southern California are colored as the species is pictured in most field guides, with wings shaded somewhere between the almost inky black of the adult yellow-foot and the slate gray of the lesser black-back (very rare on the Pacific coast). The western gulls of Oregon and Washington, however, are lighter-backed, and their wings are more obviously two-toned. Worse, they interbreed with glaucous-winged gulls regularly.

Glaucous-wing × western birds are so common where the breeding ranges of the southernmost glaucous-wings and northernmost westerns overlap that many experts consider the distinction between the two "species" more visible than biological. They are behaving more like a *cline,* a gradation of races within a single species — similar to the cline in the flickers (yellow-shafted, red-shafted, gilded-shafted) — where the birds look different to us but not to each other.

Taxonomists have been kind to birders in recent years. They've split the yellow-footed gull, the red-breasted sapsucker, Clark's grebe, and several others and so have added a number of birds to our possibilities lists. A couple of lumps and subtractions seem overdue, and the western/glaucous-wing may be one of them.

GLAUCOUS-WINGED, GLAUCOUS, AND ICELAND GULLS

Knowing the glaucous-wing's close relationship with the western gull will help you remember that it is darker than the glaucous gull at all ages (and glaucous-winged × western birds are darker still.)

The glaucous-winged is generally an easy identification simply because of its abundance. In its home territory, the shorelines and inlets of the northwestern coast, it frequently outnumbers all other gulls combined. Finding a glaucous-winged requires only that you make your way to a gull site and lift your binoculars to your eyes.

Confusion between the glaucous-winged and the glaucous is like the problems with the greater and lesser black-backs — it is due more to the similarity of names than to similarity in the field. "Glaucous-winged" is an awkward but absolutely accurate description. *The wings are grayish all the way to the tips.* For equal accuracy we'd have to rename the glaucous gull the "greater white-wing-tipped gull." It is glaucous colored only in the adult mantle and inner two-thirds of the primaries.

Away from the Pacific coast, the glaucous is the light-winged gull to expect. It is a strong flier and an aggressive explorer and wanders so frequently to all sectors of the country that it's a species every serious birder should study. It is also one of the few gulls that are more eye-catching in their first- and second-year plumages than as adults. It's possible to overlook an adult

Iceland Gull (front) and Glaucous Gull

glaucous in a crowd of herring gulls, but first- and second-year birds are more numerous than adults throughout most of the continent, and any gull chaser who scans past a large creamy or grayish white gull without saying anything should be sent back to the car for the coffee thermos.

The other creamy or grayish white large gull is the Iceland, "the lesser white-wing-tipped gull." It is lesser than the glaucous in several senses:

- It's smaller.
- It's less numerous in most areas.
- It's less likely to wander.
- Its adult plumage usually shows less white in the wing tips.

The best-known feature on the Iceland seems to be its all-black bill, an unreliable "sufficient but not necessary" distinction between it and the glaucous. Glaucous gulls never show all black bills, but Icelands have them only in their first-year plumages. Second-year and older Icelands have variably colored bills.

Glaucous and Iceland are two gulls most easily separated by subjective impression. A couple of terrible (and therefore memorable and useful) mnemonics tell the story. *The glaucous is the hawkest; the Iceland is the nice one.*

The glaucous is a much bigger bird, close or equal in size to the greater black-backed, and it radiates a raptorlike power. Its bill is large and imposing, its chest and neck are muscled like a buteo's, and it's perceptibly heavier and larger than the herring gull.

The Iceland is as dovelike as the glaucous is hawklike. Its head and bill are small; its neck and chest are thinner and more delicate; and it's perceptibly lighter and smaller than the herring gull.

The subjective difference between glaucous and Iceland is almost as great as the difference between herring gull and ring-bill.

Most North American field guides illustrate two races of the Iceland gull: the nominate race, which has white wing tips in all plumages, and the Kumlien's race, which in its adult plumages shows a few brown or gray spots at the wing tips. Probably because the whiter form is the nominate race, there is a widespread notion that the Kumlien's is the rarer form. In most areas of the United States, however, the opposite is the case.

Northeastern gull watcher Richard Heil has noted that he often hears comments such as "I had ten Iceland gulls and one was a Kumlien's." "What this probably translates into," says Heil, "is nine immatures and one adult!"

Adult Icelands with pure white wing tips are very rare in the United States, and recognizing the brown- or gray-tipped Kumlien's race is essential for those birders who want to go on to the final exam in gull watching.

THE ULTIMATE GULL

The ultimate gull — the triple somersault and four-minute mile of gull watching — is the *Larus thayeri,* Thayer's gull. This is a bird so enigmatic that taxonomists cannot decide whether or not it is a species. It is so hard to identify that maps of its range are still only rough approximations. It is a common bird in the Pacific Northwest but so difficult to separate from its closest relatives — especially the herring and Iceland — that ornithologists are not sure where else it occurs.

"Actually," claims Lyn Atherton of St. Petersburg, Florida, "identifying a Thayer's is not as difficult as people think." Atherton and her husband, Brooks, are two of the premier gull watchers in the country. In 1982 they established a national Christmas count record by locating eight lesser black-backed gulls in a single day. They have also found the first California gulls ever seen in Florida and four of the first few Franklin gulls ever seen in Florida — and they have found one Thayer's gull after another for the last several years, thereby proving almost by themselves that the species regularly strays to the

Southeast. Atherton recently explained to me what originally prompted her to search for *Larus thayeri*.

"A super gull watcher and friend of mine named Bob Barber saw what he was sure was a Thayer's near Cape Kennedy one day in 1976. He took a photograph, but the light wasn't very good, and later some people weren't convinced. Thayer's gulls don't occur in the Southeast, they said, and no one can identify them anyway. Finding another one just sounded like a challenge to me. So I started visiting the local dump in St. Pete every day to look at the herring gulls. Luckily, there were always several thousand of them there.

"Before you can identify a Thayer's gull you need to learn all the different possible plumages of the herring gull and all the possible individual differences within each plumage. Plus you have to learn to notice things like feather wear. The books say a Thayer's is slightly paler than a herring gull. But a herring gull whose feathers have worn down can look very light just before it molts. So then you have to look at other field marks, like the dark eye and the slant of the forehead. A Thayer's gull has a more rounded forehead than a herring gull. Basically what you're looking for is a dark Iceland gull. That's really what the Thayer's is, in my opinion. I've seen museum collections showing the continuum from nominate Iceland to Kumlien's to Thayer's. So it's probably not a separate species, just one end of a cline. But I don't want to make it sound like finding a Thayer's is harder than it is. Anyone who puts his mind to it can do it."

I asked her to estimate the number of hours she'd invested in the search.

"Oh, I don't know. I started going to the dump in the fall of 1976. I found my first Thayer's in January of 1978. I was working in Tampa at the time as a dental hygienist and had an hour lunch break. It was a fifteen-minute drive back and forth to the dump. That gave me half an hour each afternoon to check the gulls. I tried not to miss a single day."

"So that's a half an hour a day for a year and a half."

"Right, not counting the time I spent in the evenings studying the photographs I took every afternoon. And of course I had Fridays and weekends off. So on Fridays and Saturdays I spent the whole day at the dump. It does take some time, I admit that."

"And the moment you saw your first Thayer's, what did you do?"

"I shot two and a half rolls of thirty-six exposure film immediately. I didn't want what happened to Bob Barber to happen to me. Then I got in my Jeep to go call Brooks, drove about fifty yards, and saw another one. You see, once you know what to look for, they just jump right out at you. Three others showed up later that winter, so we had five individuals all together."

I asked Atherton why she was so fascinated by gulls.

"That's easy," she said. "They're beautiful."

"Beautiful?"

"Absolutely."

"I know some people who would disagree with you."

"It's not the garish beauty of a scarlet tanager or a rose-breasted grosbeak. It's a subtle, muted beauty. You have to look close to see it.

"These people you know," she said, "have any of them ever taken a long, careful look at a herring gull's eyelids?"

12 · THE INNER GAME

THE INNER GAME of birding is often described too simplistically. "Be careful," we are told. "Make sure you check all the field marks. Don't let your imagination get the better of you." And so on.

The truth is, birding is a delicately balanced enterprise, half sport and half science, and doing it well involves operating at the limits of your perceptual and analytical abilities. If you want to be the best birder you can be, you can't depend on any simple rules.

My wife and I were driving through south-central Florida one afternoon when I spotted a strange black-and-white hawk perched on a fence post in a cow pasture. I slowed to pull off, found a semitrailer filling my rearview mirror, and so continued on to the next exit, crossed over the road, and headed back. Jesse, who'd been sleeping, woke up. "What's the matter?"

"There's a good bird back there. Some kind of hawk I couldn't identify. Inky black wings and a light breast."

"An osprey?"

"No, there were streaks on its breast." The lightbulb over my skull flashed on. "Caracara! It has to be a caracara. It's the perfect habitat. And I even saw red in the face — and the beak. A big, hooked beak. Caracara!"

Trees in the median strip blocked our view of the pasture from the opposite side of the road. We had to drive more than a mile to the next exit to swing back again. The whole detour now totaled three or four miles, but (I rationalized happily) we had driven a lot farther than that to see birds a lot less exciting than a caracara. "I just hope it hasn't flown away," I said.

Jesse scanned with her binoculars as we approached the pasture. "There it is!" I shouted. "It's still there!"

"I don't see it."

I screeched to a halt. "It's right in front of you!" I grabbed my own binocs and jabbed at the focus.

A piece of plastic — a scrap of trashcan liner — was flapping in the wind against the fence post.

The "wings" were black all right, but the breast streaks, red face, and hooked bill had been entirely imaginary. "Well," said Jesse, "when the wind catches it, it does look something like a hawk." Then she slid her binocs back under the seat and resumed her nap.

Driving away, I made the same resolution I always make after atrocious misidentifications: *I will never call another bird wrong as long as I live.* I've got to stop guessing at birds, I told myself, I've got to stop imagining things I haven't seen, pursuing illusions, and making a fool of myself.

Twenty miles farther down the road I spotted another strange black-and-white hawk perched on a fence post in a cow pasture. No semitrailer was on my tail this time, but I hesitated for several hundred yards before I stepped on the brakes, pulled over, and shifted into reverse.

When Jesse woke up, she found me pointing at a beautiful caracara: inky black wings, streaked breast, red face, hooked beak. "Wow!" she said.

While we watched, it left the post, flew toward us, and landed in an oak tree thirty yards from the car. It preened for a few moments, its neck crest blowing in the wind, and then took off again, flap-flap-gliding over the car, over the trees in the center of the highway, and finally out of sight.

That weird and lucky experience taught me a lesson I am still trying to absorb. The fact was, I hadn't seen the second, real caracara any better than the plastic, imaginary one: *I had guessed both times.* "Strange black-and-white hawk" had been wildly wrong the first time and wonderfully correct the second. The lesson: guessing at birds, imagining things you haven't (quite) seen, pursuing illusions, and making a fool of yourself are all part of the game.

When birders confess the worst mental errors they have made, it is invariably first-impression misidentifications they mention. "I saw a medium-sized flycatcher with a yellowish breast and, before I stopped to think, I shouted 'Western kingbird!' Everybody charged over, the bird popped up, and what was it? A phoebe — an eastern phoebe. I was so humiliated I felt like throwing my binoculars in the nearest trashcan."

Yet something tangible is gained from most first-impression mistakes, *especially* the embarrassing ones. The birder who sees a yellowish breast on a medium-sized flycatcher and shouts "Western kingbird!" learns (and will probably never forget) what no earlier experience has taught him: in fall some eastern phoebes show yellow breasts. And even when nothing tangible is gained, guessing at a bird is usually worth the risk of making a fool of yourself. In my caracara experience I actually avoided the worst error I might have made: I might have driven past the real hawk. Guessing and stopping the second time was the right thing to do. Which means guessing and stopping the first time, to look at the trashcan liner, was the right thing to do. The best attitude toward first-impression misidentifications is the attitude skiers take toward tumbles: they're embarrassing but necessary. The birder who is afraid to call a bird wrong, like the skier who is afraid to fall down, progresses slowly and may never discover the upper limits of his ability.

I was standing on Hawk Mountain's North Lookout one October morning when a birder far out on the rocks jumped up and shouted, "Goshawk over Number 2!"

"No way," said a man on my left to his companion. "It can't be."

The hawk soared closer and became an ordinary red-tail. "Sorry, everybody," the first birder said, slumping back down to his seat.

"I knew it," said the naysayer. "I haven't called a hawk wrong all fall."

"Yeah," said his companion. "But how many have you called *right?*"

EXPECTING THE UNEXPECTED

Expecting the unexpected is the mental error for which beginners are most often criticized. Tongue pressed hard against cheek, Larry Balch once observed:

> The old saying, "If you don't know what you're looking for, you won't find it," doesn't apply in birding. The less you know about accipiters, for example, the easier it is to find a "Cooper's hawk." I base this statement on the number of "Cooper's hawks" reported by beginning birders as compared to those reported by more knowledgeable and experienced observers. Long-billed dowitchers are another example; these birds, too, are more easily found by the less knowledgeable.

In a similar facetious mood, Pete Dunne once confessed, "I don't know what ever happened to the birds of my youth. When I was first beginning to look at birds as a ten-year-old in

New Jersey, I could find just about any kind of bird I wanted to. All I'd have to do is see a picture of a bird, take a walk outside, and I'd find it. In those days, tri-colored blackbirds and hermit warblers were regular migrants through my backyard."

Anyone interested in quantifying the power of suggestion might consider comparing the number of reports and rumors of the thick-billed parrot in Arizona from 1966 to 1982, 1983 to 1986, and 1987 to the present. The thick-billed parrot occasionally wandered north of the Mexico border in winter during the nineteenth century but was not convincingly reported in North America from 1936 to 1986. It is rare and declining even in its home territory, a few scattered pine forests in Mexico. Still, it was the only *Psittaciformes* illustrated in the original 1966 edition of the very popular field guide *Birds of North America,* by Robbins and others. Since other parrots frequently escape from cages to survive in the wild in the warmer areas of the United States, reports of "thick-billed parrots" probably came from birders who saw escaped birds and were unaware of the thick-bill's true status. The newer, 1983 edition of *Birds of North America* illustrates ten *Psittaciformes,* all cage birds, and the thick-bill has been eliminated. However, in 1987 the U.S. Fish and Wildlife Service released thirty thick-bills in the Chirachua Mountains of Arizona in a reintroduction program. It will be interesting to see now whether the number of sightings goes up or down.

In the East the species least deserving a field guide illustration may be the corn crake. This European rail was never more than an extremely rare vagrant to North America and occurred only nine times between 1854 and 1900 and four times between 1900 and 1943. It is now declining severely in its home range. But it is illustrated in all the major field guides and closely resembles the sora, so "corn crake" reports continue. On the sightings log book of the Brigantine National Wildlife Refuge (a document Bill Boyle calls "The Brigantine Book of Lies"), this ultrararity is reported about once every two months.

The power of suggestion makes any field guide a double-edged sword. In a sense, Roger Tory Peterson invented modern birdwatching when he published the first edition of his *Field Guide to the Birds* in 1934. Until that time, birders needed years of experience and access to museum collections before they could identify the majority of birds seen on a typical day in the field. Peterson's book and the field guides that have followed have made bird identification infinitely easier and are the primary reason why birding is so popular today. It is only because of field guides that most of us are able to identify on sight so many of the birds we encounter, even species we've never previously encountered except in these books. It must also be said, however, that some of us pay a price for this easily acquired ability.

"We are living in an era of superficiality," Peterson's gruff mentor, Ludlow Griscom, once wrote. "Excellent as Peterson's guides in fact are, they are guides and not encyclopedias of our knowledge of North American birds. [There] are many real facts about North American birds which the users of Peterson's guides and other popular manuals never acquire, and it must be admitted by the fair-minded that in the old collecting days those facts were acquired by students from the constant handling of specimens."

Griscom believed that the solution to the "flood [of] incompetent sight records in the literature" was vigilant self-restraint. He explained why he and a companion once suppressed an identification for forty-two years — a sighting of a black guillemot on Long Island in December 1911:

> The guillemot was at that time the rarest of winter stragglers to Long Island and December 3 appeared too early a date. That was Item #1. Item #2: Neither of us had ever seen a guillemot alive before. Item #3: the guillemot was in full summer plumage instead of winter plumage ... and the point was also psychological: when people were known to have suppressed what they were convinced they actually saw, they were believed when they finally did publish a sight record.

Although he had no doubts about the identification, Griscom waited until 1953 to report his sighting — after reading in a new study of the guillemot that delayed molt is common to the species.

Few of us have such self-restraint, but many birders lean over backward to avoid careless identifications. Griscom would have gotten along very well with a woman I'll call Barbara, a member of a birding group to which I belonged for several years. Barbara drove the rest of us crazy. She doubted everyone's sightings, her own most of all. On any field trip her day list was always five or ten species shorter than anyone else's. The tern the rest of us had agreed was a Forster's had been too distant for Barbara ("I'm not positive I saw white in the wing tips"); the large rail in the freshwater marsh we'd agreed had to be a king just might have been a clapper ("I don't think it's right to identify anything by size and habitat"); the accipiter with the rounded tail we'd called a Cooper's could possibly have been a sharp-shin ("Tail shapes can fool you"). Inevitably, the ride home involved several heated debates as everyone in the car tried to convince Barbara that this or that identification had been a rock-solid certainty.

Once, while we were watching a kettle of turkey vultures, a peregrine falcon swooped into sight, broke up the cluster, and zoomed off. Barbara waited until the rest of us had finished jumping up and down before she announced that she couldn't count the bird. "A bird that good," she said, "deserves a longer look."

Behind her back we called her a masochist and a killjoy — and worse. But Barbara's sensibility gradually worked its way into the group's conscience. One evening after I'd skipped a field trip, another member of the group called to hoot in triumph, "We saw a *black rail* today!"

My heart sank. "Did you really see it?" I asked. "Or was it just a shadow in the grasses?"

He laughed. "I'll tell you how well we saw it. *Even Barbara counted it!*"

Barbara's judgment had become our gold standard.

LIST KEEPING

Listing is often described as the antithesis of "real" birding. There are listers on the one hand, it is said, and serious birders on the other. Listers are supposed to care only about collecting a new name for their day, year, state, or life lists; nonlisters are supposed to care about the bird itself. Since listers are competitive, nonlisters are said to be more objective, more trustworthy observers. I utterly disagree.

I'm prejudiced, I admit, but in my experience the committed, competitive listers are the better birders and the nonlisters are more often not to be trusted. It's the nonlisters who can't remember the status of the regional breeders, the peak periods for migrants, or even the last time they saw a local rarity. "Oh, I don't know," they'll tell you. "It was four or five years ago. I remember it was a cold day, but I don't think it was winter. It was probably either late fall or early spring — wait a second, maybe it was wintertime. I remember there was snow on the ground."

A nonlister who brags, "I don't waste my time checking off lists," I figure is either lazy or not very interested in birds.

Not every lister is trustworthy, of course. A few listers *are* merely collectors, and listing in its most superficial form turns some would-be birdwatchers into stenographers. Anyone who has taken a birding tour has probably seen a "list ticker" or two in action. These are the people who follow the leader everywhere, depend on the leader to find all the birds, and record every identification without question. "Sometimes I wonder why those people bother bringing their binoculars," one tour guide has said. "They hardly look at the birds. I tell them what's out there and they add it to their lists. All they really need is a pen and a piece of paper."

It's also true that many novice birders go through a period when the only birds that excite them are those they haven't yet recorded on their life lists.

"Hey, the hotline says there's a scissor-tailed flycatcher at Lily Lake!"

"Well, I've already got that bird. I saw one last year in Oklahoma."

But list ticking and the "lifers only" syndrome are symptoms of inexperience, not list keeping. Almost all serious birders keep lists, and the most self-restrained and trustworthy observers are usually the most diligent list keepers. My doubting Thomas friend Barbara was — and is — an inveterate lister; so was Ludlow Griscom. The truth is, listing goes hand in hand with serious birding.

One immediate and seldom-mentioned benefit of list keeping is that it leads you to reconsider your original identifications. Since guessing at birds is an essential strategy of good birding, first-impression errors are unavoidable. The courage to make mistakes must be matched by the courage to *admit* mistakes, however. Listing gives you the chance to prove yourself on this front. After the shouting is over and bird has flown, was your sighting good enough to count? Can you list the bird? Birders who begin to care about the quality of their lists will find themselves studying birds more carefully. If you know you're going to second-guess yourself later, when you tally up your list, you'll work harder while the bird is in sight.

Another seldom-mentioned benefit of list keeping is that it alerts you to "negative data." The hardest birds to keep track of are the birds you don't see. Without a list, you'll have only the dimmest impression of nonsightings. What species present two weeks ago seem to have migrated? What birds seem to be doing poorly this season? What habitats have you been underemphasizing? What common birds regularly elude you? Listing will help you answer all these questions.

A simple organizational system is a three-ring binder containing the checklists for each field trip. The lists can be arranged chronologically, with twelve master lists for the month totals and one master for the year. Though nonlisters may give you some grief ("How you can be bothered with such trivia?"), anyone interested in migration ought to keep a month list and, if you are out in the field often enough, even a week list. Nothing will give you a sharper sense of the bird movements in your area. Indeed, after three or four years, you'll probably have a more accurate record of the birds of your specific locality than you can find in your regional guide.

Buying copies of a checklist or photocopying it makes comparisons between lists and year-to-year analyses far simpler. Definitely not recommended (but surprisingly common) is the blank notebook system, where you write the species down in the order you find them. This method makes comparisons awkward and too time-consuming to be rewarding.

Personal computers have made long-term, multiple list keeping much easier. For IBM PC's and IBM compatibles, menu-driven listing programs are available (advertised in *American Birds, Birding,* and elsewhere); all you need to do is turn on your computer and start typing in the names of your birds.

Owners of machines not compatible with IBMs (and owners of IBMs who want to save some money) can design their own data bases with a minimum of fuss. All that's required is any conventional data base program that allows you to format your own data record, an option usually available in even the most inexpensive programs. Designing your own data record enables you to customize the format to your special interests and leave checklist blanks ("data fields") for your yard list, local park list, or nests-found-in-the-southern-half-of-the-county list.

The one trick in designing your own data base is organizing the files so that they will print out in taxonomic sequence, rather than alphabetically. Leave space breaks for the taxonomic groupings — order, family, genus, and species. With a pencil in hand, go through the sixth edition of the American Ornithologists' Union Checklist (which appeared in the supplement to *Auk* in July 1982) or the American Birding Association's *Checklist of North American Birds.* Number each order, each family within the order, each genus within the family, and each species within the genus. Then ask your program to sort by these numerical subsets. Thus the northern gannet's reference number is 4-3-2-1: fourth order, Pelicaniformes; third family, Sulidae; second genus, *Morus;* and first species, *bassanus.* The loggerhead shrike is 20-21-1-2: twentieth order, Passeriformes; twenty-first family, Laniidae; first genus, *Lanius;* and second species, *ludovicianus.* This operation sounds more complicated than it is. Penciling in the numbers and typing them into your data base requires only one rainy afternoon of work. Once you've done it, you need consult the reference number again only when you're adding a brand new species to your lists. All existing records can be called up by the bird's name.

Unless you intend to do professional data analysis, you won't need an expensive "bells and whistles" PC for your record keeping. For the last four years I've done all my long-term list keeping on a Kaypro II (64K) computer using two single-sided disks, one for the program and one for the year's records. At the end of the year, I copy the records disk to a new disk, put the original away, use a universal command to clear the past year's records from the new copy, and I'm ready to go again.

The greatest virtue of careful list keeping — electronic or manual — is its cumulative effect. The more diligently you list the birds you see and the more lists you keep, the more you will appreciate the discoveries you make. Novices are plagued by the "lifers-only" syndrome because they have no other way to measure their finds. Veteran list keepers have far more thrills available to them because their data gathering has given them the context to understand the "little discoveries" — the common yellowthroat overwintering for the second time in the last five years, the pectoral sandpiper coming north three weeks ahead of schedule, or the tufted titmouse nesting for the first time ever in the southern half of the county. The longer you keep listing, the more you'll treasure the accuracy and "purity" of your records. In the long run, despite what the critics say, listing makes you a better birder.

Jim Meritt, whose North American list is in the mid-600s and whose New Jersey state list is a spectacular 365, epitomizes the serious lister and the excellent birder. Spend a day in the field with him, and you come home a more careful observer; Jim won't count anything until he sees "the whites of its eyes," and he has the patience of a panther. We were talking one day about the Brewer's blackbird, one of the few "regular accidentals" in New Jersey that Jim has yet to spot in the state, and I asked him if the bird had begun to feel like a jinx.

"Not at all," he said. "I think a high list is a sign of old age. If you live long enough, all the birds come to you eventually."

TAKING FIELD NOTES

The first trick in taking field notes is making the process quick, convenient, and unselfconscious. How-to articles about note taking often mention the importance of field notes for "posterity." Amateur birders are cautioned to record their observations carefully ("Include the species' Latin name," "Express distances in meters," "Note the windspeed") so that the records of their field work will be taken seriously by professionals. The problem with trying to write like an ornithologist is that it leads to writer's block. If you are worried about the technical expertise and scientific tone of your notes, you'll take fewer than you should.

Unless you're a very active or lucky birder regularly finding reportable rarities, 99.9 percent of your notes will never be seen by anyone else. They are for your eyes only. If your notes are professional enough for that audience, then they are as good as they have to be.

Self-consciousness can also be a problem if you use a bound notebook or one of the various "birder's diaries" on the market. The paper in these books is thick and expensive; some of them are even gilt-edged, with colored illustrations of birds in the margins. These books too can lead to writer's block. Is my observation interesting enough to waste this good paper writing it down? Won't one of my stick-figure sketches look particularly ugly next to this professionally painted picture?

Another problem with a bound notebook is that you must do your note taking at home or take the whole book with you each time you go out. Neither strategy is satisfactory. Note taking at home means you're recording your memories hours or days later, when the details have blurred and the power of suggestion has had time to work its evil. If you take your notebook into the field, you risk losing all your past notes — and unlike your field guide, gloves, hat, and even your binoculars, your field notes are irreplaceable.

More and more birders seem to be using tape recorders for note taking. Many models are small enough to fit in a jacket pocket. For sheer speed and in-the-field convenience, these can be superior to pencil and pad. Since you can keep your eye on the bird as you record your observations, tape recorders are especially useful if your primary interest is bird behavior.

Tape recorders have some disadvantages, however. Cassettes are expensive, fill up (and wear out batteries) surprisingly quickly, and unless you have the time to transcribe your spoken comments into writing, it can be exasperating trying to relocate your previous observations of this or that species or your last trip to some particular site. Each time you consult your "notes" you must find the correct side on the correct cassette and then where on the side you made the observation you want to hear again. If you are going to use a tape recorder, try to buy one with a meter so that you can record where each day's observations begin and end.

One other disadvantage of tape-recorded observations is that they must be entirely verbal. Artist's block seems even more severe among birders than writer's block, but nothing will help you look more carefully at birds than drawing them. Some tips for nonartists appear below.

Start with large slow-moving or resting birds that you can keep in your scope — ducks, herons, gulls, shorebirds, and perched hawks. You will then be able to move your eye back and forth quickly from bird to sketchpad without having to relocate the bird after each line drawn. You might also want to bring along a folding lawn chair for your first few sketching expeditions.

Don't try to draw the whole bird in a single eye-pleasing picture. Sketch the bird in disconnected parts. Focus first on the head and try only to depict the proportions of head, bill, and eye. Skip some space and draw a single wing or a headless torso next, then go on to the tail or the legs.

Work fast and don't erase. Ignore your mistakes. If you're struggling to make any one element perfect — the curve in the bill, the shape of the eyering, the angle of the wings — the bird may fly away and leave you with nothing but that one element. It's better to draw the bird five times quickly than try to do it once well. Quality is too hard to judge in the heat of the moment. Once you have five or six attempts on paper, you can combine the best of each later at home, out of the wind and the cold.

Use full-sized paper, 8½" × 11" or larger. Small paper is easier to carry but requires finer finger movements. Full-sized paper enables you to draw with your whole arm and allows you to do larger sketches that will minimize the effect of each misdirected line.

A clipboard you can keep under your car seat or slip into your birding pack will encourage you to take out your pencil at dull moments — or in very exciting moments when a rarity needs to be documented.

Chuck Bernstein and others have argued that birders should go into the field "British style" — with binoculars, pencil, clipboard or sketchpad, and *no field guide.* If you've reached the point where the birds of your area seem to present few challenges, you should try this excellent exercise. Even the most modest of discoveries becomes a delicious double-thrill: first, as you sketch the bird and make your initial identification, and then again, back at the car or back home, when you confirm the find by matching your drawing with the field guide's. You feel you've truly earned each identification. You will also find that this practice leads you to notice features that, because they weren't necessary for field guide identification, never caught your eye before: the difference in darkness on the caps of male and female white-breasted nuthatches, the eyeline present only on breeding male blue-gray gnatcatchers, or the rufous upper flanks of the tree sparrow.

A looseleaf binder is probably the best place to keep your field notes. You can then take only your clipboard and fresh paper on each field trip and leave all your old notes at home. With a three-hole punch, you can also insert magazine clippings, maps, day lists, and other extras in the appropriate places. Your notebook will quickly become a hodgepodge of information, observations, and memories and the most evocative text in your ornithological library. Open it five years later to your coffee-stained directions to Pine Tree Pond, your notes on the day's conditions ("hazy, no wind, no-see-ums ferocious"), and your crude sketches of the Bachman's sparrow you found there, and you'll hear the bird sing again.

REPORTING RARITIES

When you find your first "good bird," the temptation is to call the local expert on the closest telephone. Unless the expert knows you, however, or the bird is so rare that an immediate stake-out is in order, it's better to report by mail. This will give you the chance to sort out your notes, triple-check all similar species, and make sure the field marks you recorded in the field (*not* those you noticed later in the field guide) were sufficient for the identification.

I learned the dangers of the telephone report in a particularly painful way one winter day in my second year of birding. Jim Horner and I were leaning against my car scanning the ducks on Payne's Prairie outside Gainesville, Florida. We were listening to "The Birdwatcher," a weekly call-in show on the university radio station, when I noticed an oddly colored hawk sitting in a bare tree. "Jim, what's this over here?" I asked.

He swung his scope around and did a classic double-take. "Holy smokes! It's a rough-leg!"

"How often do you see them on the Prairie?"

"Never! That's a state bird for me. Go call the show! We've got to get everybody down here! I'll keep it in sight."

I took another five-second look at the only rough-legged hawk I'd ever seen in my life, hopped into the car, raced to the nearest gas station, put a dime in the coin box, and heard Bill Hardy, the host of the show, say, "Hello, this is 'The Birdwatcher' and you're on the air."

"Hi - this - is - Jack - Connor - Jim - Horner - and - I - just - found - a - rough - legged - hawk - out - on - Payne's - Prairie - you - can - see - it - from - the - road - it's - standing - in - a - tree - there - right - now - we -

just-found-it-a-couple-of-minutes-ago-everyone-who-wants-to-see-it-should-come-down-here-as-fast-as-they-can!"

"Terrific!" said Dr. Hardy. "Is it a light phase or a dark phase?"

What followed was a long silence while Dr. Hardy slowly realized I didn't have the slightest idea of what he was talking about. "What's the color on the breast?" he tried to coax me. "Is it dark all the way down or only on the belly?"

"I don't know," I blurted. "But I better get back there before it flies away." Then I hung up. I was told later there was another long silence, then Dr. Hardy said, "Well now, *there's* an excited birder." Whether he believed I could identify a rough-legged hawk if I tripped over one he was kind enough not to say.

The audience for most telephone reports is only one person, but if you make a mistake and your only excuse to talk to the expert again is the discovery of another reportable bird, it may be a long time before you get a second chance to prove your credibility. Save the phone calls for superrarities. Report on paper.

The extent of the details required depends on the rarity of your find. Moderately unusual birds can be reported with reference to:

- date, site, names of the observers, and the length of observation;
- diagnostic field marks seen;
- the bird's behavior, whether diagnostic or not.

For truly rare birds you should also include:

- the weather, lighting conditions, and time of day;
- the precise location: "the north side of the parking lot," "the oak trees behind the library";
- the distance between the observers and the bird and the magnifying power of all observers' optical equipment;
- any calls or songs (if none, note "No vocalizations were heard");

- the other species present, whether size comparisons were possible, and any behavioral interactions;
- which recorded field marks enabled you to eliminate the rarity's lookalikes;
- your previous experience with the species and with its lookalikes;
- a photocopy of any notes or sketches done in the field.

If the bird was photographed, you should include the name and the address of the photographer and when the photographs will be available.

Once you've established your credibility, you can trim the length of your reports, but don't abuse this privilege. Experts may feel uncomfortable questioning you, but if they'll be including your observation in a published report or adding it to the hotline tape, they must be concerned with their own credibility. On Christmas bird counts, for example, it's not the observer who gets criticized for supplying insufficient details on rarities, it's the compiler.

Be aware that there is one notoriously frequent, universally deplored comment you should *never* make when describing a sighting: "It looked exactly like the picture in the field guide!" Too many birders think that this statement is the final, irrefutable proof that their identification was correct and that they had a good, close look. Actually, it suggests just the opposite. Anyone can make that comment about any bird on the planet, whether it's seen it or not. And more important, *no bird carefully and critically observed looks exactly like the picture in the field guide.* In fact, if you want to write a truly convincing report, you should note how field marks on the individual you observed *differed* from those on the ideal, common denominator bird pictured in your field guide. Was there any sign of molt, feather wear, or injuries? Any dirt on the bill? Any unexpected markings on the rump, belly, or crown? Any differences in the shading on the breast? Did the eyeline seem longer or shorter or paler or brighter than in the field guide? Were the cheek patches equally dark on both sides of the head? Did the bird make any calls that seemed unlike those described in the field guide? Reporting details like these is the best way to prove you got a good, close look, know what you're talking about, and saw what you say you did.

ENCOUNTERING SKEPTICISM

When you report your finds to people unfamiliar with your ability, you should be prepared for some resistance. For a variety of reasons, some justified, some not, knee-jerk skepticism runs rampant in birding circles.

Even with the bird in sight, some birders can be hard to convince. Jesse and I were feeling triumphant one August morning in 1978 at Rustler Park, Arizona. We had just found a brown-throated wren, a life bird for us, and it was putting on quite a show — hopping around in a brush pile twenty feet away — when a quintet of birders led by a bearded man came up the road to the meadow.

"There's a brown-throated wren over here," I called to them, "if you're interested." The Beard looked over at us expressionlessly, pointed out a couple of birds to his group, and then sauntered over. "It's been in this brush pile for the last fifteen minutes," I told him.

He said nothing, just scanned the branches with his binocs. "Here it is!" Jesse said as the wren hopped up.

"That," pronounced The Beard after a three-second study, "is a house wren. A brown-throated wren is much buffier." Then he sauntered away, his group in tow.

While they circled the meadow, Jesse and I returned to our field guide. We'd agreed with each other earlier that the bird was too dark to be a house wren, but we were birding in foreign territory, the Beard radiated expertise, and now the seeds of doubt had been sown. Meanwhile the wren had stopped cooperating. It was down in the bottom of the brush, out of sight. "What do you think?" I asked Jesse.

"I need another look," she said.

"Calliope hummingbird!" shouted a young man in the Beard's group. We raced over and for five minutes watched a male calliope zig and zag through the cardinal flowers and other spiky plants growing along a fence line. A second tiny hummer with yellow flanks buzzed it once or twice. "That might be a female calliope!" said the young man.

"Here's a brown-throated wren!" It was the Beard and he was pointing into *our* brush pile.

"Look out," he called as all of us ran back toward him and the bird whirled off into the woods. "There it goes."

"That's got to be the same wren we were looking at," I tried to argue.

The Beard ignored me and pointed skyward. "Band-tailed pigeons overhead!"

After a futile pursuit into the woods, Jesse and I decided to cross the brown-throated wren off our list. We'd see another, we told ourselves, and that moment of doubt after the Beard had "corrected" our identification indicated that we hadn't been positive. We wanted an untainted sighting. We never saw another, though, and a few years later, when the American Ornithologists' Union lumped the brown-throated wren with the house wren, I was perversely pleased. In fact, I was sorely tempted to write the Beard a note: "Attention: the AOU has determined the brown-throated wren is not a valid species. Please remove it from your life list at once."

Philip Parsons and Herman Weissberg of the Brookline (Massachusetts) Bird Club had a far more frustrating experience in the winter of 1975. Late on the afternoon of January 14, they were birding at the old yacht club in Newburyport harbor when they spotted a gull with a pink breast in a group of Bonapartes.

"It was only fifty yards or sixty yards away, standing on the mud flats," Parsons recalls. "And we got our scopes on it. It seemed about the same size as the Bonys, but it had a pink breast. And that wasn't the only thing that made it stand out from them. It had a short, thin bill and a pigeonlike head. We didn't know what it was."

They turned every page of their field guide, Peterson's third edition of his eastern guide, and couldn't find a picture to match the bird. There was a good reason for the omission. At the time the species had never been reported in the United States south of Alaska.

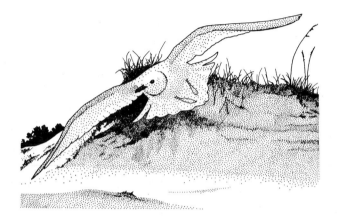

Ross' Gull

Flipping through his books at home that evening, Parsons finally came upon plate 26 of the *Audubon Water Bird Guide* and Don Eckelberry's drawing of the Ross' gull. "Once I saw that picture, I was certain about the identification and I called up [the local expert] to report it. She wrote down what I said, but I could tell she didn't believe me and our report never made the telephone hotline."

For the next several days Parsons and Weissberg tried to interest others in searching the area, but they couldn't generate any real excitement. Parsons went back alone to Newburyport on January 16 and saw the gull a second time. "Now I was positive about the ID but I still couldn't convince anybody except my friends."

On March 2, six weeks later, the bird was found again. This time it made the CBS Evening News and page 1 of *Time* and triggered the response described in the last chapter. In all the fuss, however, Parsons's and Weissberg's original report was generally unmentioned and forgotten.

"The whole thing really soured us on the birders' network," Parsons says now. "We still report our good finds, but not as often as we used to — and we don't expect to find another Ross' gull."

The prevalence of skepticism in all birders' networks keeps some people from reporting their finds at all. "They're not going to believe me anyway," many birders say, "so why should I bother to tell anybody about it?" Unfortunately, this attitude leads to frustration worse than that of Parsons and Weissberg.

James Nash saw the Newburyport Ross' gull even earlier than Parsons and Weissberg — on December 28, 1974. "That afternoon still seems like yesterday," he told me recently, "and I still feel like kicking myself about it."

Nash, too, spotted the gull in a flock of Bonys on the Newburyport mud flats. "When I saw it, it was standing alone, slightly removed from the Bonys, less than a hundred yards from me, and the pink was *bright* — far more striking than it was later in March when it was rediscovered. I knew instantly it wasn't a Bonaparte's. I could even see the black line on the neck! The possibility that it was a Ross' hit me pretty quickly, but I was all alone, I'd never heard of anyone reporting a Ross' gull, and there wasn't another birdwatcher anywhere around. I watched it for thirty minutes, and I was sure someone would come along to verify it for me. Usually, there are almost as many birders along that river as there are birds, but that day, maybe because it was the holidays, no one else was there. Finally out of desperation I got in my car and drove up and down the road looking for someone I could show the bird to. There simply wasn't anyone else birding there that day."

When Nash arrived home that night, he told his wife, "I just saw something that couldn't be what it was."

"She and my children wanted me to report it, but I just didn't want to be taken for a fool. There's so much skepticism among birders — I'm often skeptical myself about other people's rarities. Finally, I decided that with all the birders who go to Newburyport someone else was going to see it."

Nash mentioned the sighting to only one other person, a nonbirding friend at work, who two months later met Nash in the hallway and said, "I noticed that thing you saw at Newburyport has been confirmed."

"What are you talking about?" said Nash.

"That Ross' gull. It was on television last night."

"If there's one lesson I learned from that experience," says Nash, "it's that you have to have the courage to come forward, not be afraid to be taken for a quack, and insist on what your eyes have seen — no matter what the bloody skeptics are going to say."

UNEXPECTING THE EXPECTED

James Nash's mistake is not the worst a birder can make, not by a long shot. Nash saw his Ross' gull, and he knew he did. Another kind of error is more insidious and far more common. It may even be the most common mental error of all, though it is hard to recognize and seldom discussed. The birders most susceptible to it are those of us who have moved past the beginner's stage. We've learned to avoid the novice's error of expecting the unexpected, and have reached the point where we take pride in our equanimity. Our experience has taught us the simple truth that common birds are common and rare birds are rare, and we no longer get excited about every other bird that comes by. Nothing can surprise us anymore, we like to think, and so we step into a different trap.

On October 13, 1984, Jesse and I spent a couple of hours hawk watching from the pond about a quarter mile northwest of Cape May Point's lookout platform. Hurricane Josephine had passed offshore, the wind was still howling (at forty knots plus, we learned later), and the hawks were all going with it, flying from our right to our left, most of them dropping down under the break of the tree line as they came over the pond.

We decided to call it a day, stood up to go home, and Jesse pointed to a bird. "What's this coming?" she said. "It's a raven or the biggest crow I've ever seen in my life."

A glistening black corvid was sailing toward us across the water. In mental replay now I see its primaries splayed wide, its head and bill jutting forward. Unlike the kestrels, sharpies, and Cooper's we'd been watching, it was flying left to right, angling *into* the wind. At the moment, though, these unconscious observations were buried deep under one conscious and know-it-all thought: *it can't be a raven; ravens don't occur in southern New Jersey.*

It flapped as it cut past us and the stroke was so oddly stiff and flat I almost let Jesse's instincts wake me up. But — and this is the crucial thing — rather than look at all the bird was giving me, *I looked only for a way to nullify the possibility.* I noticed that the tail seemed crowlike and announced, "It's a crow. No wedge."

The bird sheered upward as it reached the trees at the end of the pond and disappeared over them, sailing straight for the hawk-watch platform. "It sure seemed big," said Jesse.

"Yeah," I said dismissively, "it did." That was that and I'd bet my best binocs that is how most intermediate birders miss most of the birds they miss. It's not expecting the unexpected that gets us in trouble; it is *expecting the expected.*

Underidentifications receive far less criticism than overidentifications because they generally go unnoticed. When a common species is mistaken for a rarity, there's a good chance a correction will follow. The mistaken observer announces the identification, other observers come running, and the error is pointed out. The dynamics are entirely different when a rarity is mistaken for something common. No one comes running, and so, ordinarily, the underidentifier's know-it-all attitude leaves him in ignorance. "Why don't I ever have any luck?" he may even find himself thinking. "Why can't I ever find something really exciting?"

Jesse and I walked down the trail, birding along the way, talking of other things, and emerged out of the woods to see Frank Nicoletti bent over the rail of the hawk-watching platform in an animated discussion with Clay Sutton, standing on the ground. Nicoletti had the walkie-talkie the hawk counters

260 · THE COMPLETE BIRDER

use to communicate with the banding stations in the fields beyond the platform. As we walked over, it crackled a message
and he threw his fist in the air. "All right! Clay, Carol just had
it come right over her! Thank you, Carol!"

"What's up?" I said.

Sutton's eyes were gleaming. "We just had the first raven at
Cape May in about fifty years. Roger Tory Peterson and James
Tanner had one here back in the thirties and now we —"

"That's amazing," I said, not daring to look at Jesse. "We
just saw a crow that looked like a raven, only it didn't have a
wedge in the tail."

"Going that way?" said Sutton, motioning. "About ten minutes ago?"

I could barely nod.

"We didn't see a wedge either, but not all ravens show that
and everything else about that bird was raven all the way."

"*Yeah!*" shouted Nicoletti, pumping his fist. "I never saw a
crow give me an eagle look before!"

I'm convinced that what most often keeps intermediate birders like me from moving up to the next level of expertise is not
weak eyesight or lack of experience. It is, plainly and simply,
lack of concentration. Not all the best birders have good eyes;
not all of them have the most years of experience. But all of
them are supremely alert. They see more because they miss less.

On one of his adventures in "participatory journalism,"
George Plimpton accompanied John Rowlett and Victor Emmanuel on a birding expedition to northern Mexico. The inten-
tion of the trip was to search for the imperial woodpecker, one
of the rarest birds in the world. What Plimpton found remarkable, however, was his companions' interest in *every* bird, no
matter how mundane. He describes one morning's drive up a
backwoods road:

[Rowlett and Emmanuel] level their shotgun blasts of enthusiasm at whatever bird they spot. . . . As we climb into the
mountains John calls out "Junco! Junco!" — perhaps the
most common bird along the road. This morning during a

halt to fill the leaking radiator with water from a roadside stream, he spent a number of minutes admiring the junco's yellow eye.

Here are two top experts not the least bit interested in posing as know-it-alls. "It would be easy to imagine them," writes Plimpton, "crouching in a hen house and observing a Rhode Island Red if there were nothing else around."

This is exactly the attitude of Clay Sutton, Frank Nicoletti, John Hintermister, Pete Dunne, Jim Meritt, David Sibley, Lyn Atherton, Bob Barber, and all the elite birders I've seen in action. They don't waste their time cursing their luck, wishing they were in some more exciting spot, or demeaning the "trash birds." They enjoy whatever birds their luck and their locale give them each day. They have maintained that part of their "beginner's mind" which keeps them looking at birds with a novice's happy intensity, and they take none for granted. In a sense, they *unexpect* the expected. Every bird is a bird to be studied, and so, when a rarity appears, there's no need to step up the concentration level to full power. They are already concentrating with all they've got.

I'm working at it, of course. At least I've learned to look at crows a lot more carefully — and I'm hoping for another chance at a raven in southern New Jersey. If you live long enough, do all the birds come to you *twice*?

BIBLIOGRAPHY

Many of the identification tips and other quoted comments in the text come from personal conversations. As several of these conversations were conducted during the heat of the battle, while some unidentifiable bird winged its way toward the horizon, the persons quoted should not be held responsible for any errors or misstatements. I take responsibility, of course, for any errors due to my own misinterpretations. The primary published sources appear below. The background sources who must go nameless here are the hundreds of birders who contribute records of their sightings to *American Birds* and the dozens of subregional editors who compile their seasonal reports. Thanks to their efforts, the bird life of North America is better understood with each passing year. May this book help swell their ranks.

Able, Kenneth P. "A migratory bird's Baedeker." *Natural History* 92:9 (September 1983), 22–29.

Armstrong, Robert H. *Guide to the Birds of Alaska.* 2d ed. Anchorage: Alaska Northwest, 1984.

Aubry, Yves. "First nests of the common black-headed gull in North America." *American Birds* 38:3 (May–June 1984), 366–367.

Bailey, Wallace. *Birds of the Cape Cod National Seashore and Adjacent Areas.* South Wellfleet, Mass.: Eastern National Park and Monument Association, 1968.

Bakker, Robert T. "Dinosaur renaissance." *Scientific American* 232:4 (April 1975), 58–78.

Balch, Lawrence G. "Some general problems of field identification." *Birding* 9:2 (March–April 1977), 53–56.

Balch, Lawrence G., H. David Bohlen, and Gerald B. Rosenband. "The Illinois Ross' gull." *American Birds* 33:2 (March 1979), 140–142.

Beaver, Joseph C. "Sonograms as an aid in bird identification." *American Birds* 30:5 (October 1976), 899–903.

Bell, Gary P., Frank J. S. Phelan, and Ron C. P. Wypkema. "The owl invasion of Amherst Island, Ontario, January–April 1979." *American Birds*, 33:3 (May 1979), 245–246.

Bellrose, Frank C. *Ducks, Geese, and Swans of North America.* Harrisburg, Pa.: Stackpole Books, 1976.

Benoit, Dick. "Eastern Great Lakes." *Newsletter of the Hawk Migration Association of North America* 11:2 (August 1986), 35–37.

Bent, Arthur Cleveland. *Life Histories of North American Birds of Prey.* New York: Dover, 1961.

Bergman, Charles A. "The glass of fashion." *Audubon* 83:6 (November 1981), 74–80.

Bernstein, Chuck. *The Joy of Birding.* Santa Barbara, Calif.: Capra Press, 1984.

Birds: Readings from Scientific American. San Francisco: W. H. Freeman, 1980.

Blankinship, David R., and Kirke A. King. "A probable sighting of 23 Eskimo curlews in Texas." *American Birds* 38:6 (November–December 1984), 1066–1067.

Bond, James. *Birds of the West Indies.* 2d ed. Boston: Houghton Mifflin, 1971.

Boyle, William J. *A Guide to Bird Finding in New Jersey.* New Brunswick, N.J.: Rutgers University Press, 1986.

Brett, James J., and Alexander Nagy. *Feathers in the Wind.* Kempton, Pa.: Hawk Mountain Association, 1973.

Brown, Leslie. *Birds of Prey: Their Biology and Ecology.* New York: A&W, 1977.

Brown, Leslie, and Dean Amadon. *Eagles, Hawks, and Falcons of the World.* New York: McGraw-Hill, 1968.

Bruun, Bertel. *Birds of Europe*. New York: McGraw-Hill, 1970.

Buckley, P. A. "Changing seasons." *American Birds* 26:3 (June 1972), 568–574.

Bull, John, and John Farrand, Jr. *The Audubon Society Field Guide to North American Birds: Eastern Region*. New York: Knopf, 1977.

Burton, John A., ed. *Owls of the World*. Milan, Italy: A&W, 1973.

Chapman, Frank M. *The Warblers of North America*. New York: Dover, 1968.

Chartier, Bonnie, and Fred Cooke. "Ross' gulls nesting at Churchill, Manitoba, Canada." *American Birds* 34:6 (November 1980), 839–841.

Clark, William S. "The field identification of accipiters in North America." *Birding* 16:6 (December 1984), 251–263.

———. "The field identification of North American eagles." *American Birds*, 37:5 (September–October 1983), 822–826.

Cronin, Edward W., Jr. *Getting Started in Bird Watching*. Boston: Houghton Mifflin, 1986.

Cruickshank, Allan D. *Birds around New York City*. New York: American Museum of Natural History, 1942.

DeBenedictus, Paul A. "The A.B.A. checklist: A review." *American Birds* 30:5 (October 1976), 913–915.

———. "The changing seasons." *American Birds* 34:2 (March 1980), 133–138.

———. "Gleanings from the technical literature." *Birding* 10:3 (June 1978), 112–116.

———. "Gleanings from the technical literature." *Birding* 10:4 (August 1978), 179–184.

Duncan, Charles D., and Ralph W. Havard. "Pelagic birds of the northern Gulf of Mexico." *American Birds* 34:2 (March 1980), 122–132.

———. "Western gull in Alabama and northwestern Florida." *American Birds* 36:5 (September 1982), 899–902.

Dunne, Peter. "Binoculars for birders." *Peregrine Observer* 7:2 (Fall 1984), 16–22.

———. "How to tell a hawk from a gull." *Newsletter of the Hawk Migration Association of North America* 10:1 (February 1985), 10.

Dunne, Peter, Debbie Keller, and Rene Kochenberger. *Hawk Watch: A Guide for Beginners*. Cape May: Cape May Bird Observatory/New Jersey Audubon Society, 1984.

Eaton, Brian. "Holiday beach — the Ontario outlook." *Newsletter of the Hawk Migration Association of North America* 10:2 (August 1985), 1–9.

Farrand, John, Jr., ed. *The Audubon Society Master Guide to Birding*. New York: Knopf, 1983.

Fish, Allen M. "California." *Newsletter of the Hawk Migration Association of North America* 11:2 (August 1986), 44–46.

Fisher, Allen C., Jr. "Mysteries of bird migration." *National Geographic* 156:2 (August 1979), 154–193.

Francis, Charles M., and Fred Cooke. "Differential timing of spring migration in wood warblers." *Auk* 103 (July 1986), 548–556.

Gill, Frank B. "Historical aspects of hybridization between blue-winged and golden-winged warblers." *Auk* 97 (January 1980), 1–18.

Gosselin, Michel, and Normand David. "Field identification of Thayer's gull in eastern North America." *American Birds* 29:6 (December 1975), 1059–1067.

Graham, Frank, Jr. *Gulls: A Social History*. New York: Random House, 1975.

Grant, Peter J. *Gulls: A Guide to Identification*. 2d ed. Vermillion, S.D.: Buteo, 1986.

Griscom, Ludlow. "Historical development of sight recognition." *Birding* 8:2 (March–April 1976), 86–90.

Harding, John J., and Justin J. Harding. *Birding the Delaware Valley Region*. Philadelphia: Temple University Press, 1980.

Hardy, John William. "A tape recording of a possible ivory-billed woodpecker call." *American Birds* 29:5 (June 1975), 647–651.

Harrington, Brian A., and David C. Twichell. "Untying the enigma of the red knot." *Living Bird Quarterly* 1:2 (Autumn 1982), 4–7.

Harrison, George H. *Roger Tory Peterson's Dozen Birding Hot Spots.* New York: Simon and Schuster, 1976.

Harrison, Hal H. *Wood Warblers' World.* New York: Simon and Schuster, 1984.

Harrison, Peter. *Seabirds: An Identification Guide.* Boston: Houghton Mifflin, 1983.

Hayes, Jim. "Ruff migration in eastern North America." *Records of New Jersey Birds* 10:1 (Spring 1984), 9.

Hayman, Peter, John Marchant, and Tony Prater. *Shorebirds: An Identification Guide to the Waders of the World.* Boston: Houghton Mifflin, 1986.

Heil, Richard S. "Northeastern maritime region." *American Birds* 37:3 (May–June 1983), 279–281.

Henry, Durrae, and David DeReamus. "Northern Appalachians." *Newsletter of the Hawk Migration Association of North America* 11:2 (August 1986), 24–27.

Hickey, Joseph J. *A Guide to Bird Watching.* Garden City, N.Y.: Doubleday, 1963.

Holt, Denver W., John P. Lortie, Blair J. Nikula, and Robert C. Humphrey. "First record of common black-headed gulls breeding in the United States." *American Birds* 40:2 (Summer 1986), 204–205.

Howell, Arthur H. *Florida Bird Life.* New York: Coward-McCann, 1932.

Jackson, Jerome A. "Biopolitics, management of federal lands, and the conservation of the red-cockaded woodpecker." *American Birds* 40:6 (Winter 1986), 1162–1168.

Jameson, William. *The Wandering Albatross.* New York: William Morrow, 1959.

Johnsgard, Paul A., and Rose DiSilvestro. "Seventy-five years of change in mallard–black duck ratios in eastern North America." *American Birds* 30:5 (October 1976), 905–908.

Johnson, Hugh M. "Looking into binoculars." *Mother Earth News* 89 (September–October 1984), 70–72.

Keller, Timothy C. "First Indiana record of the California gull." *American Birds* 37:1 (January–February 1983), 120.

Lane, James A. *A Birder's Guide to the Rio Grande Valley of Texas.* 3d ed. Denver: L&P Press, 1979.
———. *A Birder's Guide to Southeastern Arizona.* 3d ed. Denver: L&P Press, 1977.
———. *A Birder's Guide to Southern California.* 4th ed. Denver: L&P Press, 1979.
Lane, James A., and Harold R. Holt. *A Birder's Guide to Denver and Eastern Colorado.* 3d ed. Denver: L&P Press, 1979.
Lane, James A., and John L. Tveten. *A Birder's Guide to the Texas Coast.* 2d ed. Denver: L&P Press, 1974.
Leahy, Christopher W. "On the aesthetics of birding." *Birding* 10:4 (August 1978), 237–239. [Reprinted from *New York Times,* July 27, 1975.]
LeGrand, Harry. "The 1983 hawk flight at Cape May." *Peregrine Observer* 7:1 (Spring 1984), 3–5.
Lehman, Paul. "The changing seasons." *American Birds* 37:2 (March–April 1982), 150–154.
———. "The identification of Thayer's gull in the field." *Birding* 12:6 (December 1980), 198–210.
Leppert, Mark. "Southwest." *Newsletter of the Hawk Migration Association of North America* 11:2 (August 1986), 43–44.
Lockley, R. M. *Ocean Wanderers: The Migratory Sea Birds of the World.* Harrisburg, Pa.: Stackpole Books, 1973.
Lowery, George H., Jr. *Louisiana Birds.* 3d ed. Baton Rouge: Louisiana State University Press, 1974.

McKaskie, Guy, Paul DeBenedictus, Richard Erickson, and Joseph Morlan. *Birds of Northern California.* 2d ed. Berkeley, Calif.: Golden Gate Audubon Society, 1979.
Mark, David M. "Thayer's gulls from western Christmas bird counts: A cautionary note." *American Birds* 35:6 (November 1981), 898–900.
Martin, Robert F., and Sarah R. Martin. "Niche and range expansion of cave swallows in Texas." *American Birds* 32:5 (September 1978), 941–946.

Matthiessen, Peter. *The Shorebirds of North America.* Edited by Gardner D. Stout. New York: Viking, 1967.

Mayfield, Harold. "Brown-headed cowbird: Agent of extermination?" *American Birds* 31:2 (March 1977), 107–113.

Mead, Chris. *Bird Migration.* New York: Facts on File, 1983.

Meritt, Jim. "Riding ruff-shot at Pedricktown." *Philadelphia Larus: The Newsletter of the Delaware Valley Ornithological Club* 13:2 (September 1986), 1–2.

Miliotis, Paul S., and P. A. Buckley. "Ross' gull in Massachusetts." *American Birds* 29:5 (June 1975), 643–646.

Morris, Bernard. "Shoreless shorebirding." *Birding* 11:5 (October 1979), 262–265.

The National Geographic Society Field Guide to the Birds of North America. Washington, D.C.: National Geographic Society, 1983.

Olgivie, M. A., and J. T. R. Sharrock. "Binoculars and telescopes survey." *British Birds* 71 (October 1978), 429–439.

Parker, James W., and John C. Ogden. "The recent history and status of the Mississippi kite." *American Birds* 33:2 (March 1979), 119–129.

Pasquier, Roger F. *Watching Birds: An Introduction to Ornithology.* Boston: Houghton Mifflin, 1977.

Peterson, Roger Tory. "A difficult tightrope act." *Living Bird Quarterly* 3:3 (Summer 1984), 4–10.

———. *A Field Guide to the Birds.* 4th ed. Boston: Houghton Mifflin, 1980.

Peterson, Roger Tory, and Edward L. Chalif. *A Field Guide to Mexican Birds.* Boston: Houghton Mifflin, 1973.

Phillips, Allan R. "Semipalmated sandpiper: Identification, migrations, summer and winter ranges." *American Birds* 29:4 (August 1975), 799–806.

Pitelka, Frank A. *Geographic Variation and the Species Problem in the Shorebird Genus Limnodromus.* Berkeley, Calif.: University of California Press, 1950.

Plimpton, George. "Un gran pedazo de carne." *Audubon* 79:6 (November 1977), 10–25.

Pough, Richard H. *Audubon Land Bird Guide.* Garden City, N.Y.: Doubleday, 1949.

———. *Audubon Water Bird Guide.* Garden City, N.Y.: Doubleday, 1951.

Pruitt, James, and Nancy McGowan. "The return of the great-tailed grackle." *American Birds* 29:5 *(October* 1975), 985–992.

Reilly, Edgar M. *The Audubon Illustrated Handbook of American Birds.* New York: McGraw-Hill, 1968.

Remsen, J. V., Jr. "On taking field notes." *American Birds* 31:5 (September 1977), 946–953.

Richards, Keith C., and Frank B. Gill. "The 1974 mystery gull at Brigantine, New Jersey." *Birding* 8:5 (September–October 1976), 325–328.

Richardson, W. John. "Timing and amount of bird migration in relation to weather: A review." *Oikos* 30 (1978), 224–272.

Robbins, Chandler S., Bertel Bruun, and Herbert S. Zim. *Birds of North America.* 2d ed. New York: Golden Press, 1983.

Russell, Robert P., Jr. "The piping plover in the Great Lakes region." *American Birds* 37:6 (November–December 1983), 951–955.

Russell, Will. "Field identification notes." *Birding* 8:6 (November–December 1976), 347–348.

Ryff, Alan J. "The spring mystery of Sabine's gull." *Birding* 18:2 (April 1986), 83–90.

Sherman, Sandra. "Pedricktown: 'Ruff capital of North America.' " *New Jersey Audubon* 13:1 (Spring 1987), 11–14.

Smith, Rod W., and John S. Barclay. "Evidence of westward changes in the range of the American woodcock." *American Birds* 32:6 (November 1978), 1122–1127.

Stallcup, Rich. *Birds for Real.* Inverness, Calif.: Rich Stallcup, 1985.

"Sticky problems of hawk identification: A panel discussion." *Birding* 8:6 (November–December 1976), 386–404.

Stokes, Donald W. *A Guide to the Behavior of Common Birds.* Boston: Little, Brown, 1979.

Stone, Witmer. *Bird Studies at Old Cape May.* New York: Dover, 1965.

Sutton, Clay. "Coastal plain." *Newsletter of the Hawk Migration Association of North America* 9:2 (August 1984), 19–22.

———. "Mid-Atlantic." *Newsletter of the Hawk Migration Association of North America* 11:2 (August 1986), 19–24.

Sutton, Clay, and Patricia Taylor Sutton. "The spring hawk migration at Cape May, New Jersey." *Cassinia* 60 (1983), 5–18.

Terres, John K. *The Audubon Society Encyclopedia of North American Birds.* New York: Knopf, 1982.

———. *How Birds Fly.* New York: Hawthorn Books, 1968.

Veit, Richard R., and Lars Jonsson. "Field identification of smaller sandpipers within the genus *Calidris*." *American Birds* 38:5 (September–October 1984), 853–876.

Vickery, Peter D., and Robert P. Yunick. "The 1978–1979 great gray owl incursion across northeastern North America." *American Birds* 33:3 (May 1979), 242–244.

Wander, Wade. "Techniques for aging selected species of shorebirds in the field." *Records of New Jersey Birds* 10:3 (Autumn 1984), 49–55.

Weir, Ron D. "Ontario region." *American Birds* 38:3 (May–June 1984), 310–314.

Welty, Joel Carl. *The Life of Birds.* 3d ed. Philadelphia: Saunders, 1982.

Williams, Brad. "Birding Attu." *Crane* 28:2 (September 1986), 6.

Williams, Timothy C., Janet M. Williams, Leonard C. Ireland, and John M. Teal. "Autumnal bird migration over the western North Atlantic Ocean." *American Birds* 31:3 (May 1977), 251–267.

Willoughby, Hugh. "Letters to the editor." *Birding* 9:5 (October 1977), 206.

Zimmer, Kevin J. *A Birder's Guide to North Dakota.* Denver: L&P Press, 1979.

INDEX

Able, Kenneth, 67
accipiter, **137, 138**, 146–149
albatross, 62
Aleutian Islands, 76–77
Allen, Arthur, 44, 47
Amherst Island, 94
Archaeopteryx, 82
Assateague Island, 118
Atherton, Lyn, 221, 234–236
Aubry, Yves, 233
auklet, Cassin's, 68
avocet, American, **165**, 170, 176

Bailey, Wallace, 205
Bakker, Robert, 82
Balch, Larry, 188, 240
Barber, Bob, 235
Beaver, Joseph C., 40–42
Bent, Arthur Cleveland, 181
Bernstein, Chuck, 250

binoculars
  brightness measures of, **14**, 15–16
  close focus range of, 20
  designs of, 21, 22–25
  eyeglass wearers and, 18–19
  field of view of, 17–18
  magnification, 11–13
blackbird, rusty, 43
Blankinship, David, 108
bobolink, 53
booby
  blue-footed, 78
  brown, 75, 78
  masked, 75
Boyle, Bill, 241
Brady, Alan, 60, 86–87
breeding
  contracting ranges of, 103–108
  expanding ranges of, 100–103

Page numbers in boldface type refer to tables or illustrations.

breeding (*cont.*)
  niche confrontations,
    108–112, 113
  vagrants' success at, 96–97
breeding bird atlas, 98–100,
  102
"Brigantine Mystery Gull,"
  209–210
Brown, Leslie, 90–91
Buckley, P. A., 223, 224
budgerigar, 97
bulbul, red-whiskered, 2
bunting
  indigo, 100, 111
  lazuli, 111
  snow, 53
buteo, 62, 69, 85, 135, 137,
  149–152, 153
  scanning technique for,
    150–151
  typical field marks of, 153

call, *see* vocalization
Cape May, 72, 73, 75, 118
  autumn hawk count, 156
  directions to, 161
caracara, 239
cardinal, northern, 52, 100
car window mount, 35
catbird, gray, 56, 84
Central Park (N.Y.), 77, 114
Chapman, Frank M., 130
chat, yellow-breasted, 51, 122,
  126

chickadee, 52, 53, 108, 109
  black-capped, 108–109
  boreal, 87, 109
  Carolina, 108–109
  Mexican, 109
  mountain, 109
Chirichua Mountains, 74
Christmas counts, 84, 85, 94,
  253
  in summer, 98, 100
chuck-will's-widow, 113
chukar, 97
Clark, William, 143, 148
color phases, 150, 152
cormorants, 64
  double-breasted, 101
Coues, Elliot, 181
cowbird, brown-headed, 38,
  100, 105–106
crake, corn, 241
crane, 74
  whooping, 107–108
creeper, brown, 39–40, 83
crossbill, 94
  red, 87, 91
  white-winged, 87, 91
crow, 52
  common, 39
  fish, 46
cuckoo, 83
  black-billed, 51
  yellow-billed, 51
curlew
  Eskimo, 108, 176
  long-billed, 164, 165, 169,
    176

Page numbers in boldface type refer to tables or illustrations.

Davis, Tom, 181
DDT, 107
de Kiriline, L., 38
Dennis, John V., 103
dickcissel, 107
dinosaurs, 82
dipper, 48
dove, rock, 96
dowitcher
  long-billed, 53–54, 165,
    176, 179–180, 181, 240
  short-billed, 53–54, 165,
    169, 176, 179–180, 181
Dry Tortugas, 75–76
duck, 64, 68, 83
  black, 110–111
  mallard, 110–111
Duncan, Charles, 210
dunlin, 164, 165, 169, 176,
  181, 184
Dunne, Pete, 122, 133, 135,
  138, 240–241

eagle, 137
  bald, 1, 5–6, 107, 142, 143,
    144, 155, 160
  golden, 142, 143, 144, 155,
    158, 160
ecological specialization,
  103–106
egret, 108
  cattle, 95, 97, 101, 111
  reddish, 108, 150
  snowy, 111
eider, 85
  common, 85–86
  king, 85–86

Ellison, Walter, 222
Emlen, Stephen, 60
Emmanuel, Victor, 260–261

falcon, 65, 107, 135, 137, 138,
  144–146
  peregrine, 69, 144,
    145–146, 156–160
  prairie, 144, 145–146
Farallon Islands, 76, 77
feather
  evolution of, 82
  molt in gulls, 214–215
field glasses, 22
field guides
  importance of, 242
  limitations of, 134, 168,
    171, 198, 211, 242, 253
  power of suggestion of,
    241–242
field notes, 248–251
  for reporting rarities,
    252–254
finch, 52, 87, 91, 93, 94
  house, 48
  purple, 87, 91
Fish, Allen, 148
flicker, yellow-shafted, 39, 65
flycatcher, 55–56, 83
  acadian, 44, 46, 55–56, 100
  alder, 55–56
  buff-breasted, 55–56, 74
  dusky, 55–56
  gray, 55–56
  Hammond's, 55–56
  least, 55–56
  olive-sided, 44

flycatcher (*cont.*)
  red-breasted, 76
  sulphur-bellied, 74
  western, 55–56
  willow, 55–56
  yellow-bellied, 55–56
frigatebird, magnificent, 78, 97
fulmar, northern, 87

Gause's rule, 109
Gill, Frank B., 109
gnatcatcher, blue-gray, 40, 100
godwit, 174
  Hudsonian, 163, 165, 176
  marbled, 84, 164, 165, 169,
    176
Golden Gate
  autumn hawk count, 159
  directions to, 161
goose, 64, 68, 83
  Canada, 48
  snow, 150
goshawk, 87, 90, 93, 147, 148
Goshute Mountains
  autumn hawk count, 158
  directions to, 161
grackle
  boat-tailed, 48, 103
  great-tailed, 48, 103
Grant, Peter, *Gulls: A Guide
    to Identification*, 211
Griscom, Ludlow, 139,
    242–243, 245
grosbeak
  blue, 100
  evening, 44, 45, 87, 91, 94

pine, 87, 91
rose-breasted, 43–44, 100
Gross, Alfred O., 87–88
grouse, 61–62
guillemot, black, 242–243
gull, 66, 83, 108
  abundance of, 209, 244
  black-headed, 212, 218,
    219, 220–221
  Bonaparte's, 194, 195, 201,
    212, 218, 219, 220, 221
  California, 209, 212, 226,
    227–228
  distinguishing from terns,
    193–194
  distribution of, 218,
    221–223, 228, 229
  Franklin's, 195, 212, 218,
    219, 220
  glaucous, 212, 214, 226,
    227, 231–233
  glaucous-winged, 212, 226,
    231–232
  greater black-backed, 212,
    215, 226, 227–230
  Heermann's, 68, 212, 217,
    221–222
  herring, 197, 209, 212, 213,
    216, 217, 224–225, 226,
    227–230, 233
  Iceland, 212, 214, 226, 227,
    233–234
  ivory, 82, 212, 219, 221
  laughing, 194, 198, 201,
    212, 218, 219, 220, 221
  lesser black-backed, 209,
    212, 226, 227–231

Page numbers in boldface type refer to tables or illustrations.

little, 212, 218, 219,
220–221
mew, 209, 212, 225,
227–228
plumages of, 209, 211, 212,
213, 214–218, 219
population dynamics of,
215–217
ring-billed, 197, 212, 216,
224–225, 226, 227, 233
Ross', 82, 212, 219, 221,
222–224, 256
Sabine's, 61, 74, 194, 208,
212, 214, 218, 219
taxonomy of, 231
Thayer's, 209, 212, 226,
234–236
western, 209, 210, 212, 226,
227, 230–231
yellow-footed, 78, 212, 226,
228, 230, 231
gyrfalcon, 89, 92–93

Haas, Frank, 145
habitat loss, 106–107
Hardy, William, 251–252
harrier, northern, 106, 137,
138, 139, 140, 154–160
Harrington, Brian, 66
Harrison, Peter, 202, 211, 222
Hauchuca Mountains, 74
hawk
autumn migration counts of,
154–159
black, 151
broad-winged, 69, 85, 151,
152, 154–157, 159, 160
color phases of, 150, 152

Cooper's, 138, 147–148,
154–160, 240
ferruginous, 140, 146, 150,
151, 152, 153
gray, 151
Harris', 149, 151
identification by flight style
of, 136–138, 139, 141,
142–149
irruptions of, 87, 89–93
plumages of, 134, 148, 150
red-shouldered, 85, 148,
149, 151, 152, 154–156,
159, 160
red-tailed, 69, 148, 150,
151, 152, 153, 154–160
rough-legged, 87, 88, 93,
150, 151, 152, 153
sharp-shinned, 69, 147, 148,
154–160
short-tailed, 150–151
Swainson's, 62–63, 64, 85,
137, 146, 148, 150, 151,
152, 153, 158
white-tailed, 139–140, 151
zone-tailed, 11, 141–142,
151
Hawk Migration Association
of North America, 153
Hawk Mountain, 240
autumn hawk count, 155
directions to, 161
Heil, Richard, 234
heron, 108, 111
little blue, 111
tri-colored, 100
Hintermister, John, 2,
130–132, 163
Hoffman, Steve, 74–75

Holiday Beach
  autumn hawk count, 154
  directions to, 160
Horner, Jim, 131, 251
Howell, Arthur H., *Florida Bird Life,* 152
hummingbird, 63, 86
  Anna's, 48, 86
  berylline, 74
  black-chinned, 63, 86
  buff-bellied, 63
  magnificent, 74
  ruby-throated, 86
  rufous, 63, 86
hybridization
  blue × Stellar's jay, 113
  blue-winged × golden-winged warbler, 109–110
  glaucous × western gull, 231
  indigo × lazuli bunting, 111

ibis, 64
  glossy, 97, 100, 112
  white, 100
  white-faced, 112
insectivores, 82–83
introduced species, 97
irruptives, 87–94

jaegers, 78
jay, 52
  blue, 56, 100, 113
  Stellar's, 113
Johnsgard, Paul A., and Rose

DiSilvestro, 110–111
Johnsson, Lars, 186

kestrel, American, 144, 145, 145, 146, 154–160
killdeer, 38, 53, 164, 165, 169, 176
King, Kirke, 108
kingbird, eastern, 38, 39–40
kingfisher, belted, 43
kinglet, 84
Kiptopeke Beach, 73–74
  autumn hawk count, 157
  directions to, 161
kites, 101, 139–140
  black-shouldered, 102, 139
  hook-billed, 101–102
  Mississippi, 102, 139, 140
  snail, 104, 105, 139
  swallow-tailed, 102, 139
kittiwake, 194, 217, 219, 221
  black-legged, 212, 221–222
  red-legged, 212, 221–222
knot, red, 66, 164

Lake Havasu, 78
Lane, James, *Birder's Guide to Southern California,* 78
Lawiewski, R. C., 63
Leahy, Christopher, 223
Leddy, Linda, 66
LeGrand, Harry, 69
Lehman, Paul, 52
limpkin, 104, 105

Page numbers in boldface type refer to tables or illustrations.

list keeping, 244–247
Little, Randolph, 46–47,
    52–53
"longlegs," 175, 176, 177–182
longspurs, 53
loon, common, 48

martin, purple, 85
Matthiessen, Peter, 163
Mayfield, Harold, 106
Mead, Chris, 58
Mead, Frank, 36–37
Mellon, Rick, 198
Meritt, Jim, 79, 247–248
merlin, 65, 144, 145, 156–160
migration
    corridor effect, 74–75
    distance covered, 61, 115,
        116
    effect of food preferences on,
        64–66, 82–83, 115
    effect of physiology on,
        61–64
    flyways, 71
    funnel effect, 72
    of hawks in autumn,
        154–160
    influence of geography on,
        70–79
    influence of weather on,
        66–70, 82, 115, 117, 118,
        121
    islands and oases, 75–80
    "leapfrogging," 86
    navigation during, 60
    peninsular effect, 73
    radar studies of, 79
    routes, 59–64, 65, 70–80,
        122
    "short-stopping," 83
    timing of, 120, 121
    V-formation flight, 64
Miliotis, Paul, 222
Millsap, Brian, 102
mockingbird, 38, 51, 84, 100
Moscatello, Brian, 81

Nabokov, Vladimir, 8
Nash, James, 257–258
National Geographic Society
    Field Guide to the Birds
    of North America, 85
Nicoletti, Frank, 188, 259
nighthawk
    Antillean, 54, 113
    common, 54, 61, 113
nightjars, 83
noddy
    brown, 75
    black, 75
nuthatch, 52, 53
    pgymy, 87
    red-breasted, 43, 45

"Old One-Foot," 210–211
optical equipment
    Bushnell/Bausch & Lomb,
        24, 25–26, 30
    Leitz, 24, 27
    Nikon, 25
    Zeiss, 23, 24, 26–27
    see also binoculars, car
        window mount, shoulder

optical equipment (*cont.*)
   stock, spotting scope,
     tripod
osprey, 65, 107, 137, **155–158**
ovenbird, 46, 51, 100, **119**,
   126
owl, 16
   barred, 50, **113**
   boreal, 43, 93
   great gray, 90, 94
   great horned, 50, 87, 90
   hawk, 93
   pygmy, 87
   short-eared, 106
   snowy, 87–88, **88, 89,** 90,
     93
   spotted, **113**
   western screech, 54
   whiskered screech, 54
oystercatcher, 84, 170
   American, **164,** 169, **176**
   black, **164,** 169, **176**

Padalino, Jack, 147
parrot, thick-billed, 241
Parsons, Philip, 254–255
partridge, gray, 97
Pedricktown, N.J., 78–79
"peep," 174, **176,** 185–186,
   187, 188, 189, 190
peewee
   eastern wood-, 51, 54, 100,
     113
   western wood-, 54, **113**
pelagic birds, 35, 78, 86

pelican, 64, 68, 87, 97, 107
penguin, emperor, 82
Peterson, Roger Tory, 72
   A Field Guide to the Birds,
     44, 152, 221, 242
phalarope
   red, 86, **165,** 169, 174, **176**
   red-necked, 78, 86, **165,**
     169, 174, **176**
   Wilson's, **165, 176,** 180
pheasant, ring-necked, 43,
   56–57, 97
Phillips, Alan R., 54, 186–189
pipit
   Sprague's, 53
   water, 53
pitch, *see* VOCALIZATION
Pitelka, Frank, 179
plover, 86, 107, **170,** 171–173,
   176
   black-bellied, 53, 86, **164,**
     165, 167, 168, 169, 173,
     176
   lesser golden, 53, 65–66, 86,
     163, **164, 165,** 166, 168,
     169, 172, 173, **176**
   mountain, 164, **165,** 169,
     172, **176**
   semipalmated, **164, 165,**
     172–173, **176**
   snowy, 53, 107, **164,** 169,
     172–173, **176**
   Pacific golden, 86
   piping, 53, 106–107, **164,**
     172–173, **176**
   Wilson's, **164,** 172, **176**

Page numbers in boldface type refer to tables or illustrations.

plumages
    of gulls, 209, 211, 212, 213,
        214–215, 216, 217–218
    of hawks, 134, 148, 150
    of shorebirds, 167–169
    of terns vs. gulls, 193
    of warblers, 121–123
"plump," 175, 176, 177,
    182–185
Point Pelee, 72
poor-will, 83
Porro, M., 22
porro prism binoculars, 21,
    22–23
postbreeding wanderers, 97
Pough, Richard, *Audubon
    Water Bird Guide,* 188,
    256
ptarmigan, 61–62

quail, 61–62

rail, 16
    Virginia, 43
    yellow, 43
raven, common, 39, 88–89,
    237, 258, 259, 260
redpolls, 94
    common, 87
    hoary, 87
redstart, American, 100, 122,
    126
Reilly, Edgar M., 42, 206
reverse porro prisms, 21,
    24–25
Richardson, John W., "Timing

and amount of bird
    migration in relation to
    weather," 70
Robbins, Chandler S., 99
    Birds of North America, 38,
        39, 241
robin, American, 52
roof prism binoculars, 21,
    24–25
Rowlett, John, 260–261
rubythroat, Siberian, 76
ruff, 78–79
Ruskin, John, 70
Russell, Will, 204
Ryff, Alan J., 74

Salton Sea, 78
sanderling, 163, **164**, 166,
    169, **176**, 185
sandpiper, 66, 171, 174, **175**,
    176–190
    Baird's, 165, 166, **176**, 184,
        186, 187, 188, 189, 190
    buff-breasted, 164, **165**,
        176, 183–184
    curlew, 174
    least, 165, 169, **176**, 182,
        185, 186, 187, 188, **189**
    pectoral, **165**, 176, 184–185
    purple, **164**, 166, 169, 175,
        176, 182–183
    rock, **164**, 169, **176**,
        182–183
    semipalmated, **164**, 165,
        176, 186, 187, 188, **189**
    solitary, **165**, **176**, 180–181

sandpiper (*cont.*)
  spotted, **164, 165, 168, 169,** **176,** 182
  stilt, **165,** 166, **168, 169,** **176,** 179, 181–182
  Terek, 76–77
  upland, 107, **165,** 169, **176,** 177–178
  western, 54, **164, 165,** 169, **176,** 186, 187, 188, **189,** 190
  white-rumped, 65–66, **163,** **164, 165,** 166, **176,** 186, 187, 188, 189, 190
San Padre Island, 115
sapsucker
  red-breasted, 64–65
  Williamson's, 64–65
  yellow-bellied, 64–65, 87
shearwater, 62, 71
  Audubon's 86–87
  black-vented, 86
  Manx, 86–87
  short-tailed, 86
  sooty, 86, 87
Shellford, V. E., 87
shorebirds
  basic principles of identification of, 164–171
  flight style, 167
  habitat preference of, **164–165,** 166, 172, 177, 178, 179, 181–184
  inland occurrence of, 164–166
  migration of, 163, 166, 174

plumages of, 167–169
taxonomy of, 169–171
vocalizations of, 53–54
shoulder stock, 30, 35
shrike, 90, 93, 94
  northern, 87, 89
siskin, pine, 87, 91, **92,** 94
skimmer, black, 78
skua, 71
  great, 81, 86
  South Polar, 86
snipe, common, 53, **165,** **176,** 179
song, *see* VOCALIZATION
sonograms, 38–40, **41, 42**
sparrow
  chipping, **41**
  Eurasian tree, 97
  field, **41,** 51
  grasshopper, **40,** 51, 107
  Henslow's, 51, 107
  house, 97
  lark, 107
  sharp-tailed, 107
  song, 38
  swamp, 51
  vesper, 51, 107
  white-throated, **36,** 52
spoonbill, roseate, 97
spotting scope, 13–14, **15,** 28–32, 35
  field of view of, 28
  fixed focus vs. zoom, 28–30
  limitations of, 28–29
Stallcup, Rich, 44, 198
starling, 56, 97

Page numbers in boldface type refer to tables or illustrations.

stilt, black-necked, **165,** 169,
170, **176**
stint, Temminck's, 76
Stone, Witmer, 43
stork, wood, 78, 97
storm petrel, 62, 71
surfbird, **164,** 169, **176,**
182–183
Sutton, Clay, 135, 146, 260
swallow, 85
barn, **58,** 61
cave, 113
cliff, 113
tree, 85
violet-green, 85
swan, 64, 83
mute, 97
trumpeter, 54
tundra, 54

tanager
scarlet, 44
summer, 100
tattler, wandering, **164, 176,**
178–179
taxonomy
of shorebirds, 169–171
of terns and gulls, 192
recent splits in, 230, 231
tern, 84, 106
arctic, 61, 64, 84, **194, 201,**
202–203, 205–206
black, 191, **194,** 195, 200,
201
bridled, **194,** 195, 198–199,
201
Caspian, 69, 84, **193, 194,**

196–197, **201,** 205
common, 78, 84, **194, 201,**
202–207
distinguishing from gulls,
193–194
elegant, 68, 69, 113, **194,**
197–198, **201**
Forster's, 84, **193, 194,** 200,
201, 202–206
gull-billed, **193, 194,** 195,
199–200, **201**
identification sequence, 192,
201
least, 106, **194,** 195–196,
201
roseate, **193, 194, 201,**
202–203
royal, 84, 113, **194,**
196–198, 200, **201,** 205
sandwich, **194,** 195,
199–200, **201,** 202, 207
size classes of, 194–195
sooty, 75, **194,** 195,
198–199, **201**
Terres, John K., 43
thrasher, brown, 38, 56, 84
thrush, 53, 84–85
eye-browed, 76
gray-cheeked, 84–85
hermit, 84–85
Swainson's, 52, 84–85
wood, 43, 51
titmouse, 52, 53
plain, 48
tufted, 48, 100
towhee, rufous-sided, 44, **45**
tripod, 32, 33, 34
trogon, elegant, 74

tropicbird, white-tailed, 75
tubenose, 62
turnstone
 black, **164**, 169, **176**, 183
 ruddy, **164**, 169, **176**, 183

vocalization
 contextual clues for, 47–49
 field birds, 53
 migrating birds, 51–52
 mimicry of, 57
 mnemonic translation of,
  43–47
 night, 50–51
 number per day, 38
 phonetic translation of,
  42–43
 pitch of, 38, 39–40
 shorebirds, 53–54
 winter, 52–53

warbler, 53, 72, 83
 basic principles of
  identification of, 125–130
 bay-breasted, 118, **119**, 120,
  122–123
 black-and-white, 120, 122,
  126
 blackburnian, 40, 117, 118,
  119, 122
 blackpoll, 40, 115–116, **119**,
  120, 122–123
 black-throated blue, **119**,
  122
 black-throated green, 38, 44,
  119, 120, 122

blue-winged, 39, 40, 109,
 110, **119**, 122
Canada, 118, **119**
Cape May, 40, 126
cerulean, 118, **119**, 122
chestnut-sided, **119** 122
Connecticut, **114**, **119**, 120,
 130, 131
expansion west of, 100–101
fall plumages of, 122
golden-cheeked, 104–105,
 106
golden-winged, 39, 40, 109,
 110
Grace's, **119**
habitat preferences of,
 116–118
hermit, 117, **119**, 124
hooded, 118, 120
Kentucky, 118, **119**
Kirtland's, 38, 104–105,
 106, 125
MacGilvray's, **119**
magnolia, 44, 118, **119**, 126
migration of, 115–116,
 117–118, 120, 121–122
mourning, 118, **119**, 120
Nashville, 40, 47, 124
northern parula, 100–101,
 121, 122, **126**
olive, 74
orange-crowned, **119**,
 124–125
palm, **119**, 120, 124
pine, 120, 124
prairie, **41**, 120, 122
prothonotary, 40, **119**, 122

Page numbers in boldface type refer to tables or illustrations.

stratigraphic preferences of,
    118, **119**, 120
Swainson's, **119**
Tennessee, 40, 47, **119**
Townsend's, **119**, 124
Wilson's, 118
worm-eating, 40, **41**, **119**
yellow, 44, 46, 114, 120,
    126
yellow-rumped, 115, 120,
    124, 125, **126–127**
yellow-throated, 120, 122
waterthrush, **119**
Louisiana, 40, 120, 122,
    129, 130
northern, 48, 122, **129**, 130
waxwing
bohemian, 87, 94
cedar, 87
Weissberg, Herman, 254–255
whimbrel, **164, 165**, 176
whip-poor-will, 50–51, 113
Wilds, Claudia, 178, 199
willet, 53, 84, **165**, 167, 169,
    176, 177
Williams, Brad, 76–77

Willoughby, Hugh, 130
woodcock, American,
    102–103, **165**, 169, 174,
    176
woodpecker, 52, 64–65, 83
black-backed, 87
ivory-billed, 103, 104
Lewis', 65
pileated, 39
red-bellied, **7**, 100
red-cockaded, 104
three-toed, 87
wren, 52
Bewick's, 40
Carolina, 84
house, 254–255
winter, 48

yellowlegs, 53, 84
greater, **165**, 169, **176**, 178
lesser, 65–66, **165**, 166,
    169, **175, 176**, 178, 181
yellowthroat, common, 114,
    119, 124, **126**